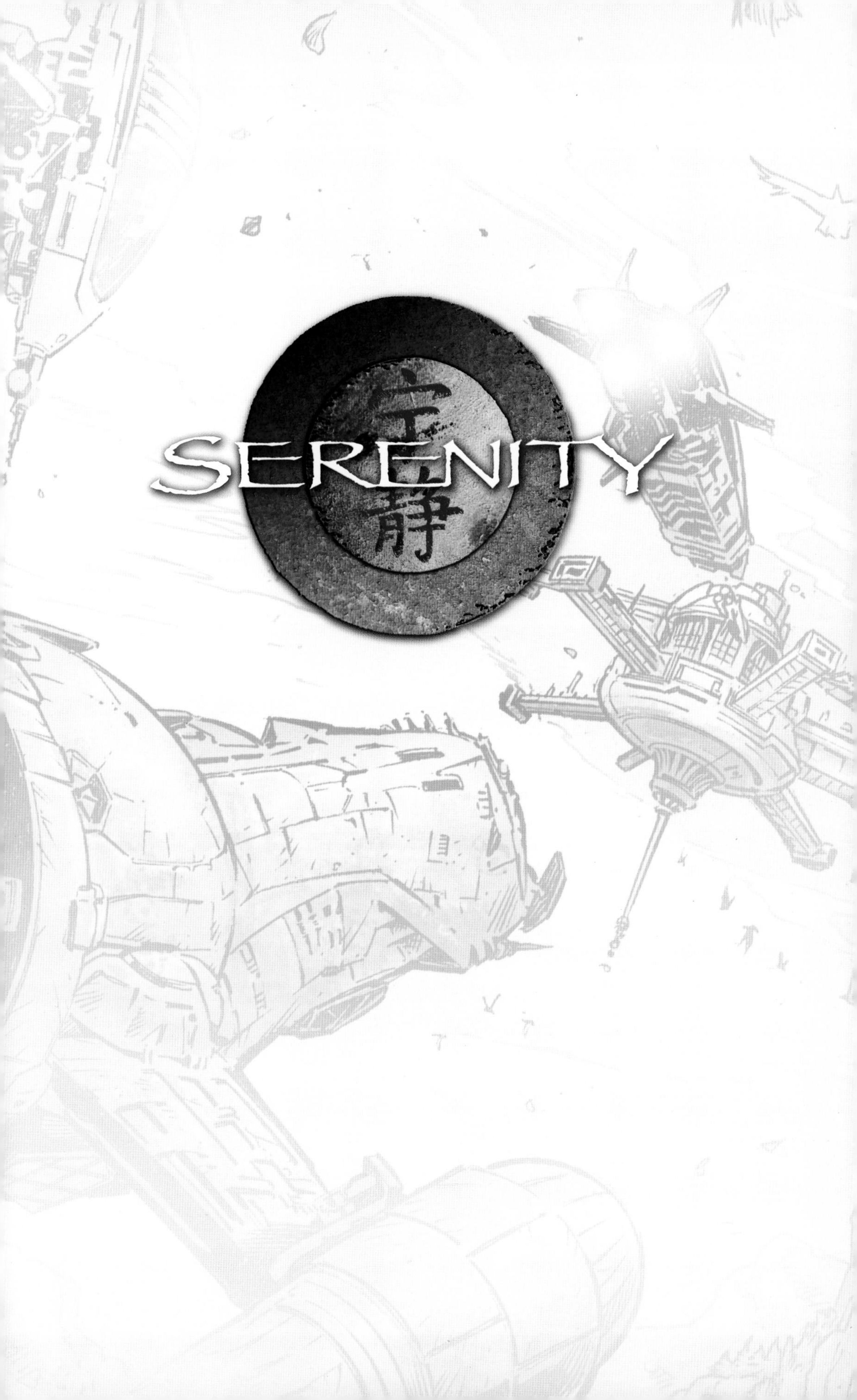
SERENITY

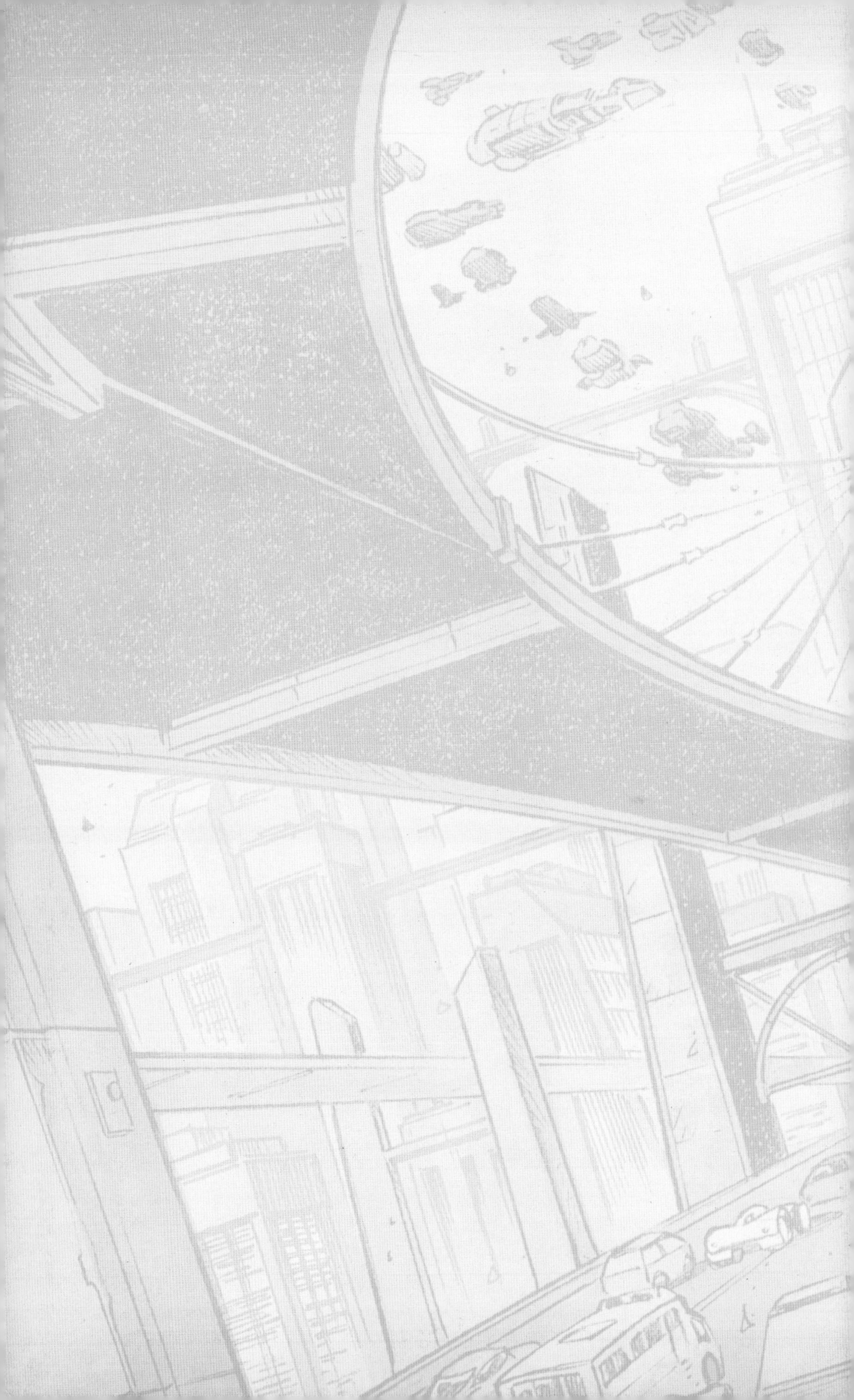

SERENITY

宁静

BETTER DAYS
AND OTHER STORIES

FEATURING
JOSS WHEDON

BRETT MATTHEWS

WILL CONRAD

ZACK WHEDON

PATTON OSWALT

CHRIS SAMNEE

JIM KRUEGER

PATRIC REYNOLDS

FRONT COVER ART
JO CHEN

DARK HORSE BOOKS®

PRESIDENT & PUBLISHER
MIKE RICHARDSON

EDITORS
SCOTT ALLIE & SIERRA HAHN

ASSISTANT EDITOR
FREDDYE LINS

COLLECTION DESIGNER
JUSTIN COUCH

SPECIAL THANKS to CINDY CHANG at UNIVERSAL STUDIOS
AND BRENDAN WRIGHT at DARK HORSE COMICS.

NEIL HANKERSON Executive Vice President · TOM WEDDLE Chief Financial Officer · RANDY STRADLEY
Vice President of Publishing · MICHAEL MARTENS Vice President of Book Trade Sales · ANITA NELSON
Vice President of Business Affairs · MICHA HERSHMAN Vice President of Marketing · DAVID SCROGGY
Vice President of Product Development · DALE LAFOUNTAIN Vice President of Information Technology
DARLENE VOGEL Senior Director of Print, Design, and Production · KEN LIZZI General Counsel
DAVEY ESTRADA Editorial Director · SCOTT ALLIE Senior Managing Editor · CHRIS WARNER
Senior Books Editor · DIANA SCHUTZ Executive Editor · CARY GRAZZINI Director of Print
and Development · LIA RIBACCHI Art Director · CARA NIECE Director of Scheduling

Published by Dark Horse Books
A division of Dark Horse Comics, Inc.
10956 SE Main Street
Milwaukie, OR 97222

DarkHorse.com

To find a comics shop in your area, call the
Comic Shop Locator Service toll-free at (888) 266-4226.

First edition: October 2008
Second edition: September 2011

ISBN 978-1-59582-739-5

1 3 5 7 9 10 8 6 4 2
Printed at Midas Printing International, Ltd., Huizhou, China

TABLE OF CONTENTS

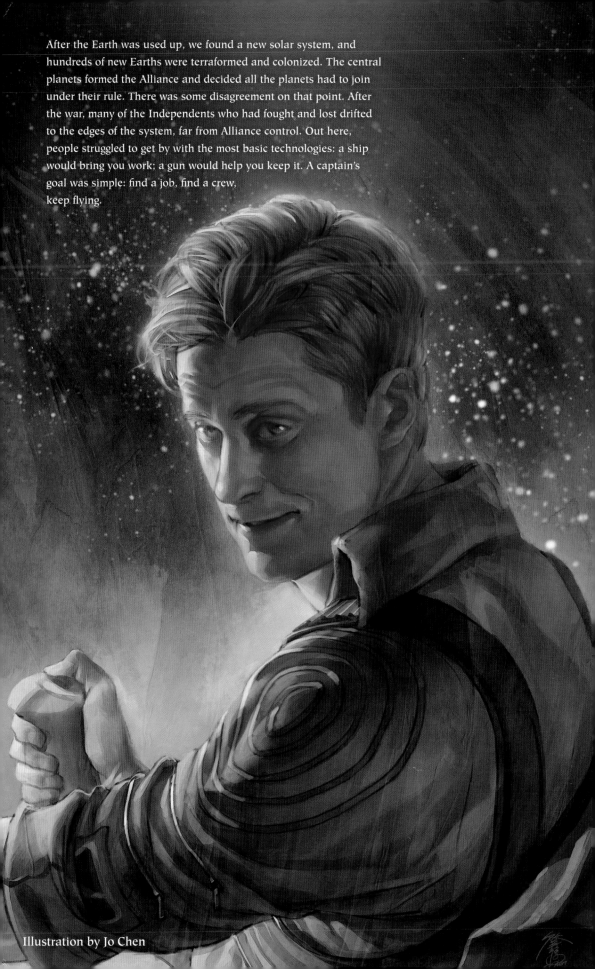

After the Earth was used up, we found a new solar system, and hundreds of new Earths were terraformed and colonized. The central planets formed the Alliance and decided all the planets had to join under their rule. There was some disagreement on that point. After the war, many of the Independents who had fought and lost drifted to the edges of the system, far from Alliance control. Out here, people struggled to get by with the most basic technologies: a ship would bring you work; a gun would help you keep it. A captain's goal was simple: find a job, find a crew,
keep flying.

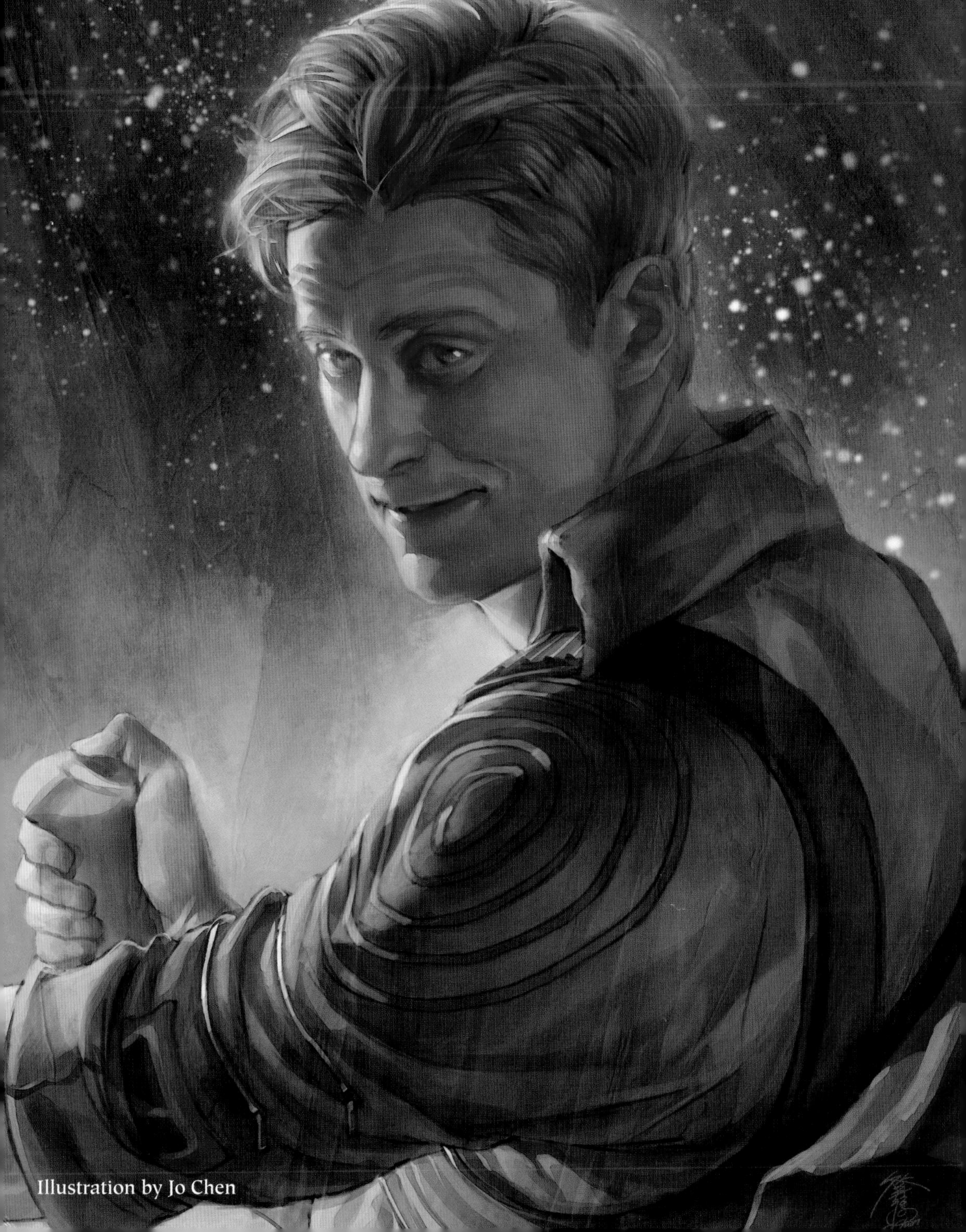

Illustration by Jo Chen

BETTER DAYS

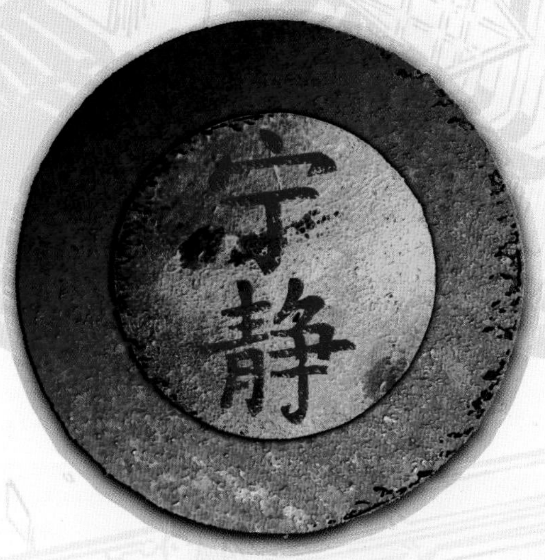
宁静

STORY
JOSS WHEDON and BRETT MATTHEWS

ART
WILL CONRAD

COLORS
MICHELLE MADSEN

LETTERS
MICHAEL HEISLER

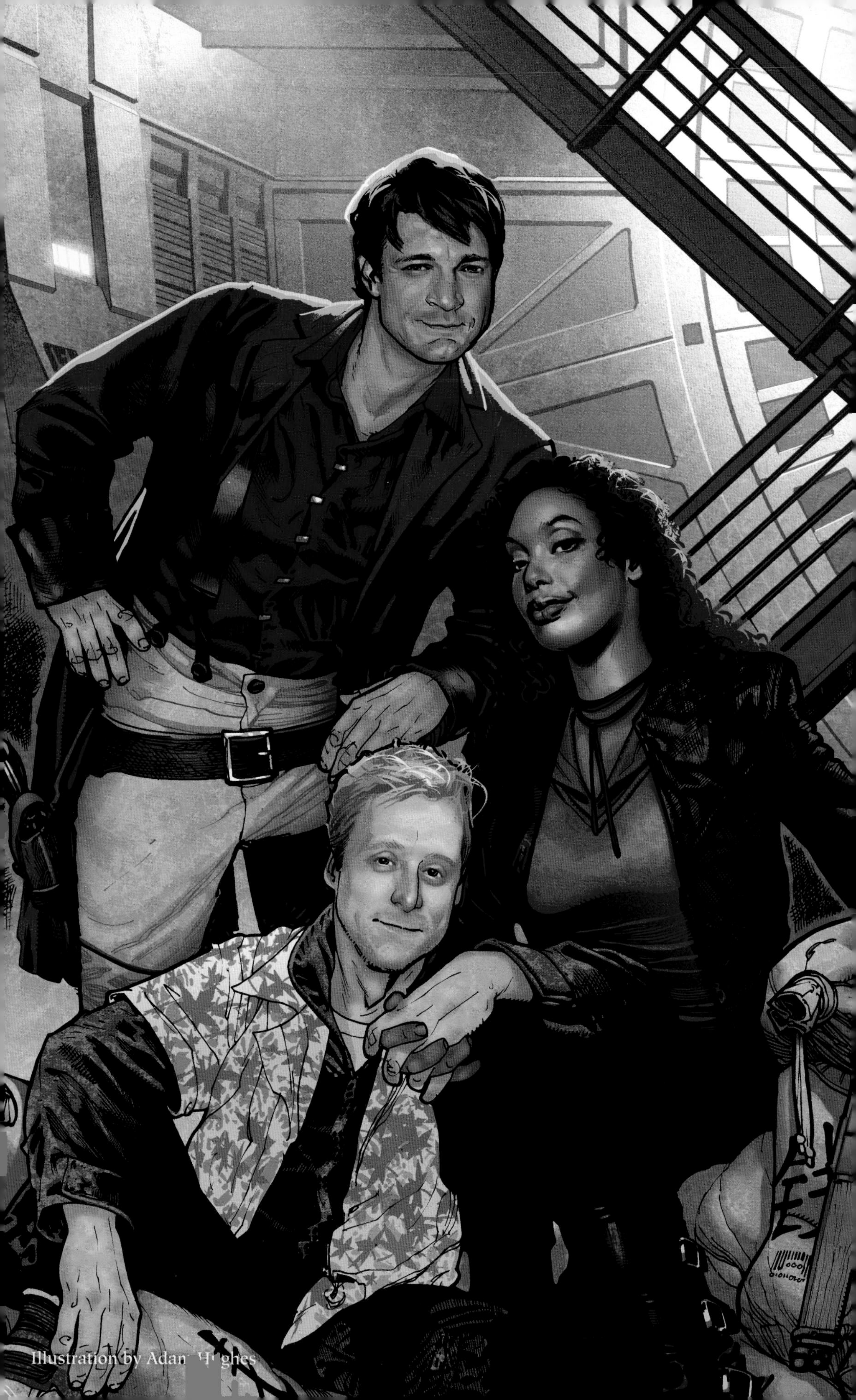

Illustration by Adam Hughes

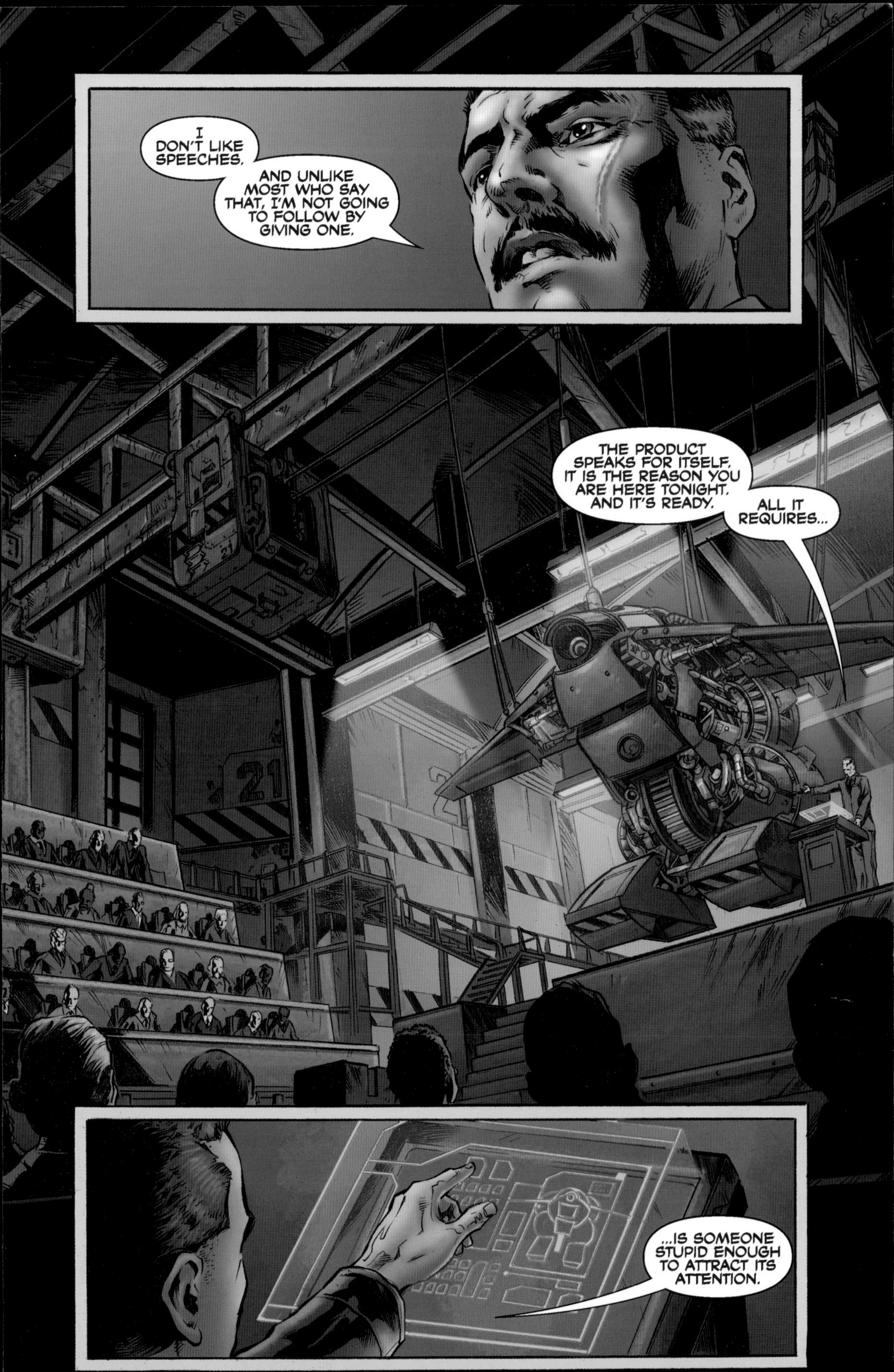
I DON'T LIKE SPEECHES.
AND UNLIKE MOST WHO SAY THAT, I'M NOT GOING TO FOLLOW BY GIVING ONE.
THE PRODUCT SPEAKS FOR ITSELF. IT IS THE REASON YOU ARE HERE TONIGHT. AND IT'S READY.
ALL IT REQUIRES...
...IS SOMEONE STUPID ENOUGH TO ATTRACT ITS ATTENTION.

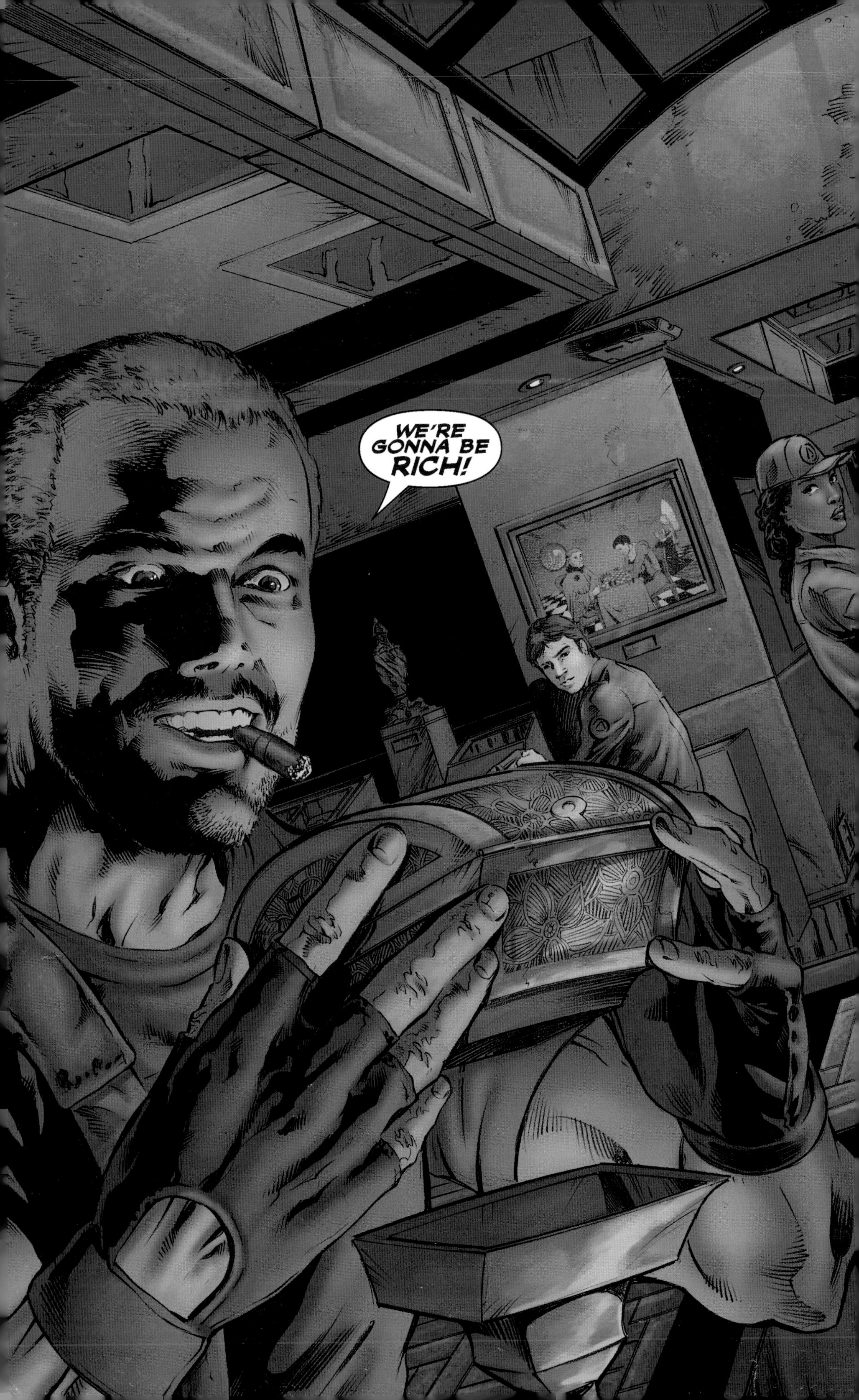
WE'RE GONNA BE RICH!

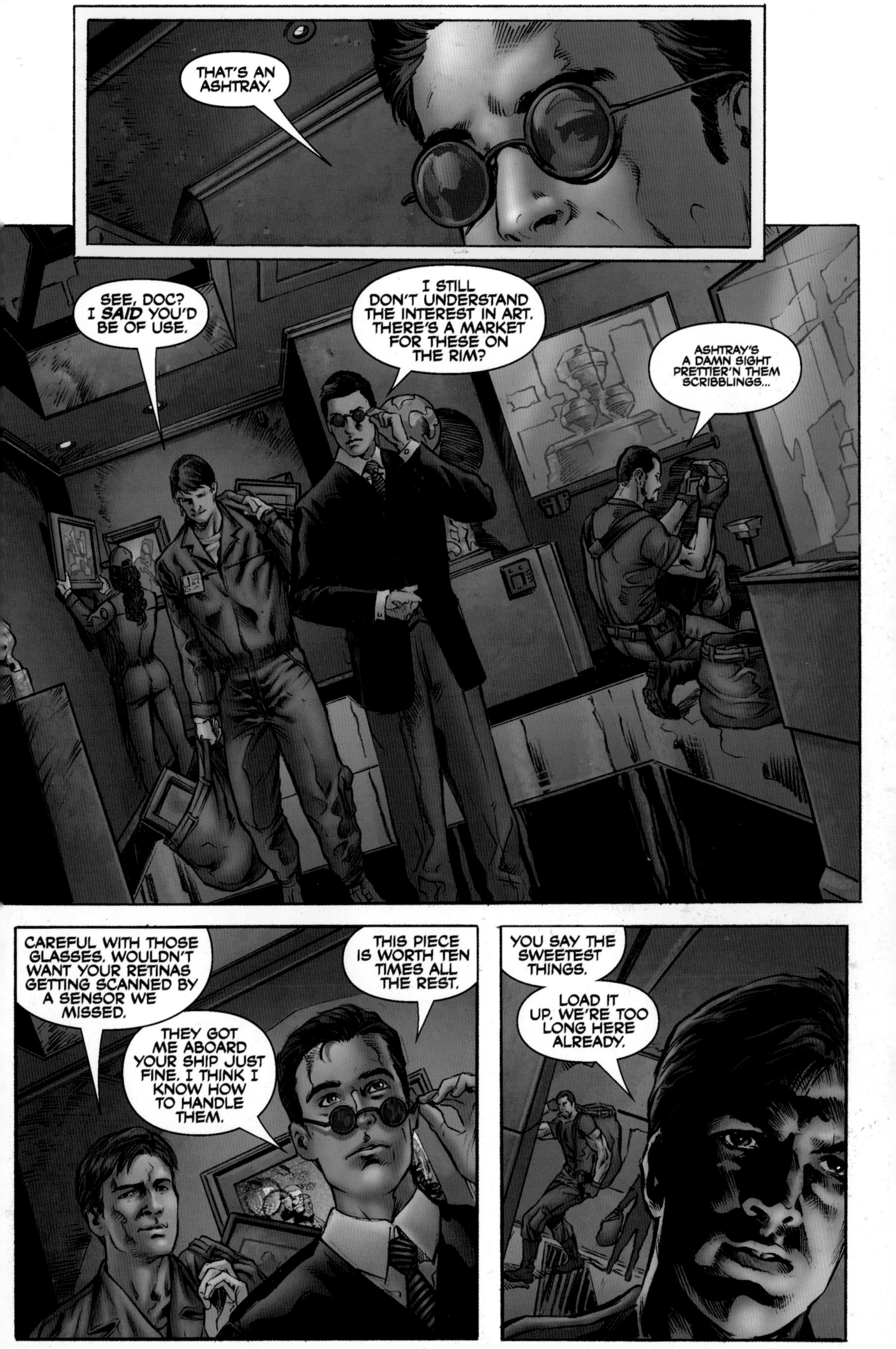
THAT'S AN ASHTRAY.
SEE, DOC? I *SAID* YOU'D BE OF USE.
I STILL DON'T UNDERSTAND THE INTEREST IN ART. THERE'S A MARKET FOR THESE ON THE RIM?
ASHTRAY'S A DAMN SIGHT PRETTIER'N THEM SCRIBBLINGS...
CAREFUL WITH THOSE GLASSES. WOULDN'T WANT YOUR RETINAS GETTING SCANNED BY A SENSOR WE MISSED.
THEY GOT ME ABOARD YOUR SHIP JUST FINE. I THINK I KNOW HOW TO HANDLE THEM.
THIS PIECE IS WORTH TEN TIMES ALL THE REST.
YOU SAY THE SWEETEST THINGS.
LOAD IT UP. WE'RE TOO LONG HERE ALREADY.

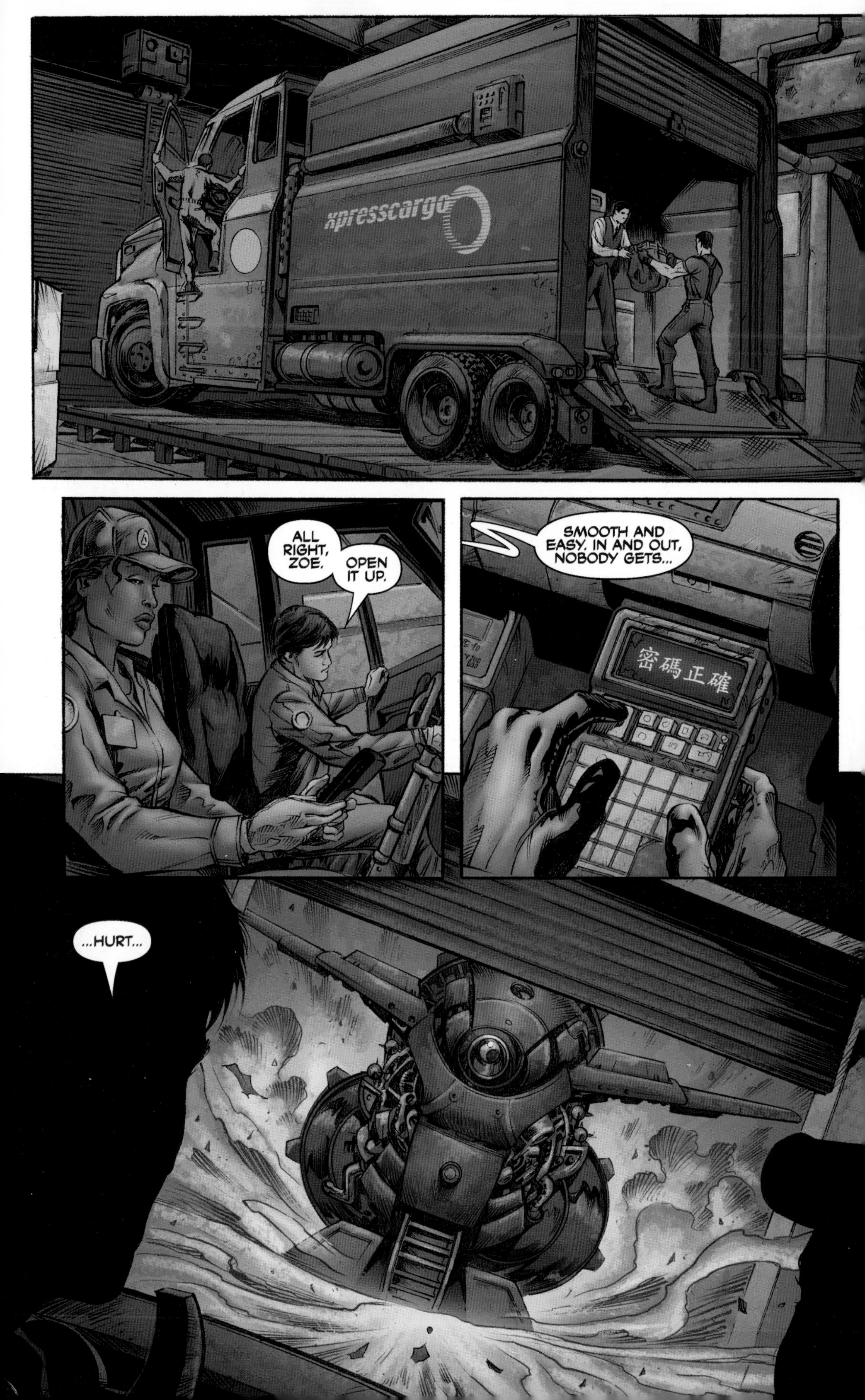
xpresscargo
ALL RIGHT, ZOE.
OPEN IT UP.
SMOOTH AND EASY. IN AND OUT, NOBODY GETS...
密碼正確
...HURT...

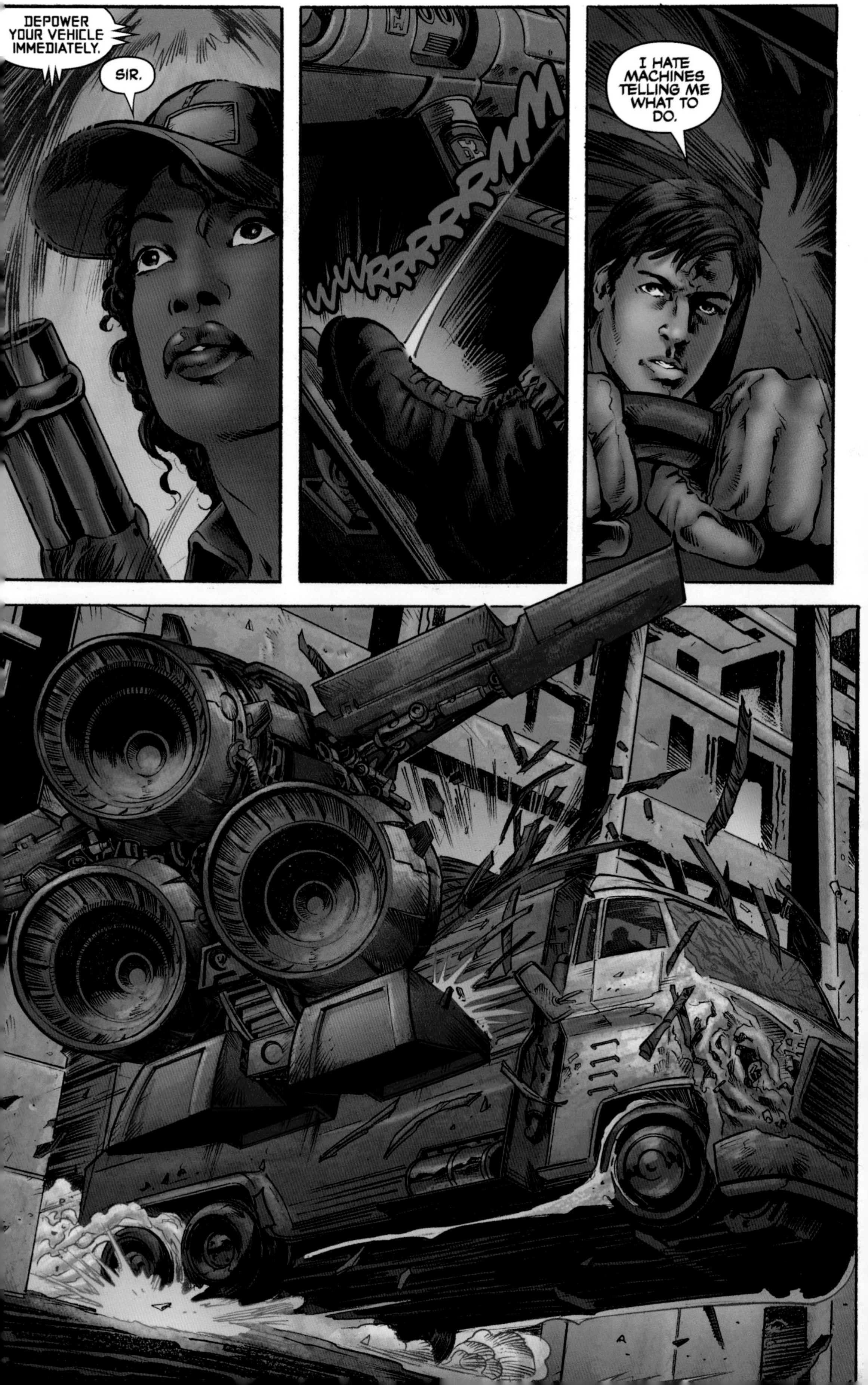
DEPOWER YOUR VEHICLE IMMEDIATELY.
SIR.
WVVRRRRRRMM
I HATE MACHINES TELLING ME WHAT TO DO.

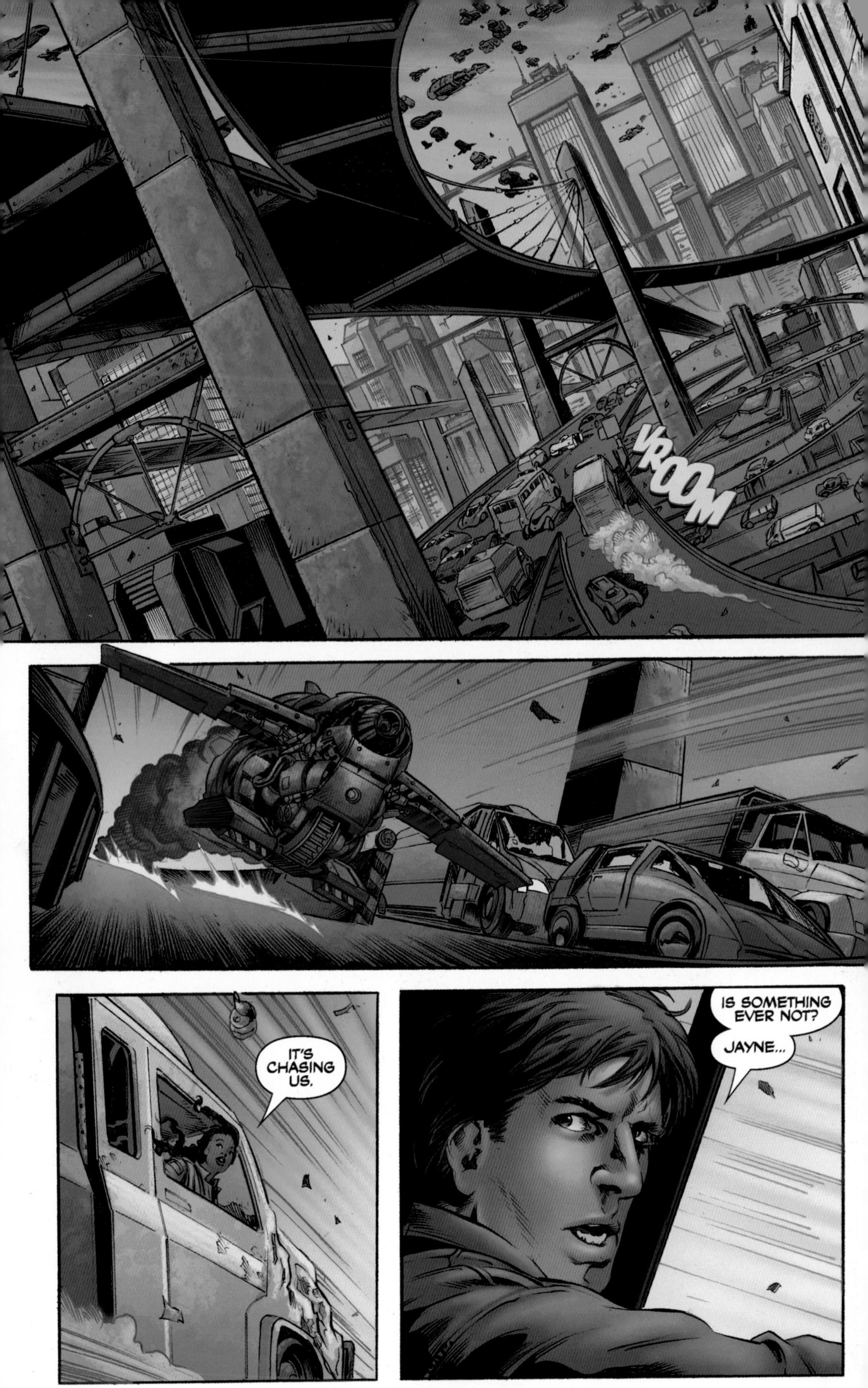
VROOM
IT'S CHASING US.
IS SOMETHING EVER NOT?
JAYNE...

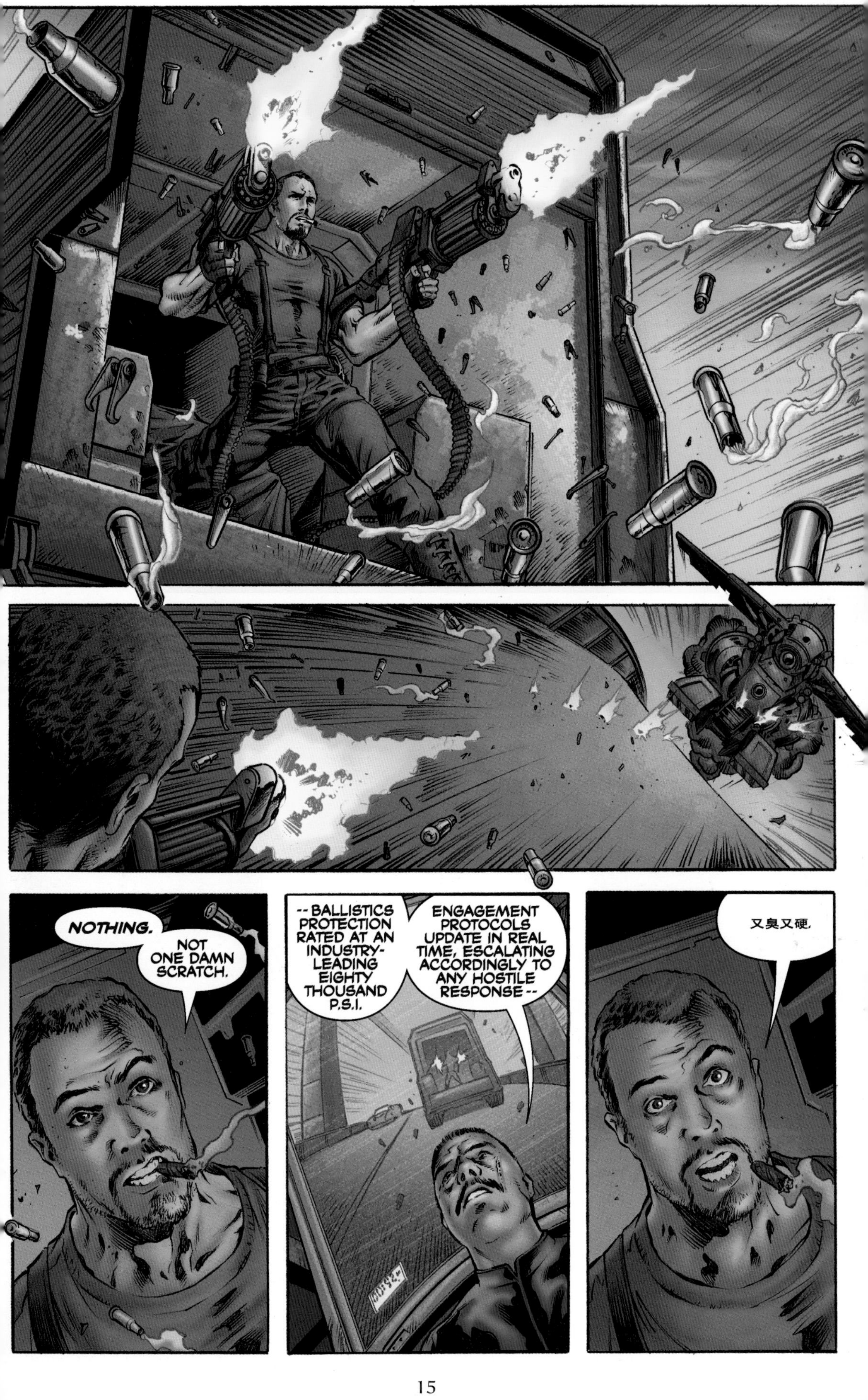
NOTHING.
NOT ONE DAMN SCRATCH.
-- BALLISTICS PROTECTION RATED AT AN INDUSTRY-LEADING EIGHTY THOUSAND P.S.I.
ENGAGEMENT PROTOCOLS UPDATE IN REAL TIME, ESCALATING ACCORDINGLY TO ANY HOSTILE RESPONSE --
又臭又硬,

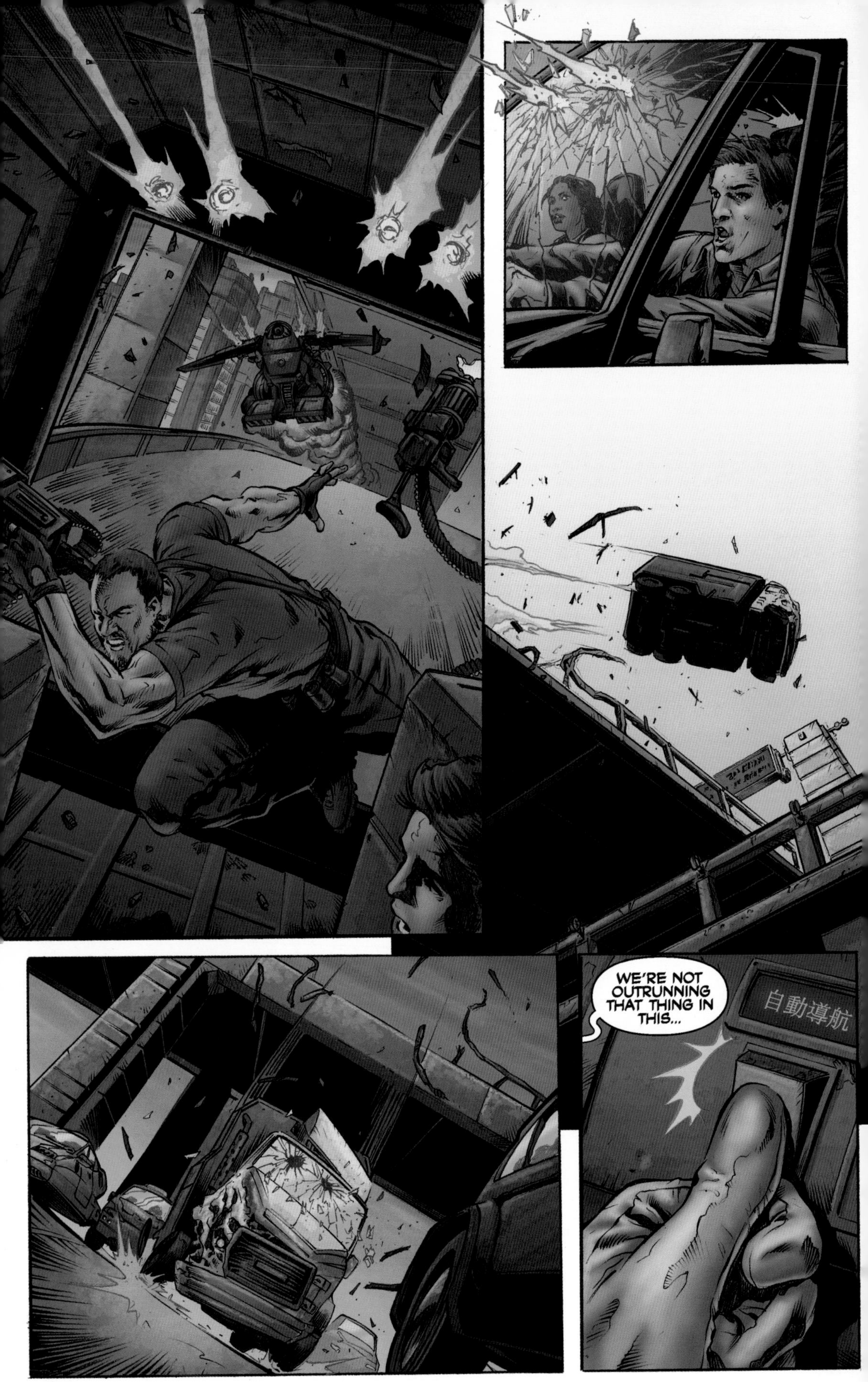
WE'RE NOT OUTRUNNING THAT THING IN THIS...
自動導航

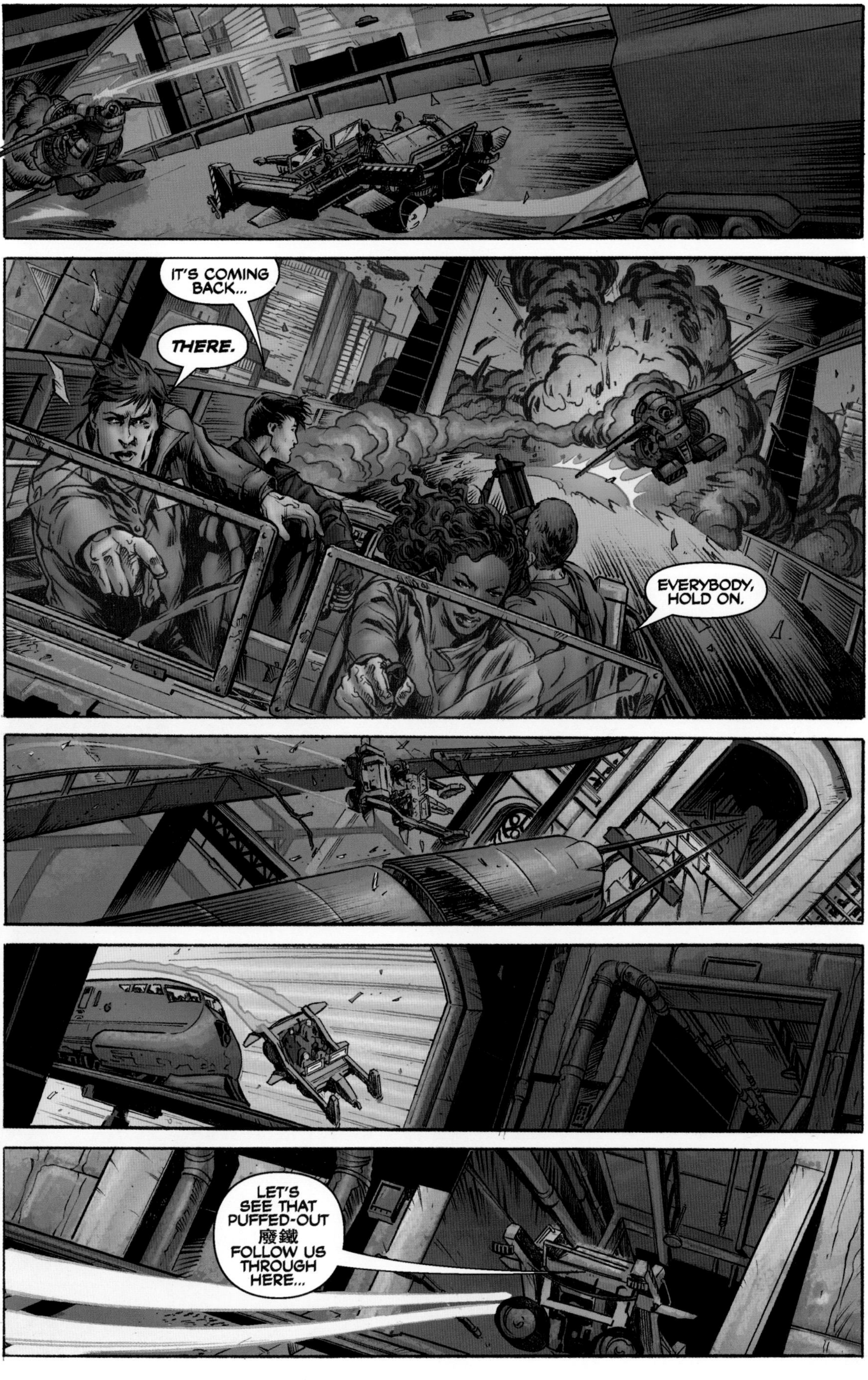
IT'S COMING BACK...
THERE.
EVERYBODY, HOLD ON.
LET'S SEE THAT PUFFED-OUT 廢鐵 FOLLOW US THROUGH HERE...

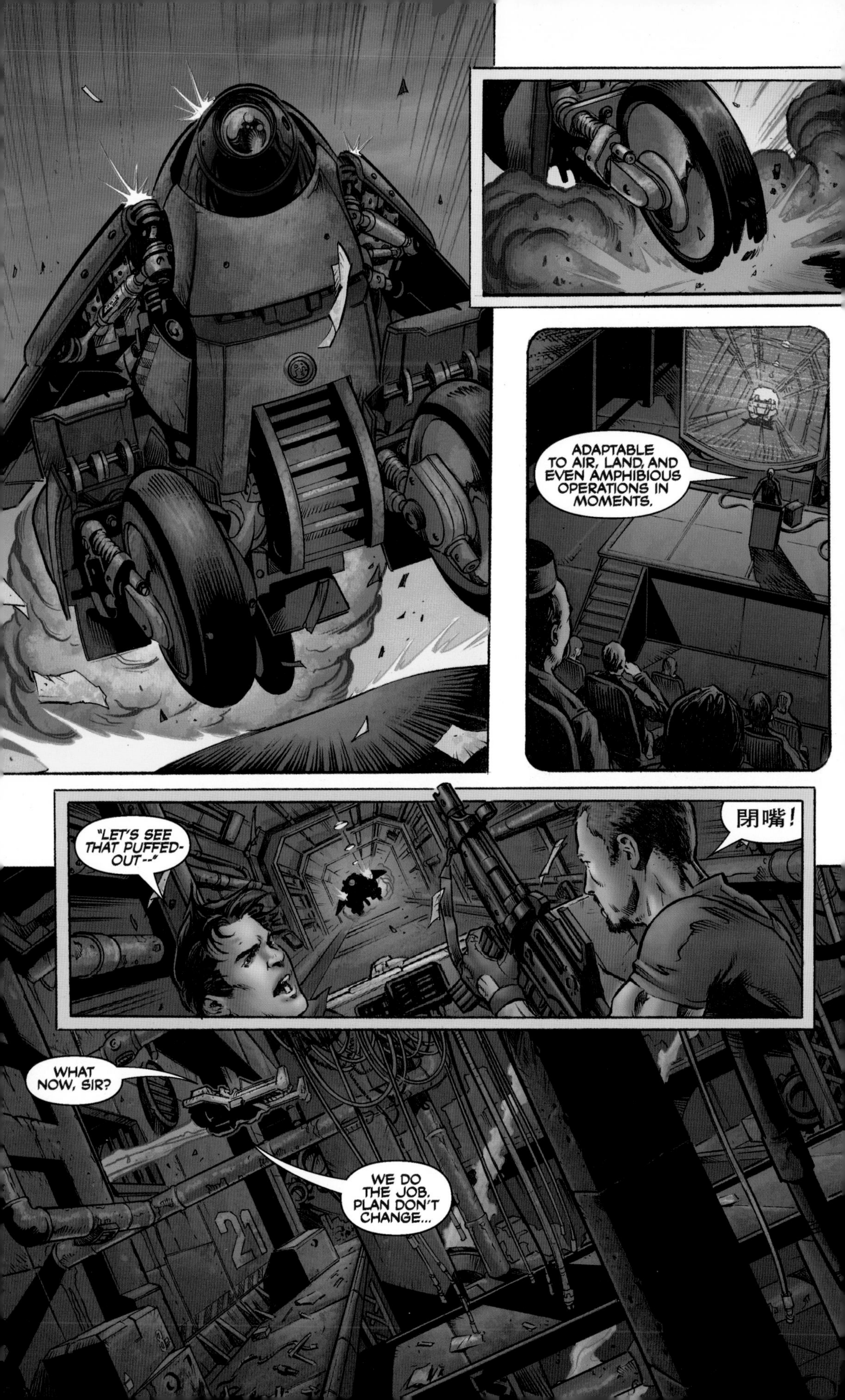
ADAPTABLE TO AIR, LAND, AND EVEN AMPHIBIOUS OPERATIONS IN MOMENTS.
"LET'S SEE THAT PUFFED-OUT--"
閉嘴!
WHAT NOW, SIR?
WE DO THE JOB. PLAN DON'T CHANGE...

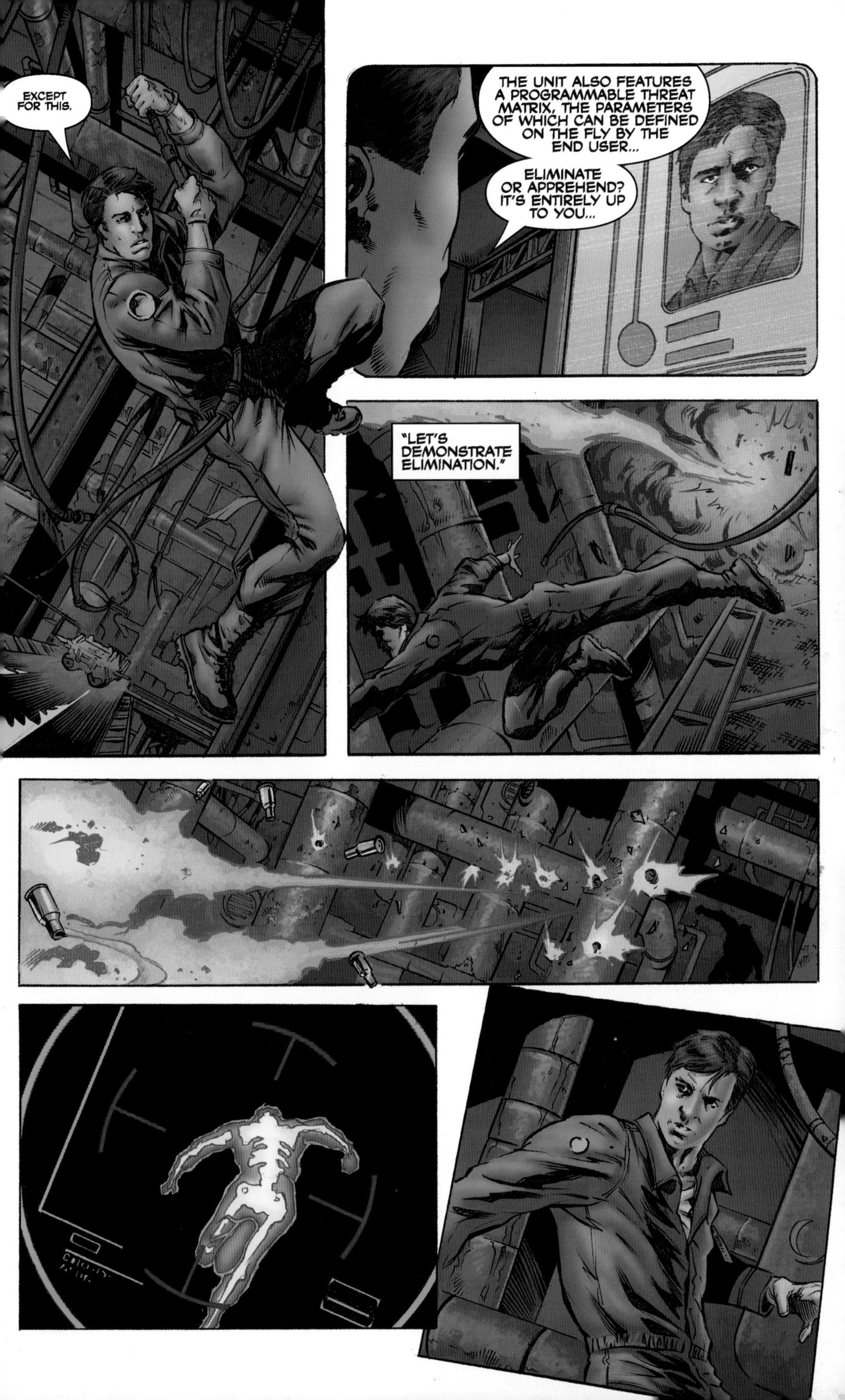
EXCEPT FOR THIS.
THE UNIT ALSO FEATURES A PROGRAMMABLE THREAT MATRIX, THE PARAMETERS OF WHICH CAN BE DEFINED ON THE FLY BY THE END USER...
ELIMINATE OR APPREHEND? IT'S ENTIRELY UP TO YOU...
"LET'S DEMONSTRATE ELIMINATION."

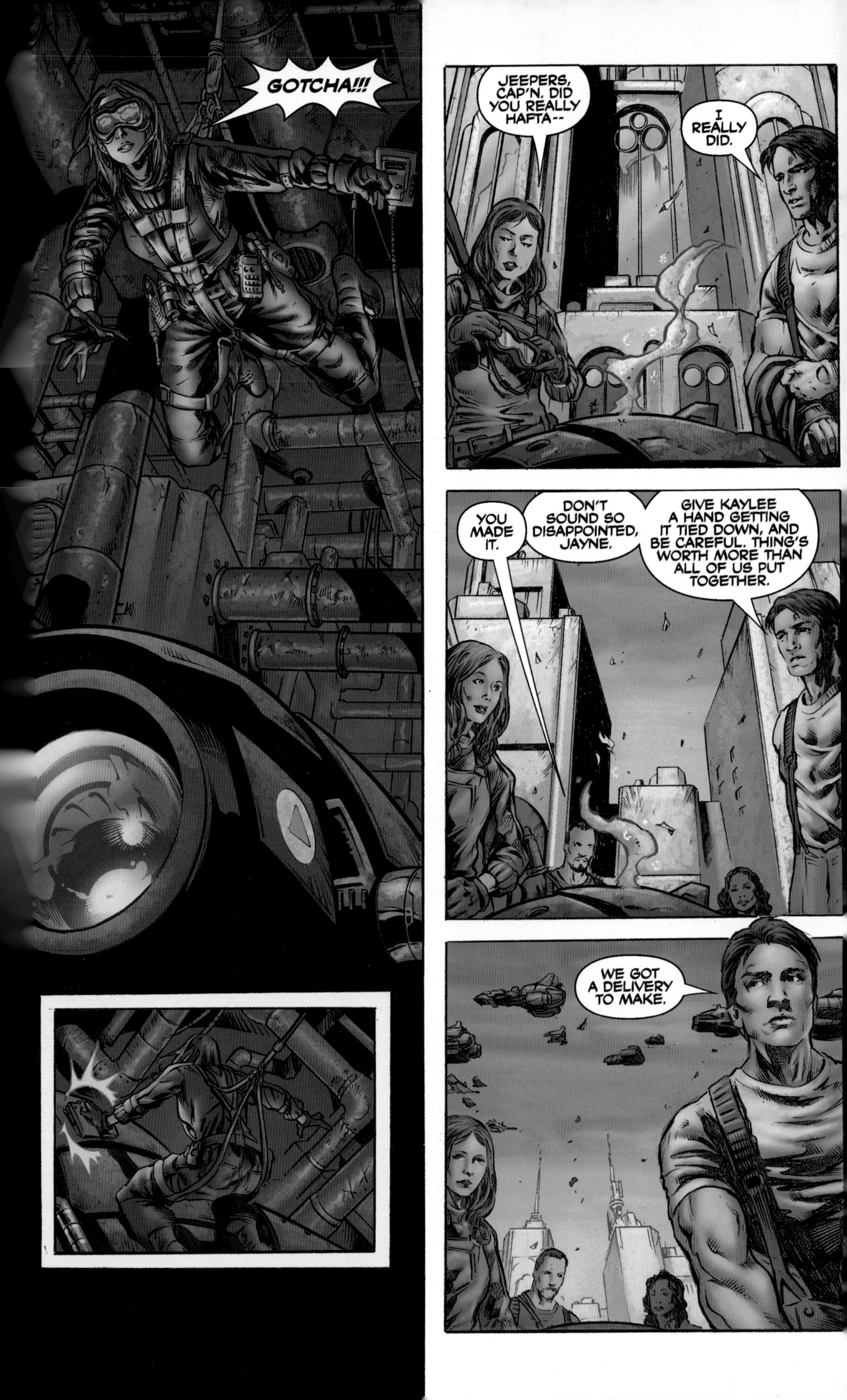
GOTCHA!!!
JEEPERS, CAP'N, DID YOU REALLY HAFTA--
I REALLY DID.
YOU MADE IT.
DON'T SOUND SO DISAPPOINTED, JAYNE.
GIVE KAYLEE A HAND GETTING IT TIED DOWN, AND BE CAREFUL. THING'S WORTH MORE THAN ALL OF US PUT TOGETHER.
WE GOT A DELIVERY TO MAKE.

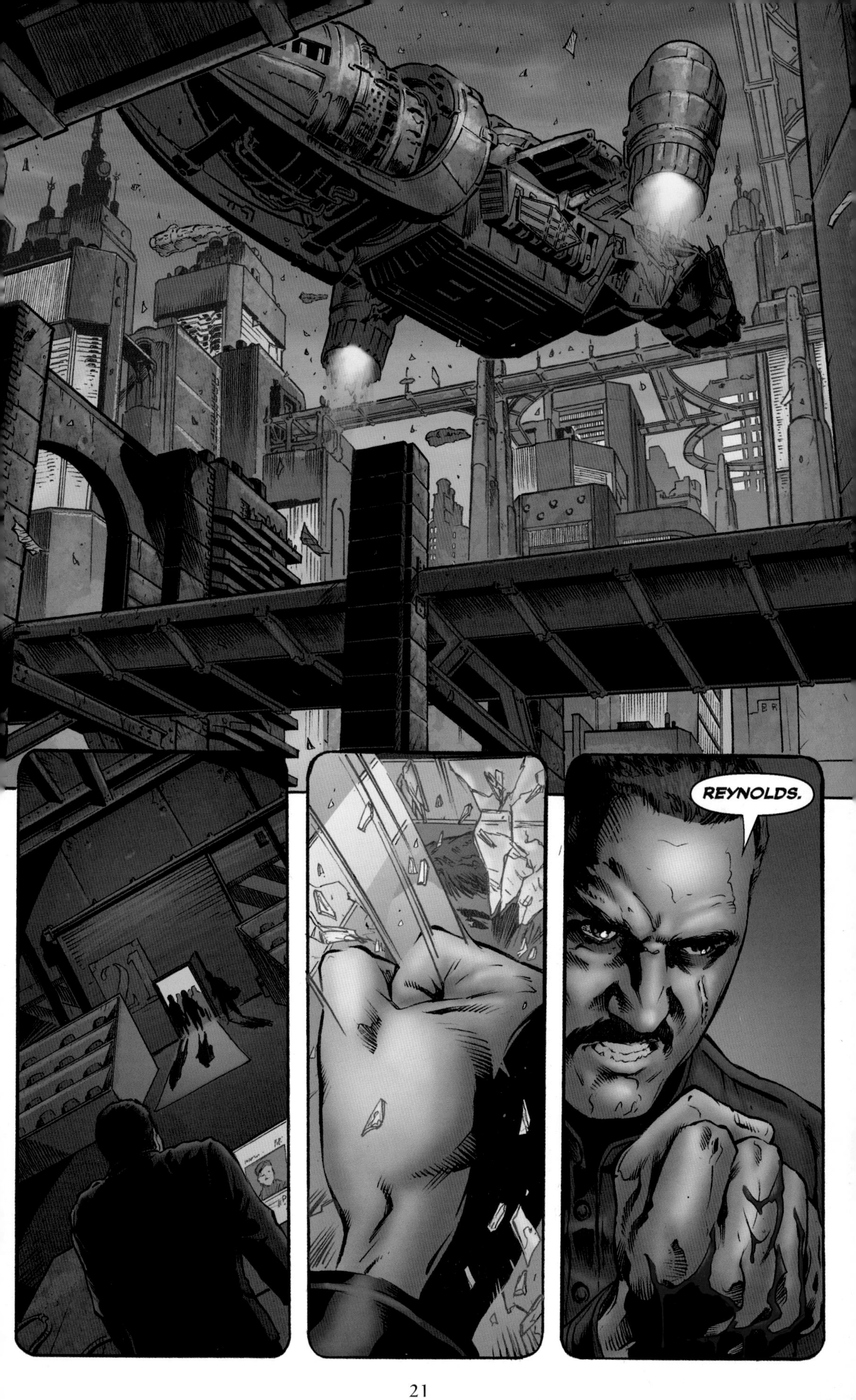
REYNOLDS.

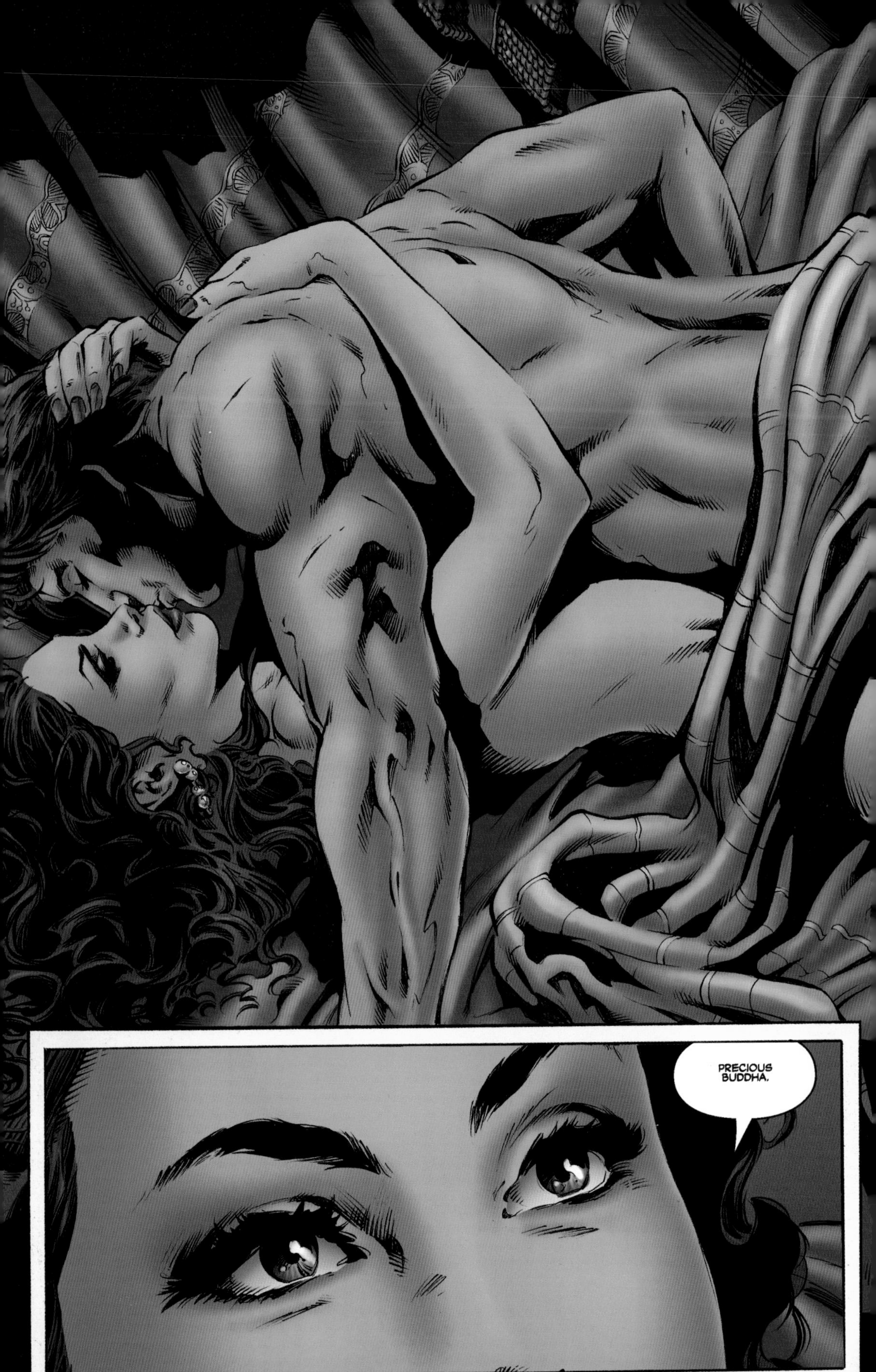
PRECIOUS BUDDHA,

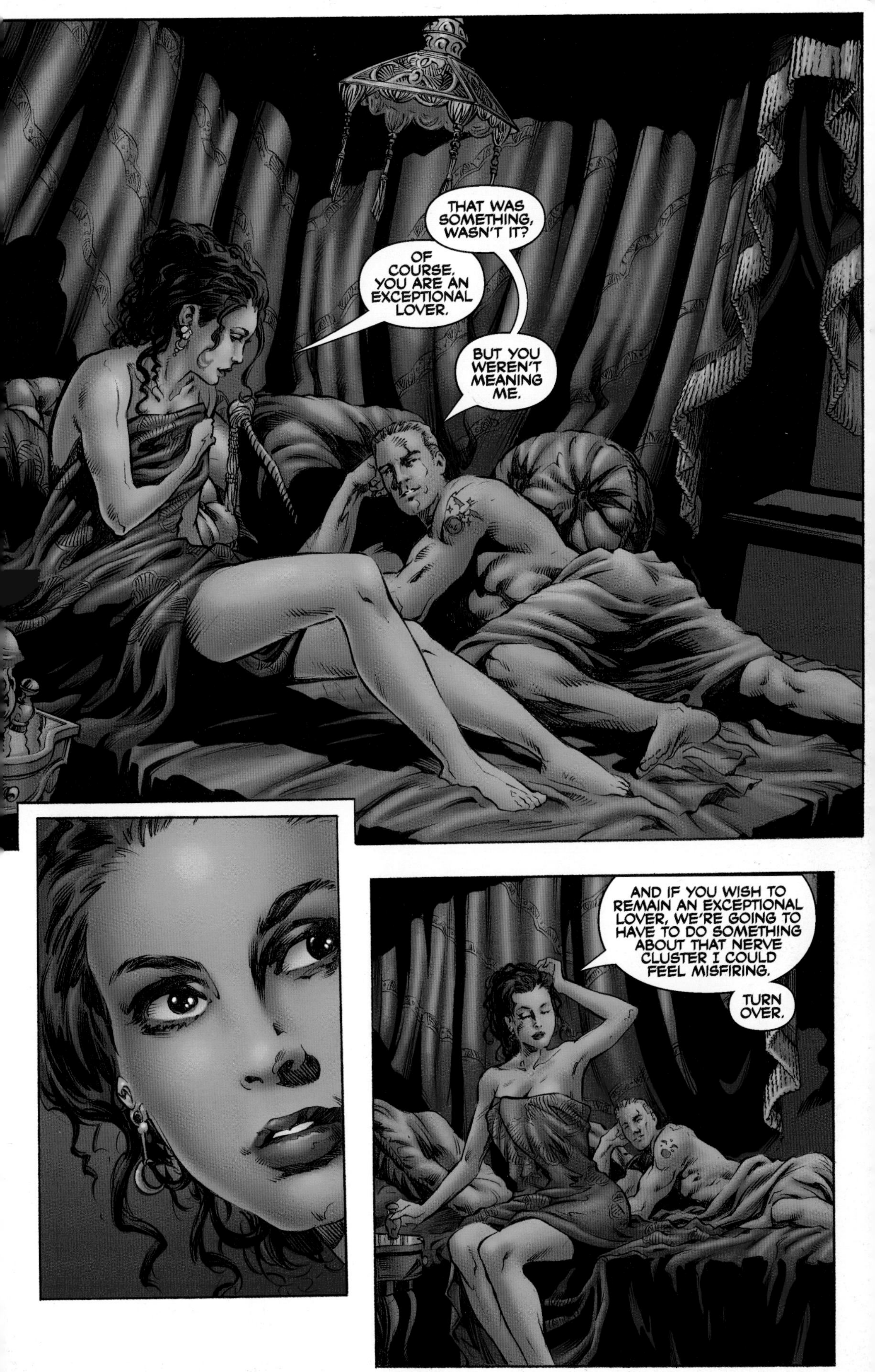
THAT WAS SOMETHING, WASN'T IT?
OF COURSE. YOU ARE AN EXCEPTIONAL LOVER.
BUT YOU WEREN'T MEANING ME.
AND IF YOU WISH TO REMAIN AN EXCEPTIONAL LOVER, WE'RE GOING TO HAVE TO DO SOMETHING ABOUT THAT NERVE CLUSTER I COULD FEEL MISFIRING.
TURN OVER.

I DON'T HOLD IT AGAINST YOU.

BEST NOT TO DWELL ON AN OLD SOLDIER LIKE ME. OR HIS WOUNDS.

THERE'S MUCH MORE TO YOU THAN THAT, EPHRAIM.

AND AS I EXPECTED, YOU'RE COMPLETELY OUT OF ALIGNMENT.

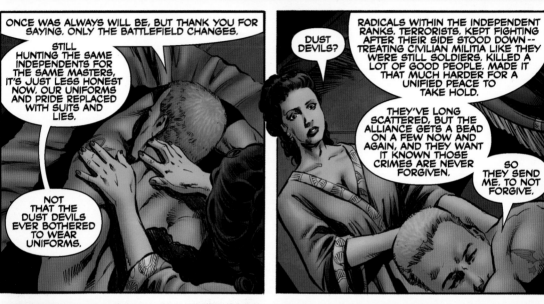

ONCE WAS ALWAYS WILL BE, BUT THANK YOU FOR SAYING. ONLY THE BATTLEFIELD CHANGES.

STILL HUNTING THE SAME INDEPENDENTS FOR THE SAME MASTERS, IT'S JUST LESS HONEST NOW. OUR UNIFORMS AND PRIDE REPLACED WITH SUITS AND LIES.

NOT THAT THE DUST DEVILS EVER BOTHERED TO WEAR UNIFORMS.

DUST DEVILS?

RADICALS WITHIN THE INDEPENDENT RANKS, TERRORISTS, KEPT FIGHTING AFTER THEIR SIDE STOOD DOWN -- TREATING CIVILIAN MILITIA LIKE THEY WERE STILL SOLDIERS, KILLED A LOT OF GOOD PEOPLE. MADE IT THAT MUCH HARDER FOR A UNIFIED PEACE TO TAKE HOLD.

THEY'VE LONG SCATTERED, BUT THE ALLIANCE GETS A BEAD ON A FEW NOW AND AGAIN, AND THEY WANT IT KNOWN THOSE CRIMES ARE NEVER FORGIVEN.

SO THEY SEND ME. TO NOT FORGIVE.

I'M SURPRISED YOU DON'T KNOW THE TERM. "DUST DEVILS" IS SPOKEN WITH PRIDE OUT HERE ON THE RIM. LOCAL HEROES TO SOME FOOLS, YOU KNOW THE TYPE:

HEADSTRONG, SUSPICIOUS, USUALLY SOME KIND OF PETTY THIEF --

KKRAKK

THANKS FOR THE ADJUSTMENT. I FEEL A WORLD BETTER ALREADY.

ANYTIME.

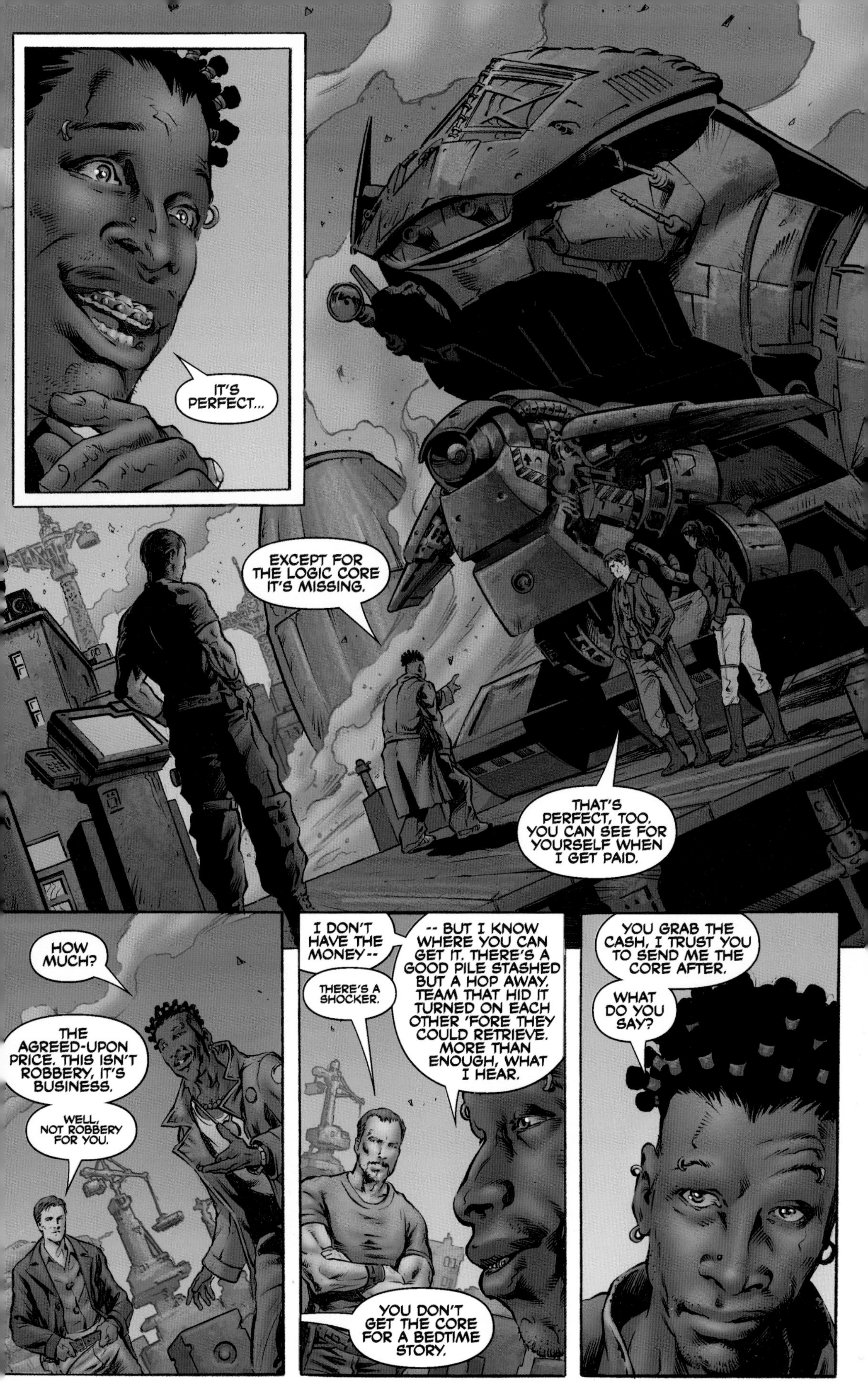
IT'S PERFECT...
EXCEPT FOR THE LOGIC CORE IT'S MISSING.
THAT'S PERFECT, TOO. YOU CAN SEE FOR YOURSELF WHEN I GET PAID.
HOW MUCH?
THE AGREED-UPON PRICE. THIS ISN'T ROBBERY, IT'S BUSINESS.
WELL, NOT ROBBERY FOR YOU.
I DON'T HAVE THE MONEY--
THERE'S A SHOCKER.
-- BUT I KNOW WHERE YOU CAN GET IT. THERE'S A GOOD PILE STASHED BUT A HOP AWAY. TEAM THAT HID IT TURNED ON EACH OTHER 'FORE THEY COULD RETRIEVE. MORE THAN ENOUGH, WHAT I HEAR.
YOU DON'T GET THE CORE FOR A BEDTIME STORY.
YOU GRAB THE CASH, I TRUST YOU TO SEND ME THE CORE AFTER.
WHAT DO YOU SAY?

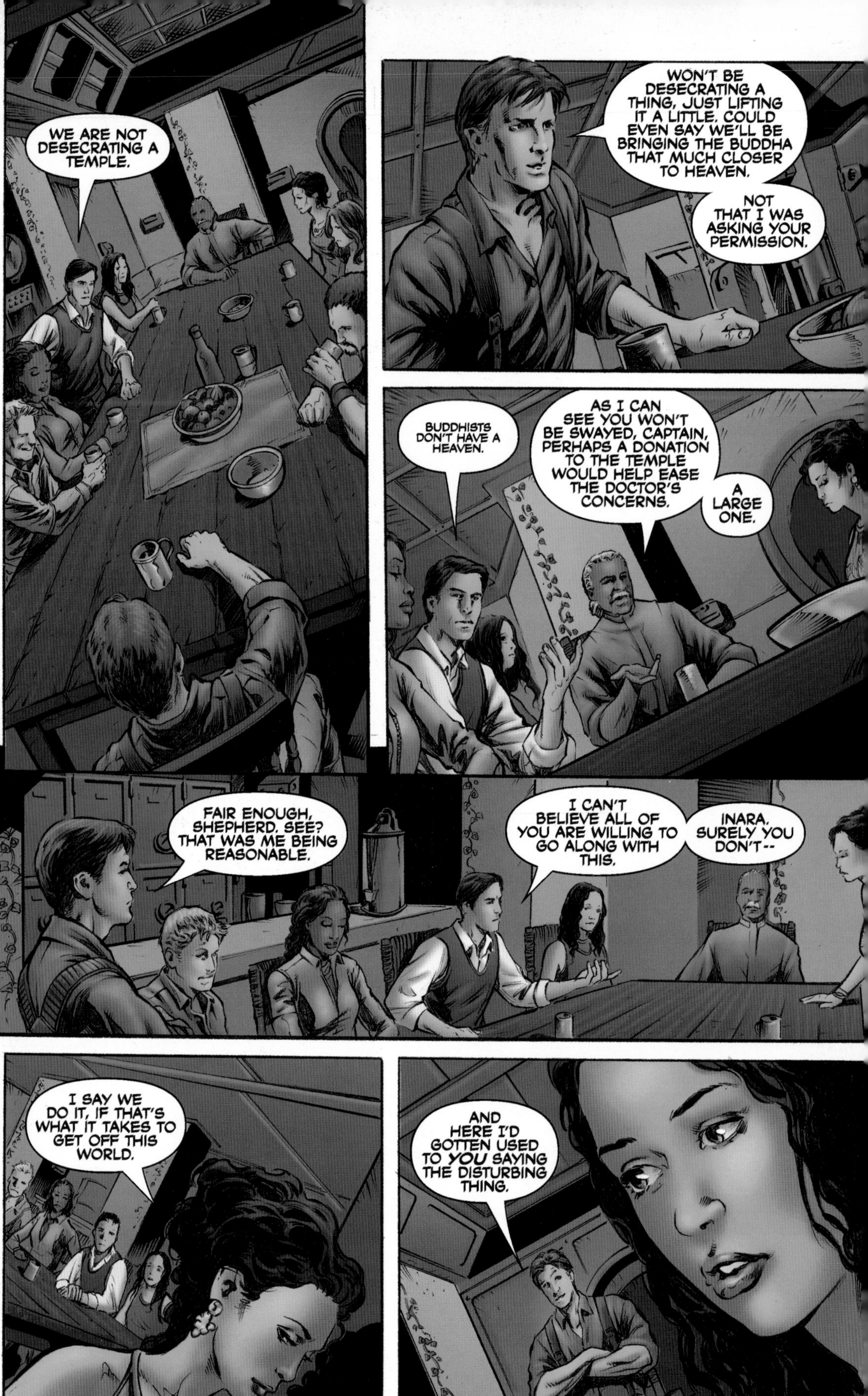
WE ARE NOT DESECRATING A TEMPLE.
WON'T BE DESECRATING A THING, JUST LIFTING IT A LITTLE. COULD EVEN SAY WE'LL BE BRINGING THE BUDDHA THAT MUCH CLOSER TO HEAVEN.
NOT THAT I WAS ASKING YOUR PERMISSION.
BUDDHISTS DON'T HAVE A HEAVEN.
AS I CAN SEE YOU WON'T BE SWAYED, CAPTAIN, PERHAPS A DONATION TO THE TEMPLE WOULD HELP EASE THE DOCTOR'S CONCERNS.
A LARGE ONE.
FAIR ENOUGH, SHEPHERD. SEE? THAT WAS ME BEING REASONABLE.
I CAN'T BELIEVE ALL OF YOU ARE WILLING TO GO ALONG WITH THIS.
INARA, SURELY YOU DON'T--
I SAY WE DO IT, IF THAT'S WHAT IT TAKES TO GET OFF THIS WORLD.
AND HERE I'D GOTTEN USED TO YOU SAYING THE DISTURBING THING.

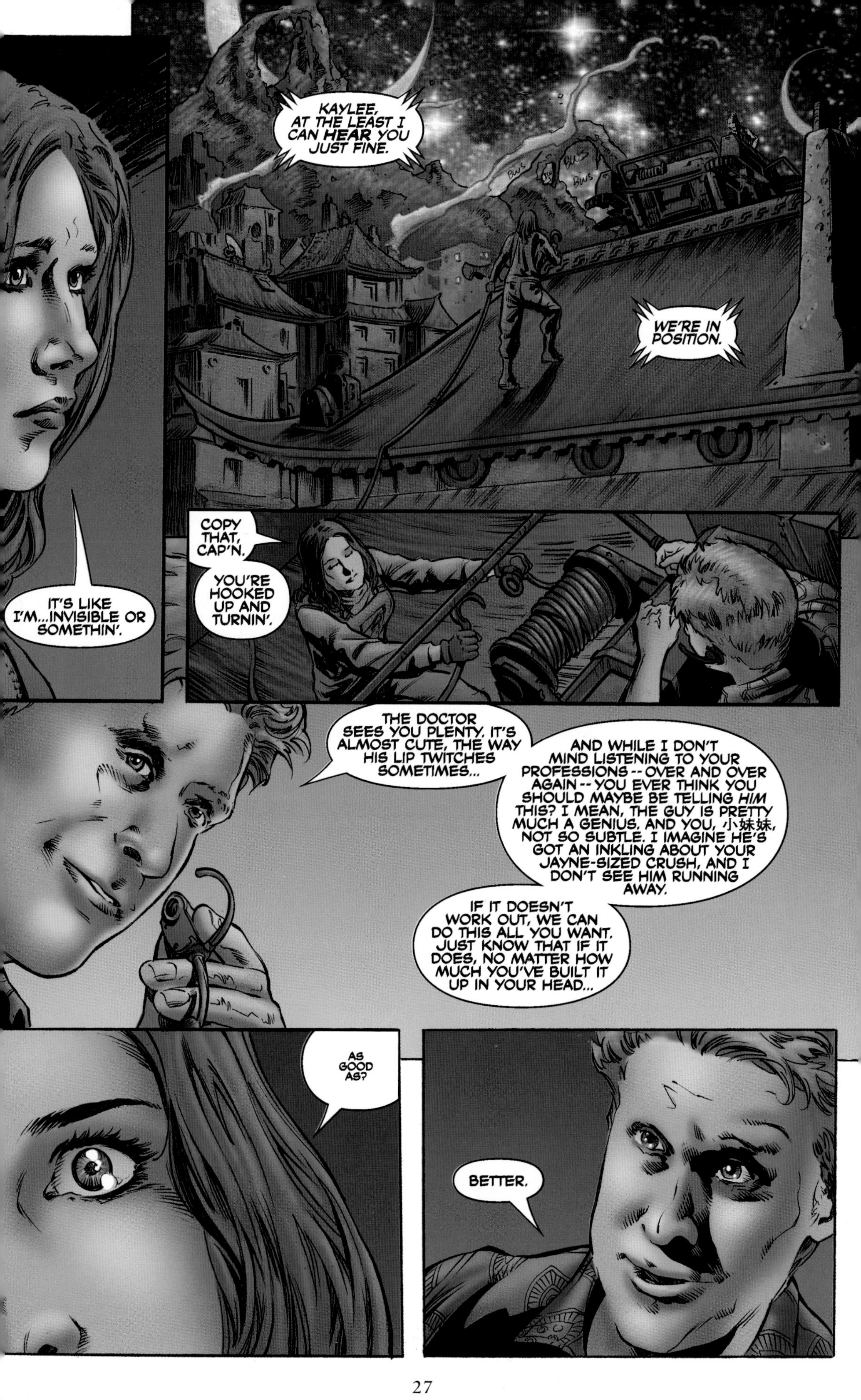
IT'S LIKE I'M...INVISIBLE OR SOMETHIN'.
KAYLEE, AT THE LEAST I CAN **HEAR** YOU JUST FINE.
WE'RE IN POSITION.
COPY THAT, CAP'N.
YOU'RE HOOKED UP AND TURNIN'.
THE DOCTOR SEES YOU PLENTY. IT'S ALMOST CUTE, THE WAY HIS LIP TWITCHES SOMETIMES...
AND WHILE I DON'T MIND LISTENING TO YOUR PROFESSIONS -- OVER AND OVER AGAIN -- YOU EVER THINK YOU SHOULD MAYBE BE TELLING *HIM* THIS? I MEAN, THE GUY IS PRETTY MUCH A GENIUS. AND YOU, 小妹妹, NOT SO SUBTLE. I IMAGINE HE'S GOT AN INKLING ABOUT YOUR JAYNE-SIZED CRUSH, AND I DON'T SEE HIM RUNNING AWAY.
IF IT DOESN'T WORK OUT, WE CAN DO THIS ALL YOU WANT. JUST KNOW THAT IF IT DOES, NO MATTER HOW MUCH YOU'VE BUILT IT UP IN YOUR HEAD...
AS GOOD AS?
BETTER.

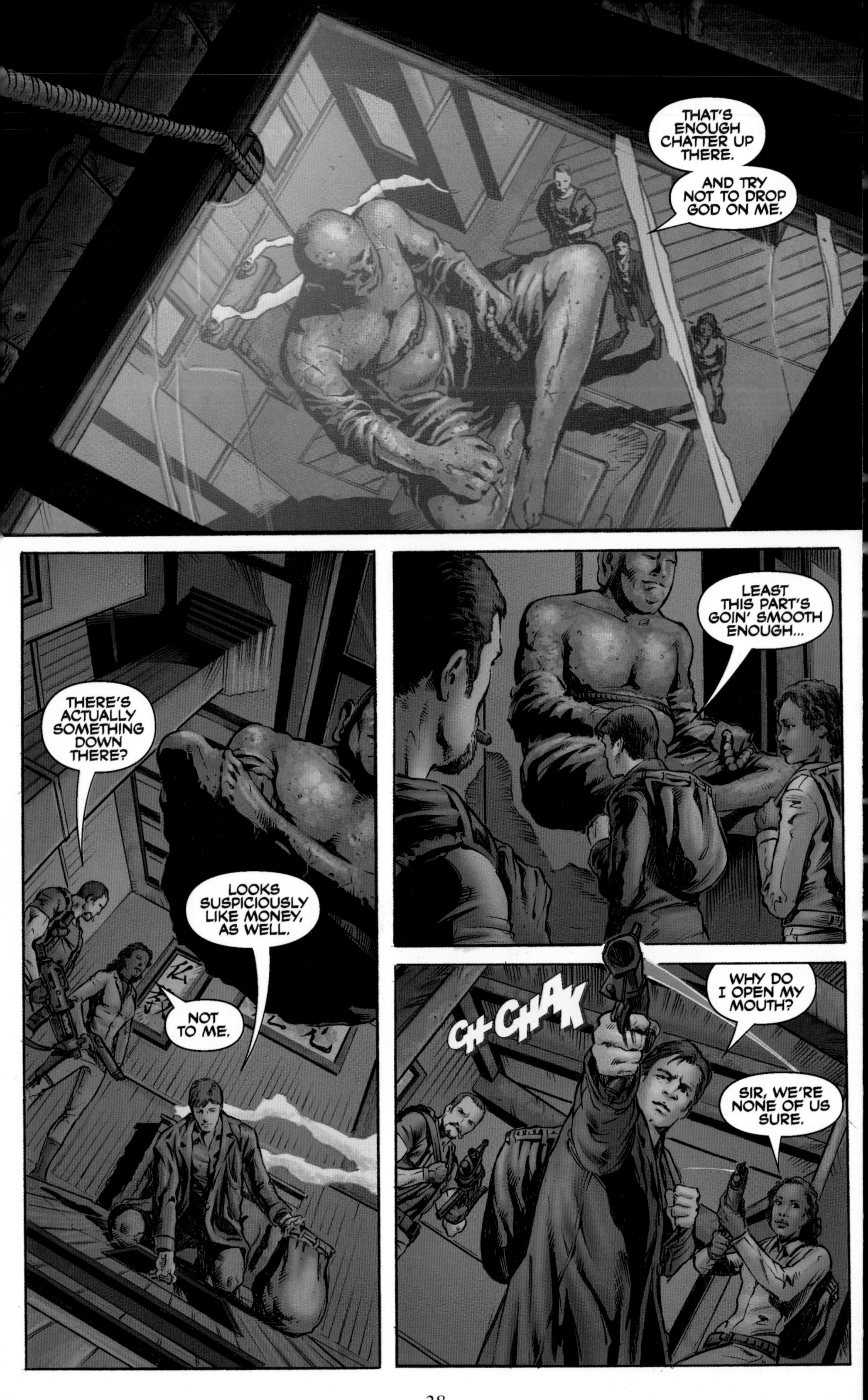
THAT'S ENOUGH CHATTER UP THERE.
AND TRY NOT TO DROP GOD ON ME.
THERE'S ACTUALLY SOMETHING DOWN THERE?
LOOKS SUSPICIOUSLY LIKE MONEY, AS WELL.
NOT TO ME.
LEAST THIS PART'S GOIN' SMOOTH ENOUGH...
CH-CHAK
WHY DO I OPEN MY MOUTH?
SIR, WE'RE NONE OF US SURE.

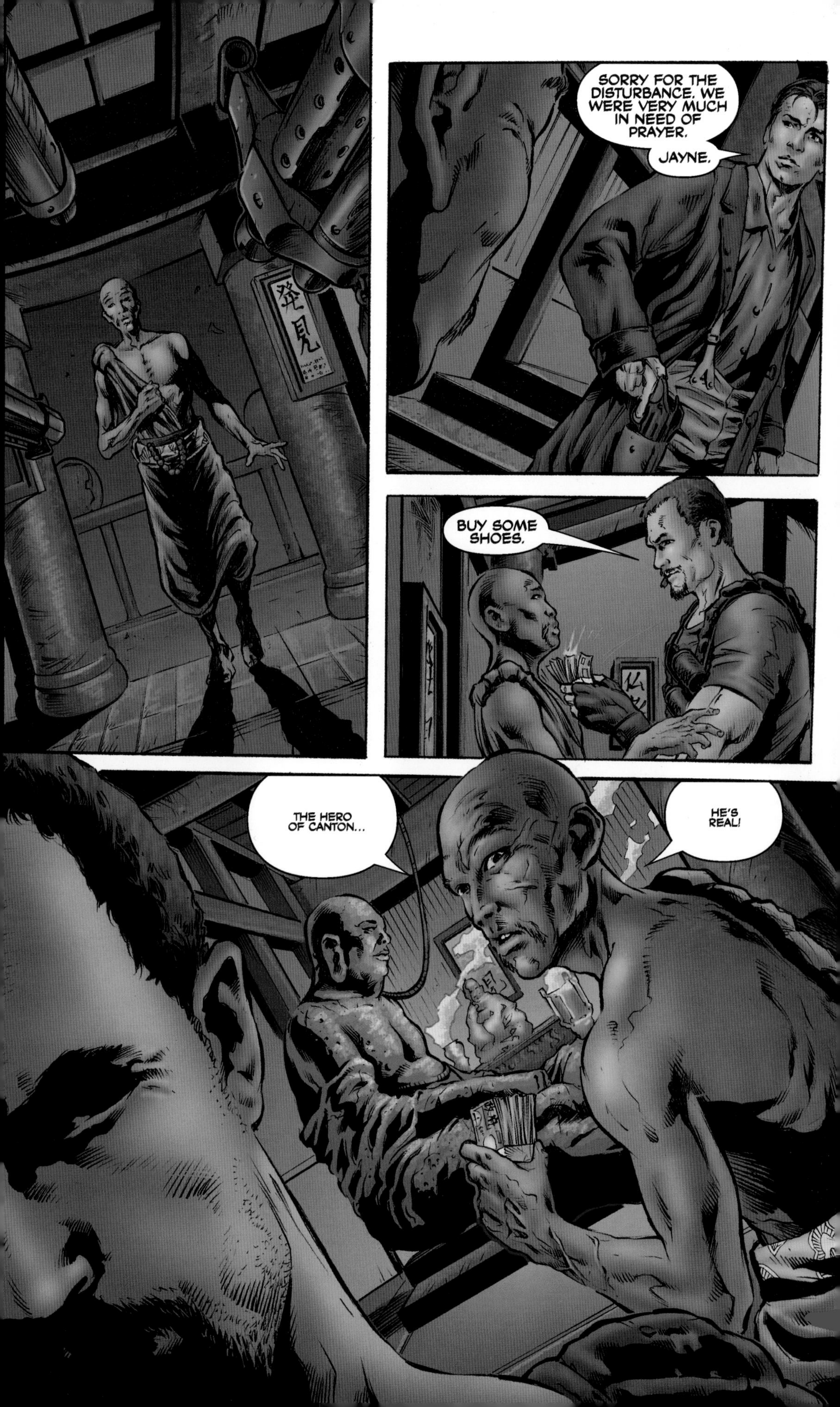
SORRY FOR THE DISTURBANCE. WE WERE VERY MUCH IN NEED OF PRAYER.
JAYNE.
BUY SOME SHOES.
THE HERO OF CANTON...
HE'S REAL!

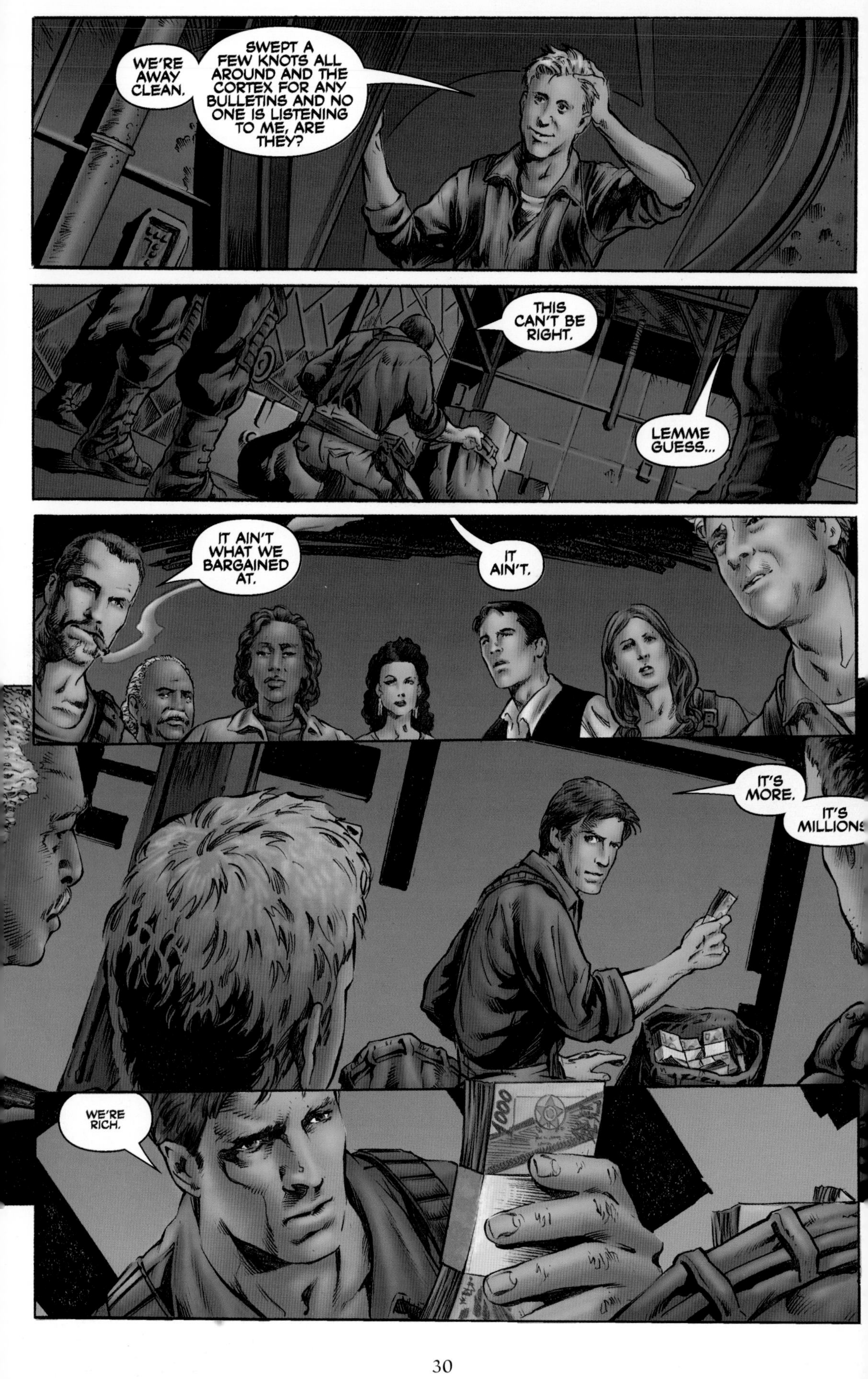
WE'RE AWAY CLEAN.
SWEPT A FEW KNOTS ALL AROUND AND THE CORTEX FOR ANY BULLETINS AND NO ONE IS LISTENING TO ME, ARE THEY?
THIS CAN'T BE RIGHT.
LEMME GUESS...
IT AIN'T WHAT WE BARGAINED AT.
IT AIN'T.
IT'S MORE.
IT'S MILLIONS
WE'RE RICH.

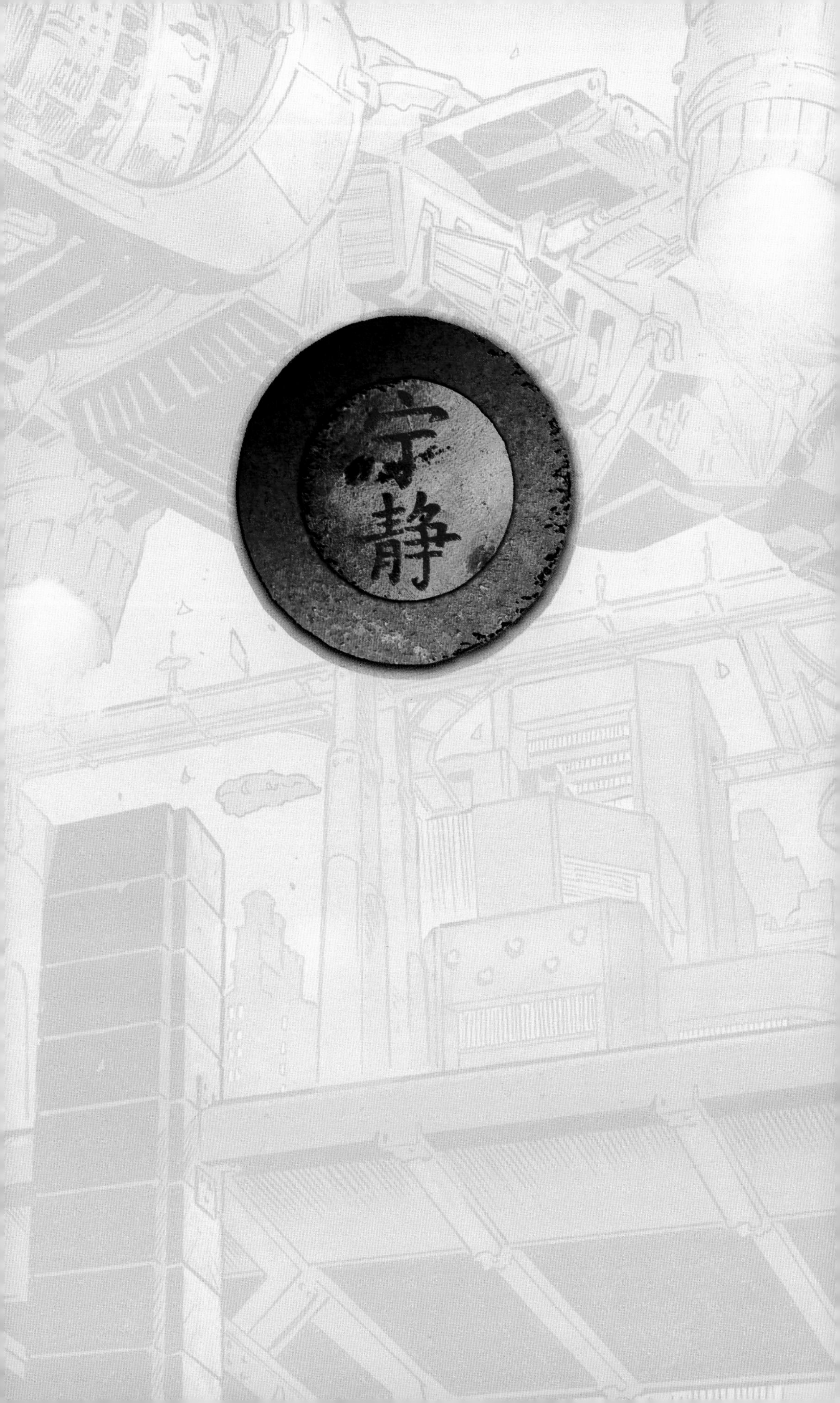

守静

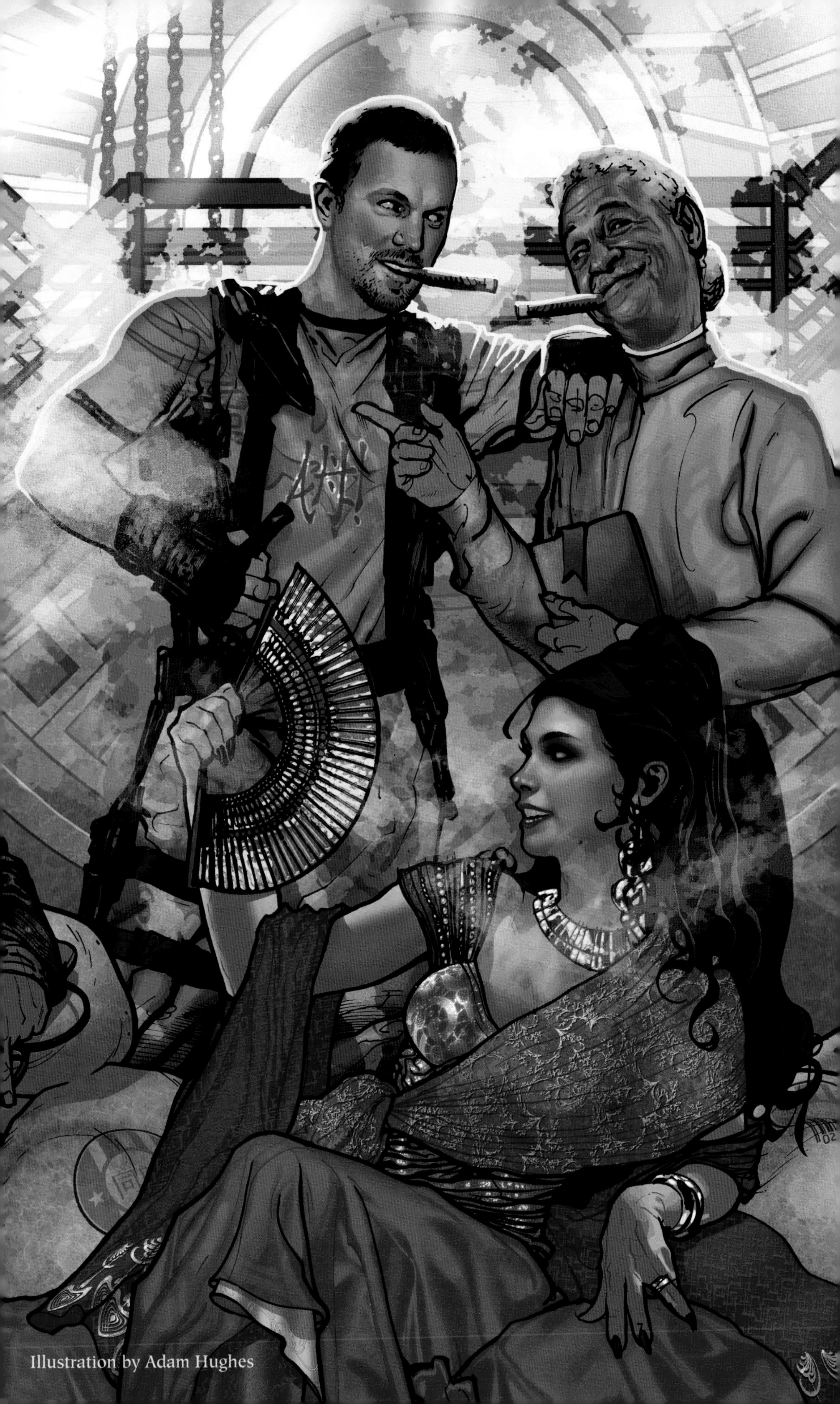

Illustration by Adam Hughes

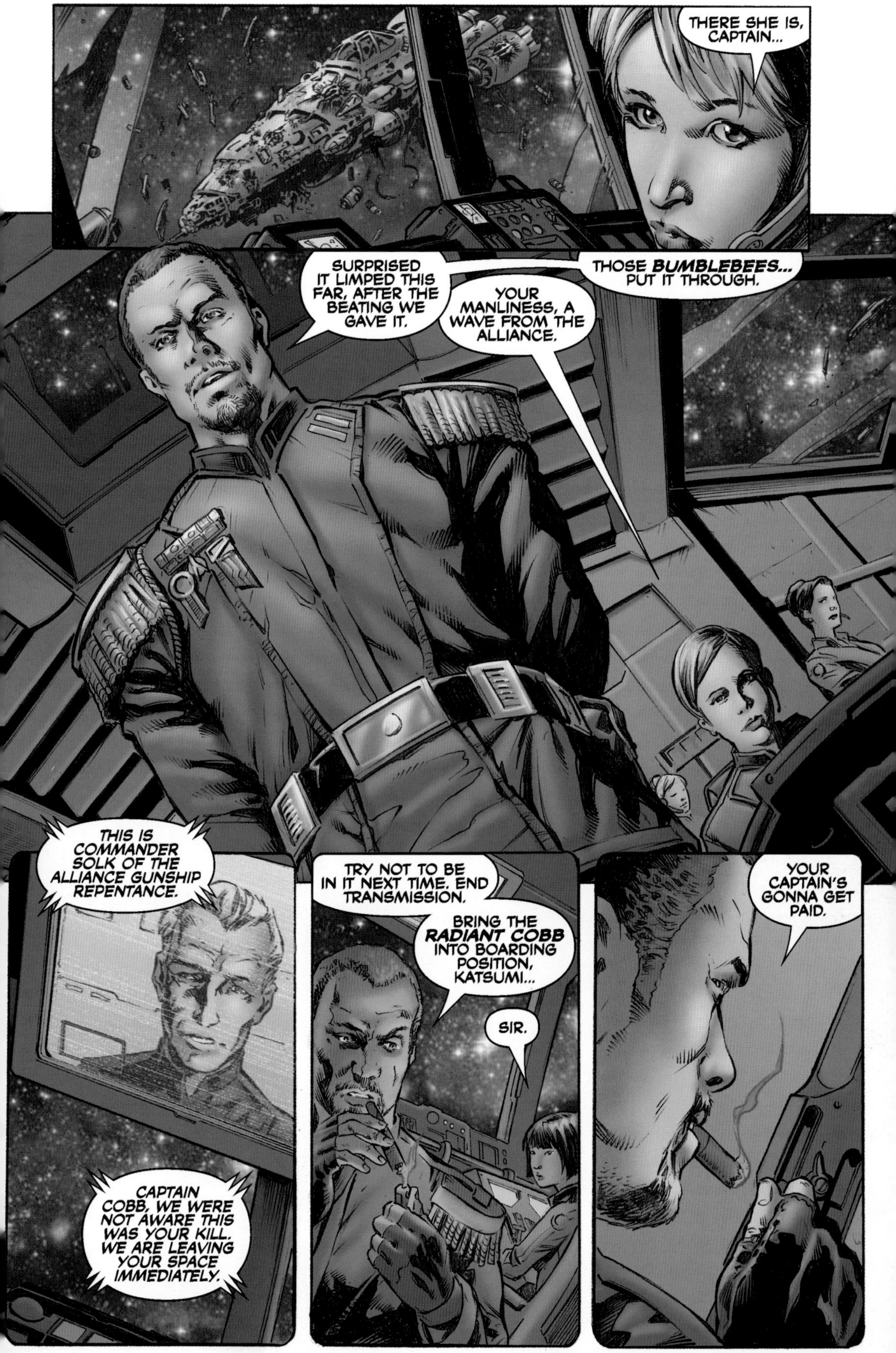

THERE SHE IS, CAPTAIN...
SURPRISED IT LIMPED THIS FAR, AFTER THE BEATING WE GAVE IT.
THOSE BUMBLEBEES... PUT IT THROUGH.
YOUR MANLINESS, A WAVE FROM THE ALLIANCE.
THIS IS COMMANDER SOLK OF THE ALLIANCE GUNSHIP REPENTANCE.
CAPTAIN COBB, WE WERE NOT AWARE THIS WAS YOUR KILL. WE ARE LEAVING YOUR SPACE IMMEDIATELY.
TRY NOT TO BE IN IT NEXT TIME. END TRANSMISSION.
BRING THE RADIANT COBB INTO BOARDING POSITION, KATSUMI...
SIR.
YOUR CAPTAIN'S GONNA GET PAID.

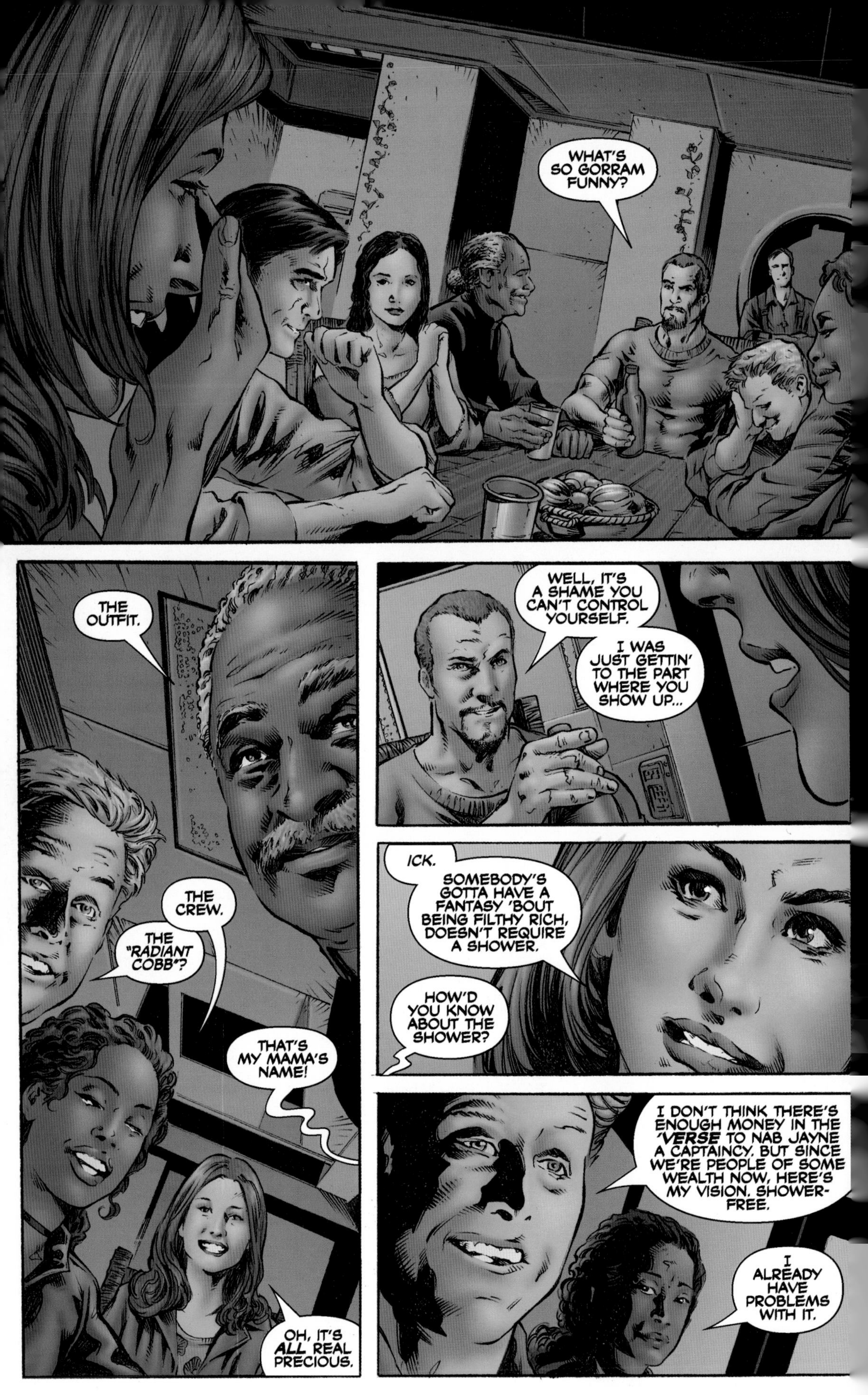
WHAT'S SO GORRAM FUNNY?
THE OUTFIT.
THE CREW.
THE "RADIANT COBB"?
THAT'S MY MAMA'S NAME!
OH, IT'S ALL REAL PRECIOUS.
WELL, IT'S A SHAME YOU CAN'T CONTROL YOURSELF.
I WAS JUST GETTIN' TO THE PART WHERE YOU SHOW UP...
ICK.
SOMEBODY'S GOTTA HAVE A FANTASY 'BOUT BEING FILTHY RICH, DOESN'T REQUIRE A SHOWER.
HOW'D YOU KNOW ABOUT THE SHOWER?
I DON'T THINK THERE'S ENOUGH MONEY IN THE 'VERSE TO NAB JAYNE A CAPTAINCY. BUT SINCE WE'RE PEOPLE OF SOME WEALTH NOW, HERE'S MY VISION. SHOWER-FREE.
I ALREADY HAVE PROBLEMS WITH IT.

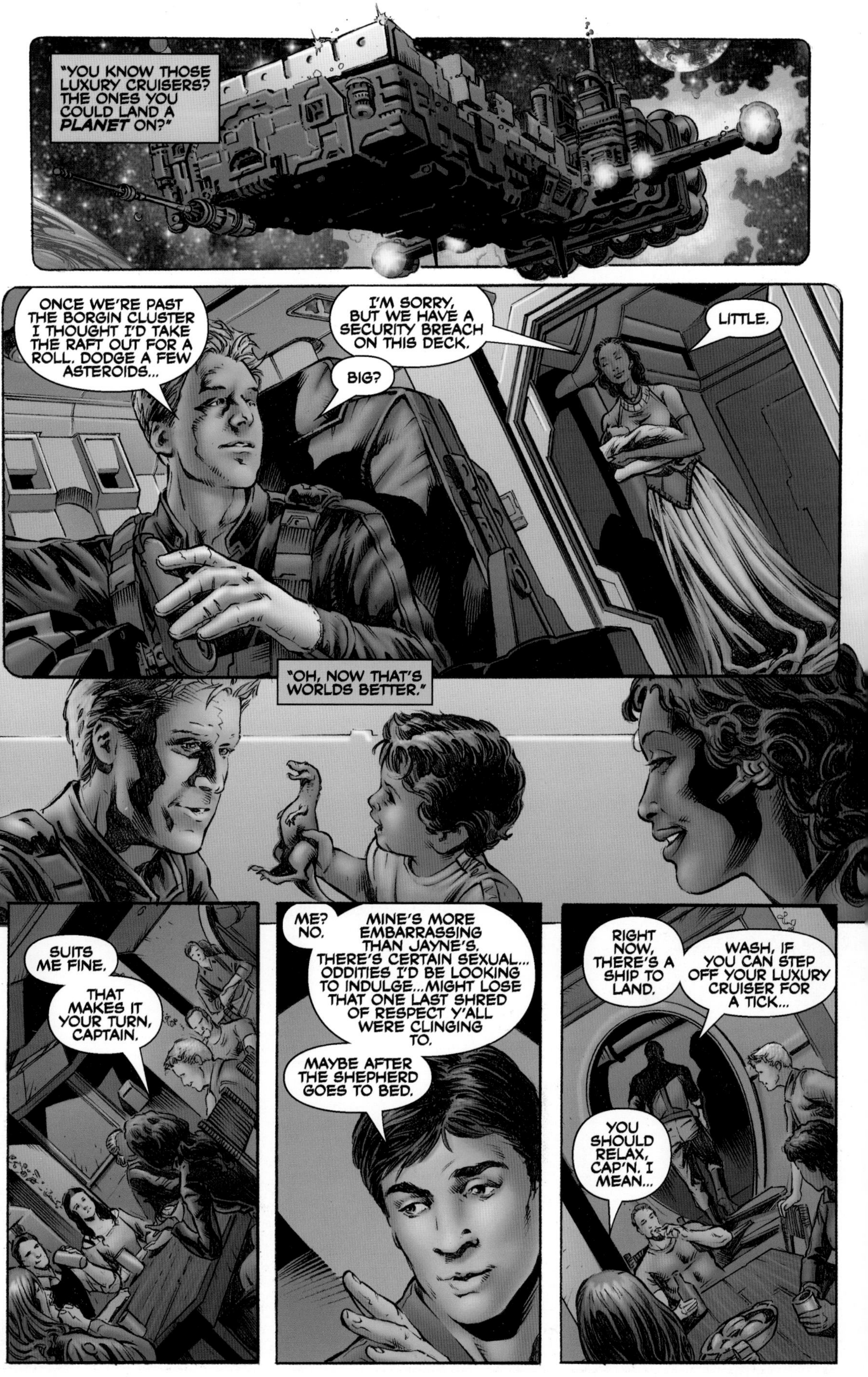
"YOU KNOW THOSE LUXURY CRUISERS? THE ONES YOU COULD LAND A PLANET ON?"
ONCE WE'RE PAST THE BORGIN CLUSTER I THOUGHT I'D TAKE THE RAFT OUT FOR A ROLL. DODGE A FEW ASTEROIDS...
I'M SORRY, BUT WE HAVE A SECURITY BREACH ON THIS DECK.
BIG?
LITTLE.
"OH, NOW THAT'S WORLDS BETTER."
SUITS ME FINE.
THAT MAKES IT YOUR TURN, CAPTAIN.
ME? NO.
MINE'S MORE EMBARRASSING THAN JAYNE'S. THERE'S CERTAIN SEXUAL... ODDITIES I'D BE LOOKING TO INDULGE...MIGHT LOSE THAT ONE LAST SHRED OF RESPECT Y'ALL WERE CLINGING TO.
MAYBE AFTER THE SHEPHERD GOES TO BED.
RIGHT NOW, THERE'S A SHIP TO LAND.
WASH, IF YOU CAN STEP OFF YOUR LUXURY CRUISER FOR A TICK...
YOU SHOULD RELAX, CAP'N. I MEAN...

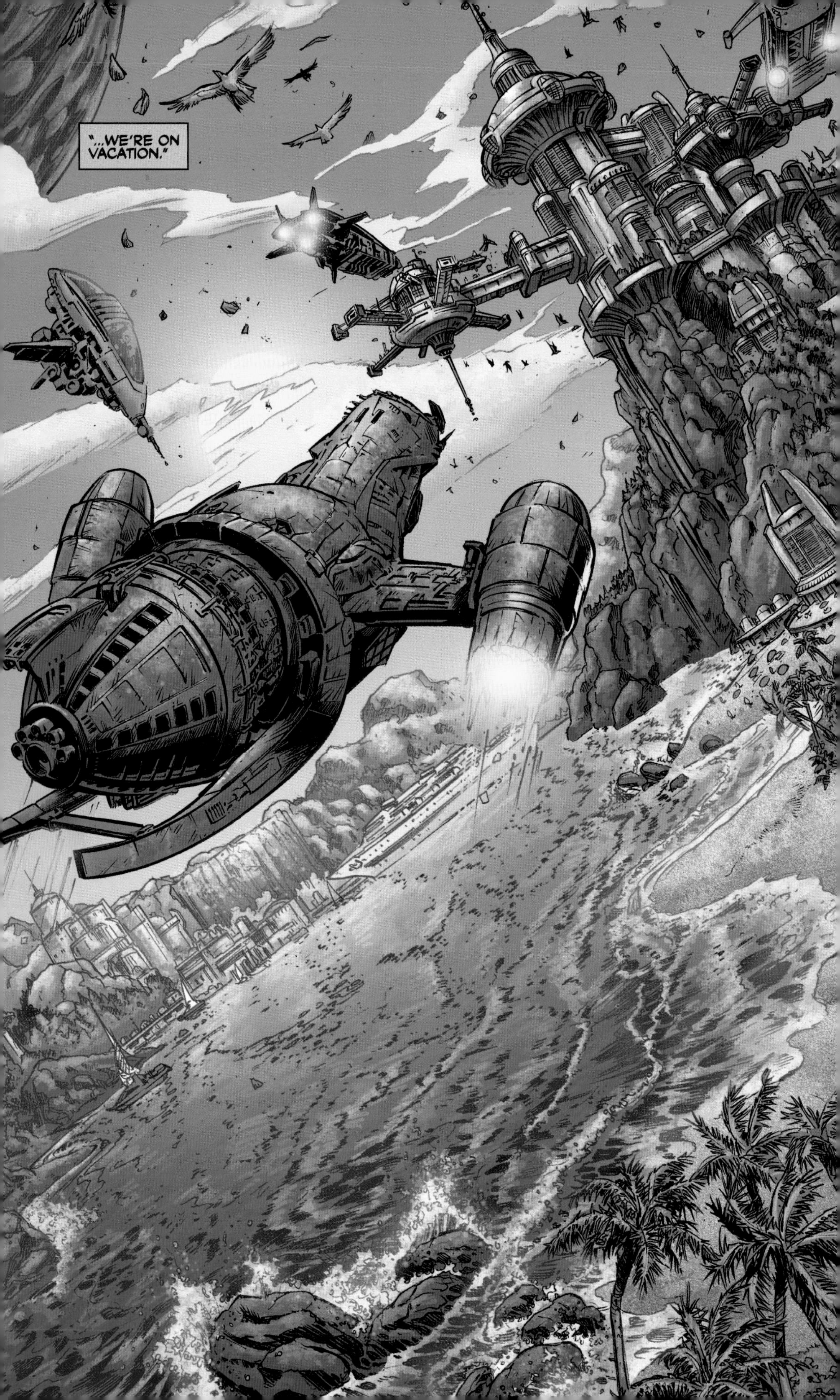
"...WE'RE ON VACATION."

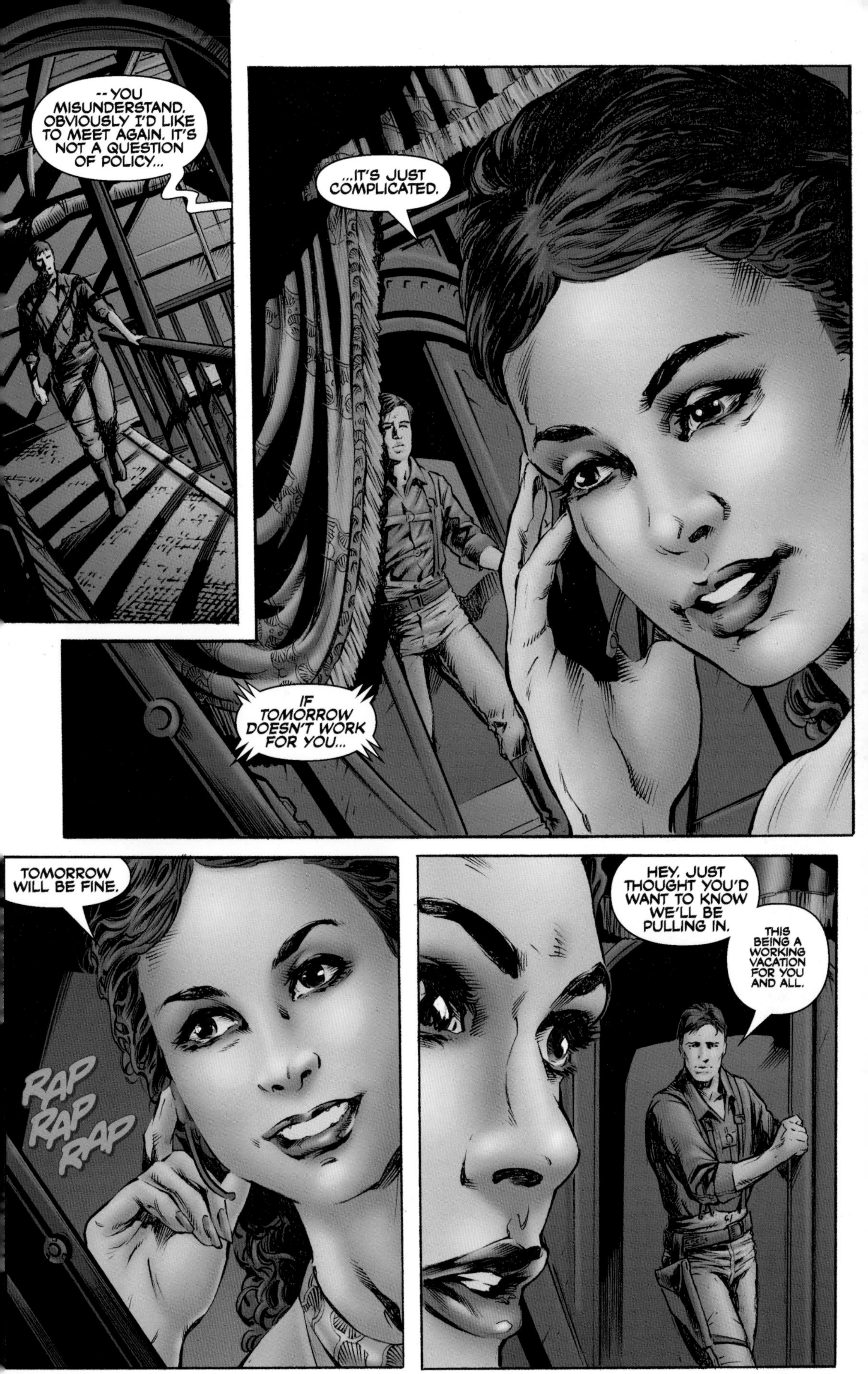
--YOU MISUNDERSTAND. OBVIOUSLY I'D LIKE TO MEET AGAIN. IT'S NOT A QUESTION OF POLICY...
...IT'S JUST COMPLICATED.
IF TOMORROW DOESN'T WORK FOR YOU...
TOMORROW WILL BE FINE.
RAP RAP RAP
HEY. JUST THOUGHT YOU'D WANT TO KNOW WE'LL BE PULLING IN.
THIS BEING A WORKING VACATION FOR YOU AND ALL.

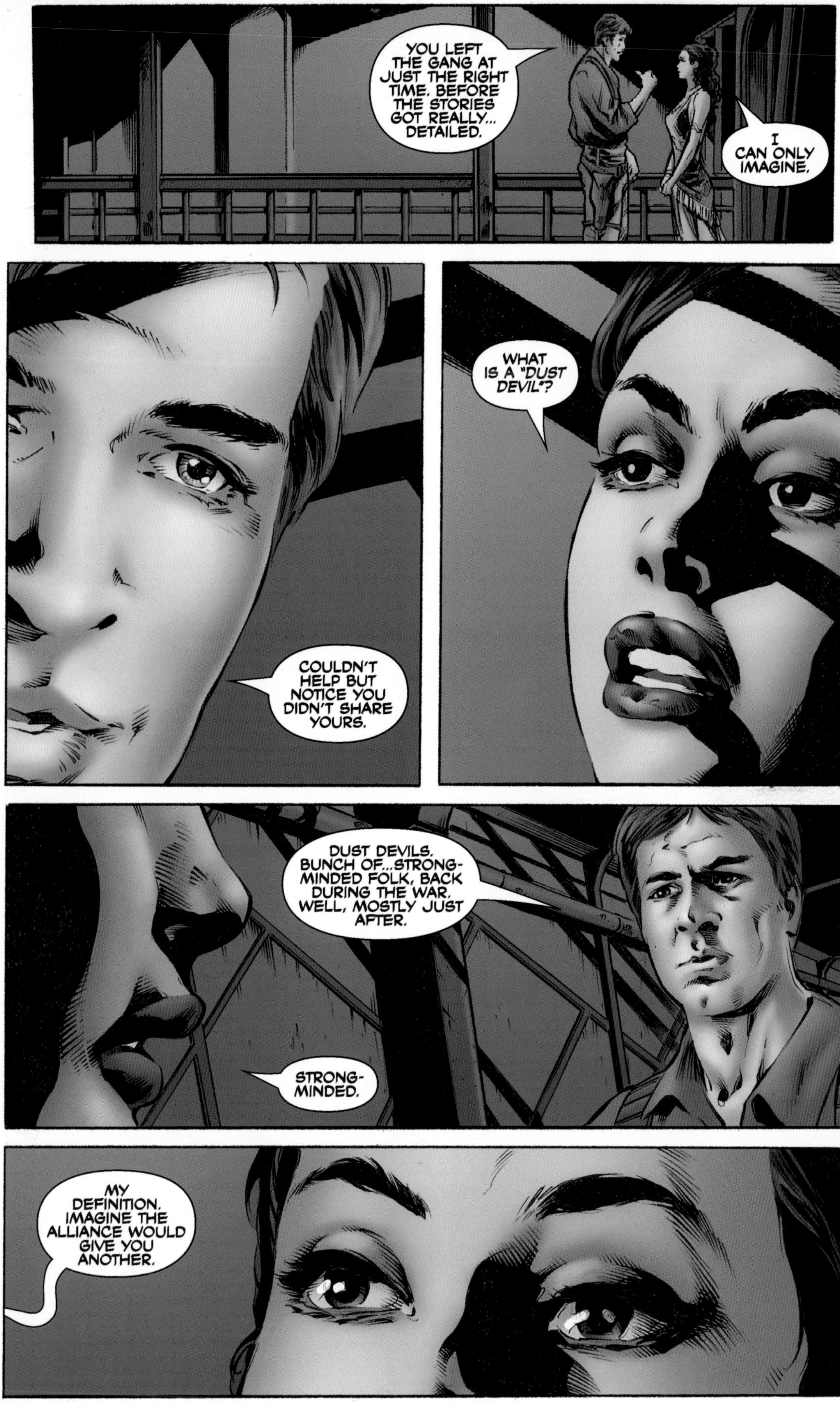
YOU LEFT THE GANG AT JUST THE RIGHT TIME. BEFORE THE STORIES GOT REALLY... DETAILED.
I CAN ONLY IMAGINE.
COULDN'T HELP BUT NOTICE YOU DIDN'T SHARE YOURS.
WHAT IS A "DUST DEVIL"?
DUST DEVILS. BUNCH OF...STRONG-MINDED FOLK, BACK DURING THE WAR. WELL, MOSTLY JUST AFTER.
STRONG-MINDED.
MY DEFINITION. IMAGINE THE ALLIANCE WOULD GIVE YOU ANOTHER.

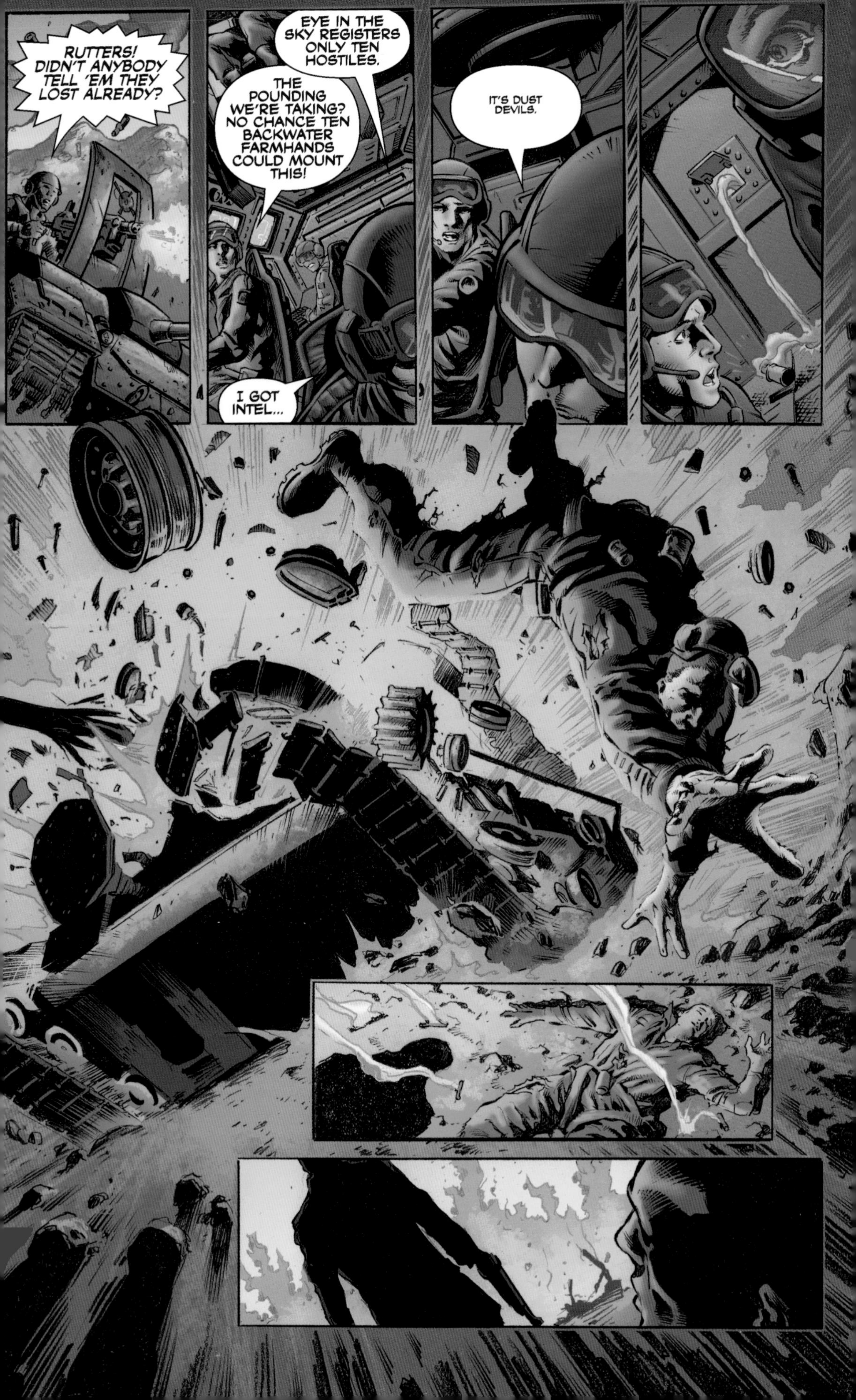
RUTTERS! DIDN'T ANYBODY TELL 'EM THEY LOST ALREADY?
EYE IN THE SKY REGISTERS ONLY TEN HOSTILES.
THE POUNDING WE'RE TAKING? NO CHANCE TEN BACKWATER FARMHANDS COULD MOUNT THIS!
I GOT INTEL...
IT'S DUST DEVILS.

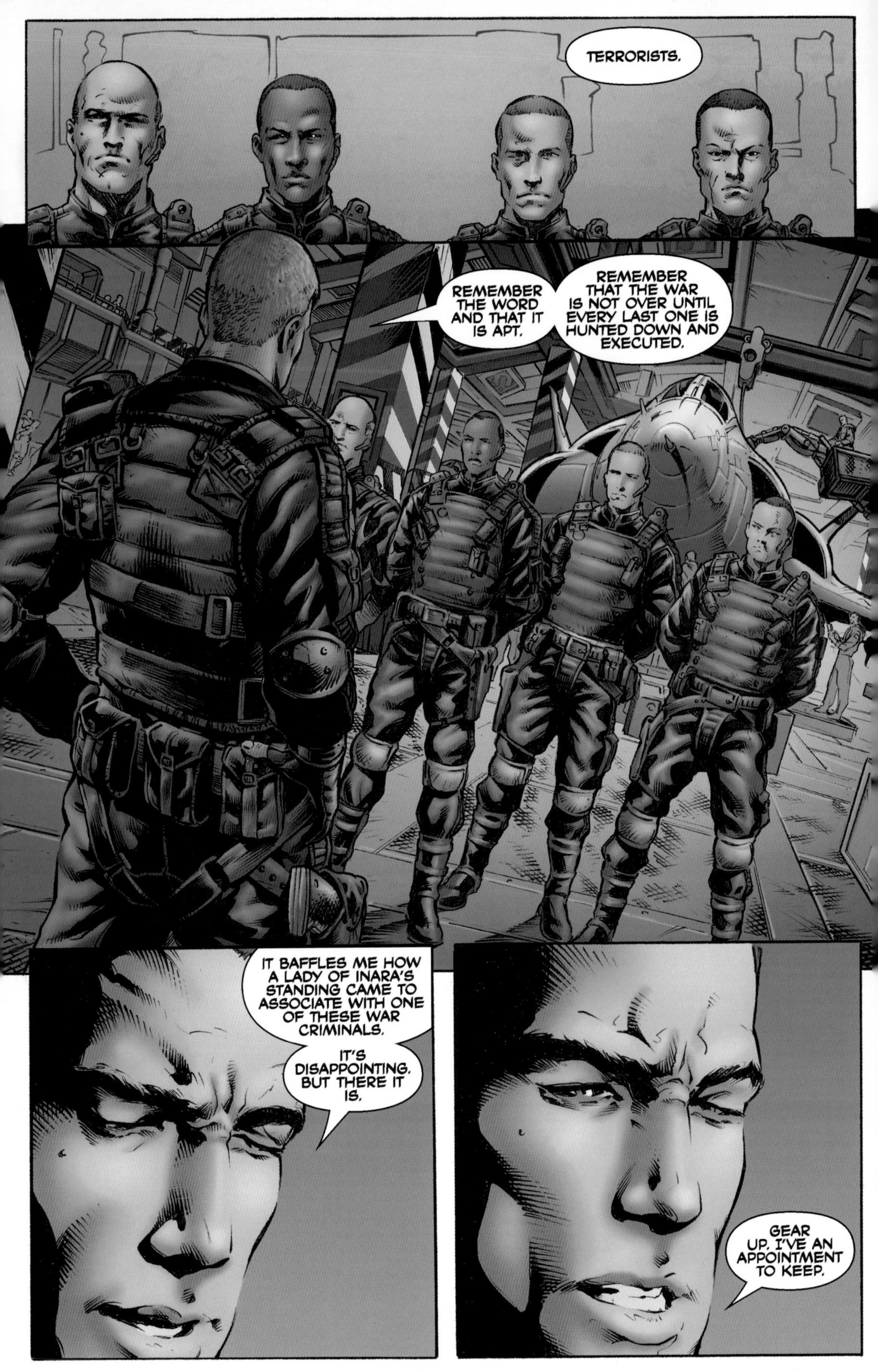

TERRORISTS.
REMEMBER THE WORD AND THAT IT IS APT.
REMEMBER THAT THE WAR IS NOT OVER UNTIL EVERY LAST ONE IS HUNTED DOWN AND EXECUTED.
IT BAFFLES ME HOW A LADY OF INARA'S STANDING CAME TO ASSOCIATE WITH ONE OF THESE WAR CRIMINALS.
IT'S DISAPPOINTING, BUT THERE IT IS.
GEAR UP. I'VE AN APPOINTMENT TO KEEP.

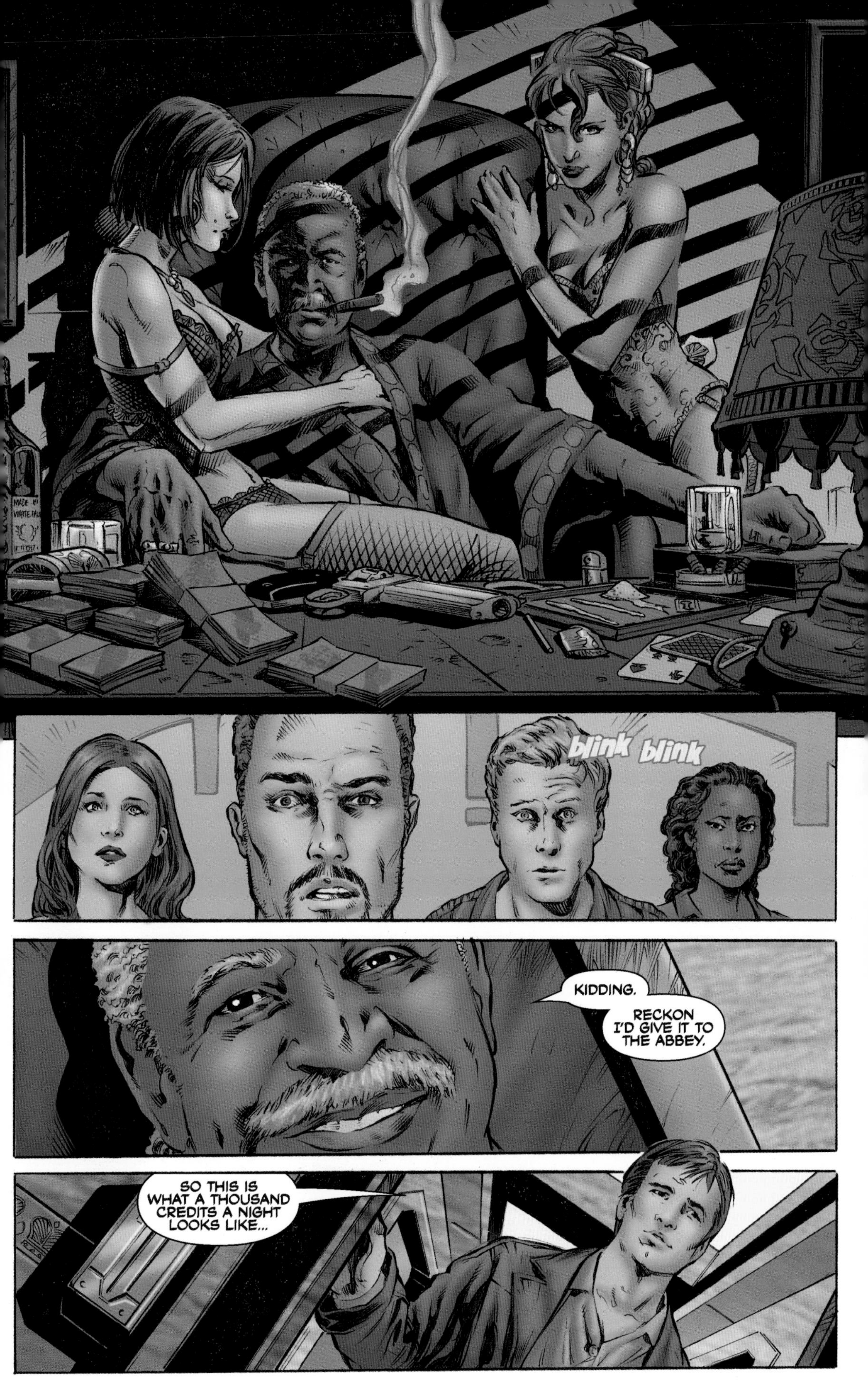
MADE IN WHITEFALL
blink blink
KIDDING.
RECKON I'D GIVE IT TO THE ABBEY.
SO THIS IS WHAT A THOUSAND CREDITS A NIGHT LOOKS LIKE...

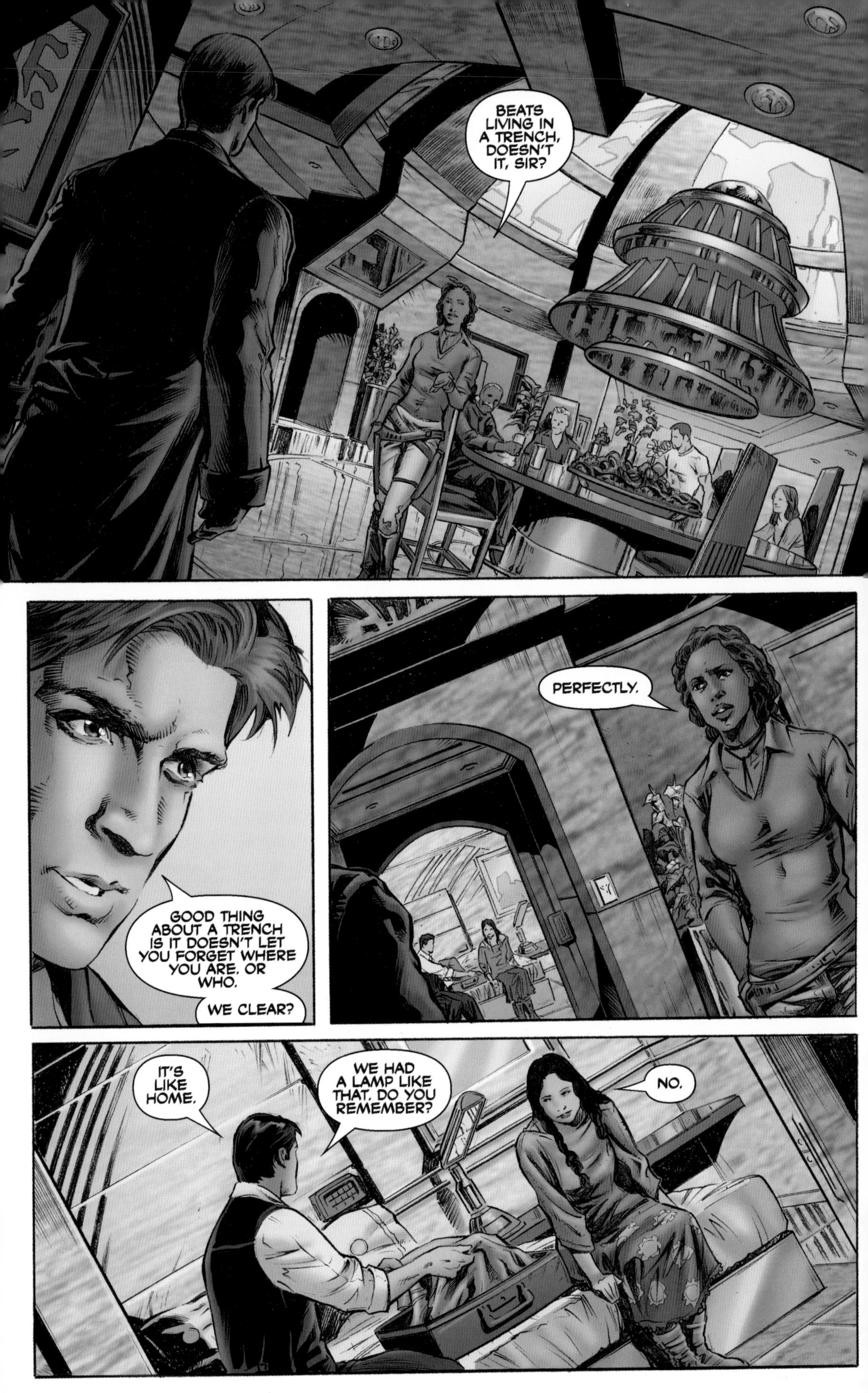
BEATS LIVING IN A TRENCH, DOESN'T IT, SIR?
GOOD THING ABOUT A TRENCH IS IT DOESN'T LET YOU FORGET WHERE YOU ARE. OR WHO.
WE CLEAR?
PERFECTLY.
IT'S LIKE HOME.
WE HAD A LAMP LIKE THAT. DO YOU REMEMBER?
NO.

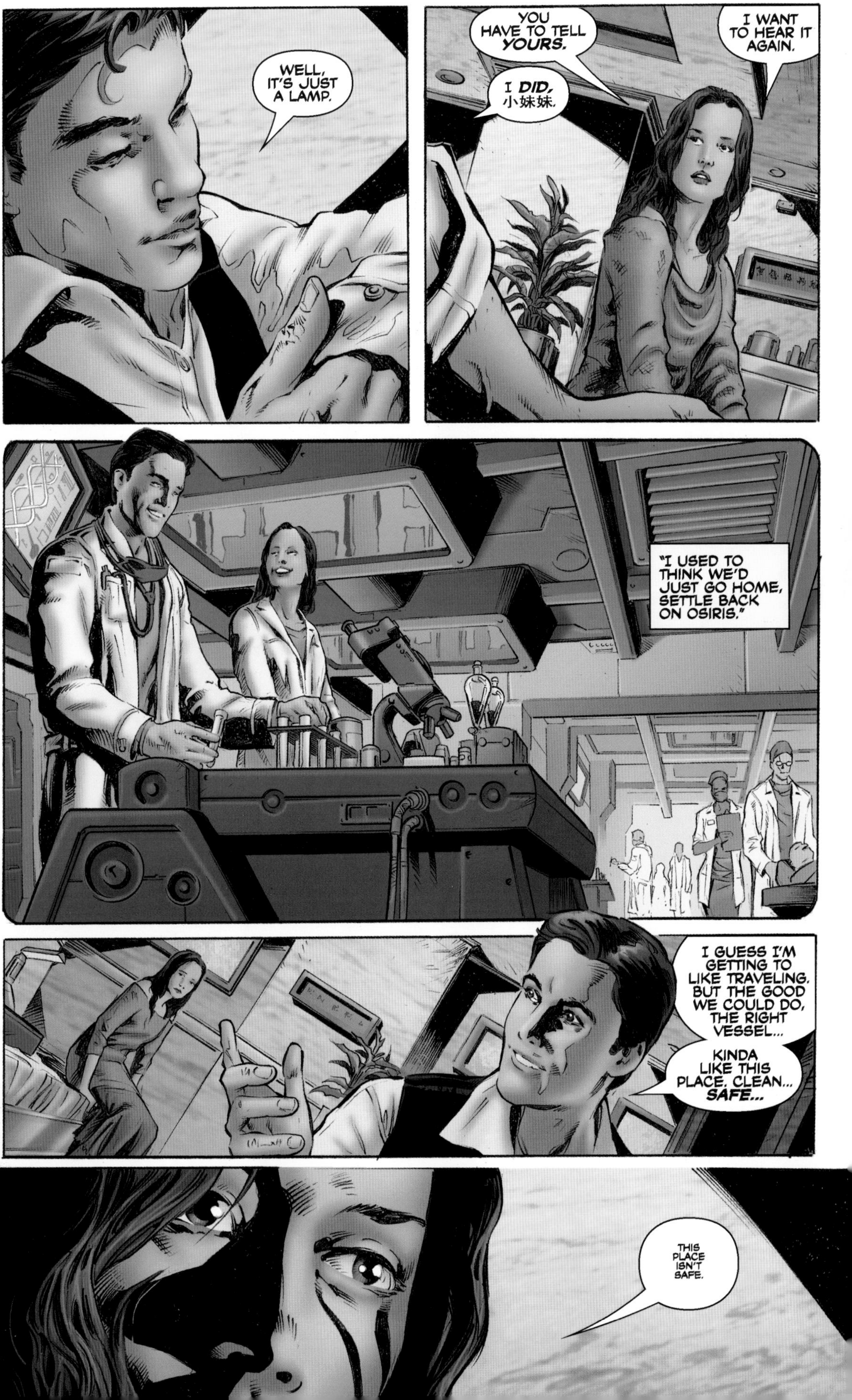
WELL, IT'S JUST A LAMP.
YOU HAVE TO TELL YOURS.
I DID, 小妹妹.
I WANT TO HEAR IT AGAIN.
"I USED TO THINK WE'D JUST GO HOME, SETTLE BACK ON OSIRIS."
I GUESS I'M GETTING TO LIKE TRAVELING. BUT THE GOOD WE COULD DO, THE RIGHT VESSEL...
KINDA LIKE THIS PLACE. CLEAN... SAFE...
THIS PLACE ISN'T SAFE.

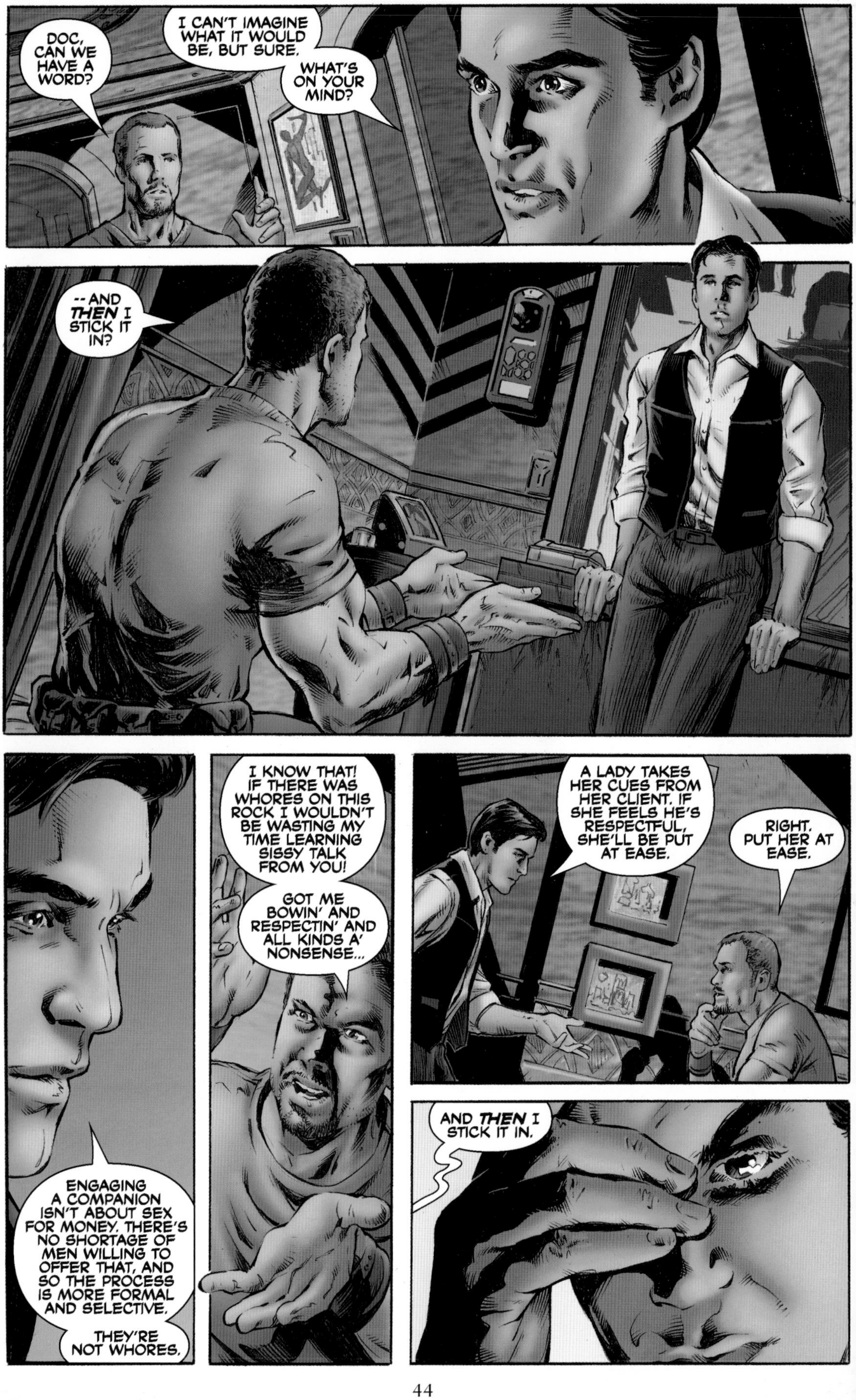
DOC, CAN WE HAVE A WORD?
I CAN'T IMAGINE WHAT IT WOULD BE, BUT SURE.
WHAT'S ON YOUR MIND?
--AND THEN I STICK IT IN?
ENGAGING A COMPANION ISN'T ABOUT SEX FOR MONEY. THERE'S NO SHORTAGE OF MEN WILLING TO OFFER THAT, AND SO THE PROCESS IS MORE FORMAL AND SELECTIVE.
THEY'RE NOT WHORES.
I KNOW THAT! IF THERE WAS WHORES ON THIS ROCK I WOULDN'T BE WASTING MY TIME LEARNING SISSY TALK FROM YOU!
GOT ME BOWIN' AND RESPECTIN' AND ALL KINDS A' NONSENSE...
A LADY TAKES HER CUES FROM HER CLIENT. IF SHE FEELS HE'S RESPECTFUL, SHE'LL BE PUT AT EASE.
RIGHT. PUT HER AT EASE.
AND THEN I STICK IT IN.

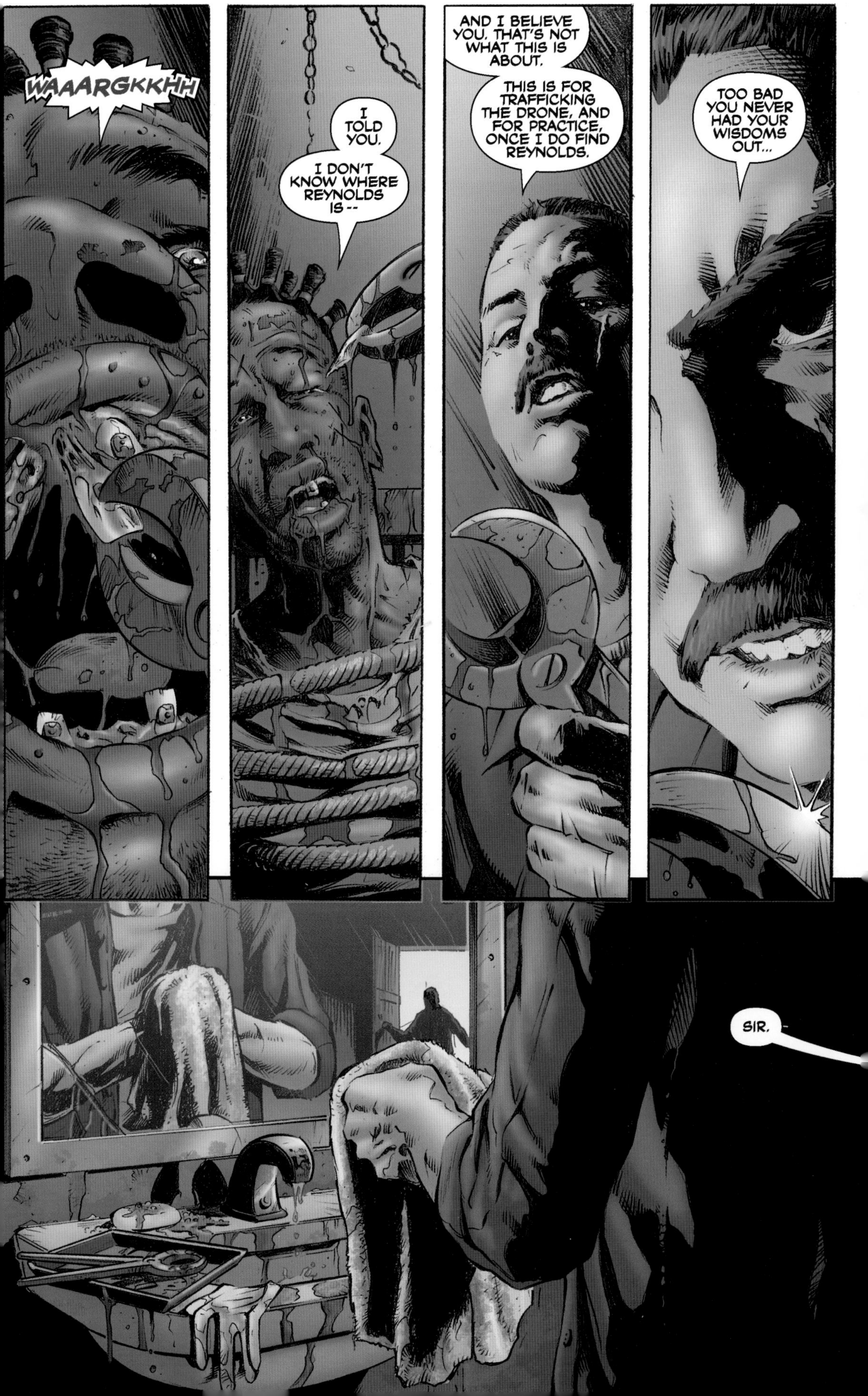
WAAARGKKHH
I TOLD YOU,
I DON'T KNOW WHERE REYNOLDS IS --
AND I BELIEVE YOU. THAT'S NOT WHAT THIS IS ABOUT.
THIS IS FOR TRAFFICKING THE DRONE, AND FOR PRACTICE, ONCE I DO FIND REYNOLDS.
TOO BAD YOU NEVER HAD YOUR WISDOMS OUT...
SIR. -

ARE YOU AWARE THE DRONE WAS DESIGNED TO EXPEL MICROSCOPIC TRACKING BEACONS UPON UNEXPECTED SHUTDOWN OR SYSTEM FAILURE?

SIR...

YOU'VE GOT A HIT.

YES. A COUPLE HUNDRED BEACONS MOVING IN UNISON. A SHIP.

MOVEMENT CEASED AT PELORUM, A RESORT WORLD. CARBON SCORING AT THE POINT OF DEPARTURE SUGGESTS--

FIREFLY CLASS?

IT CHECKS.

PELORUM.

YOU'D BETTER BRING YOUR SUNBLOCK, THEN.

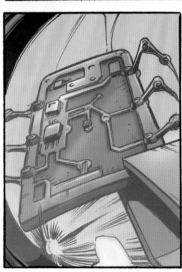

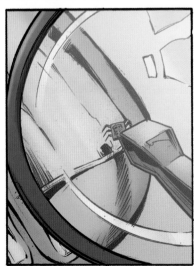

IT'S NOTHING FANCY OR ANYTHING...

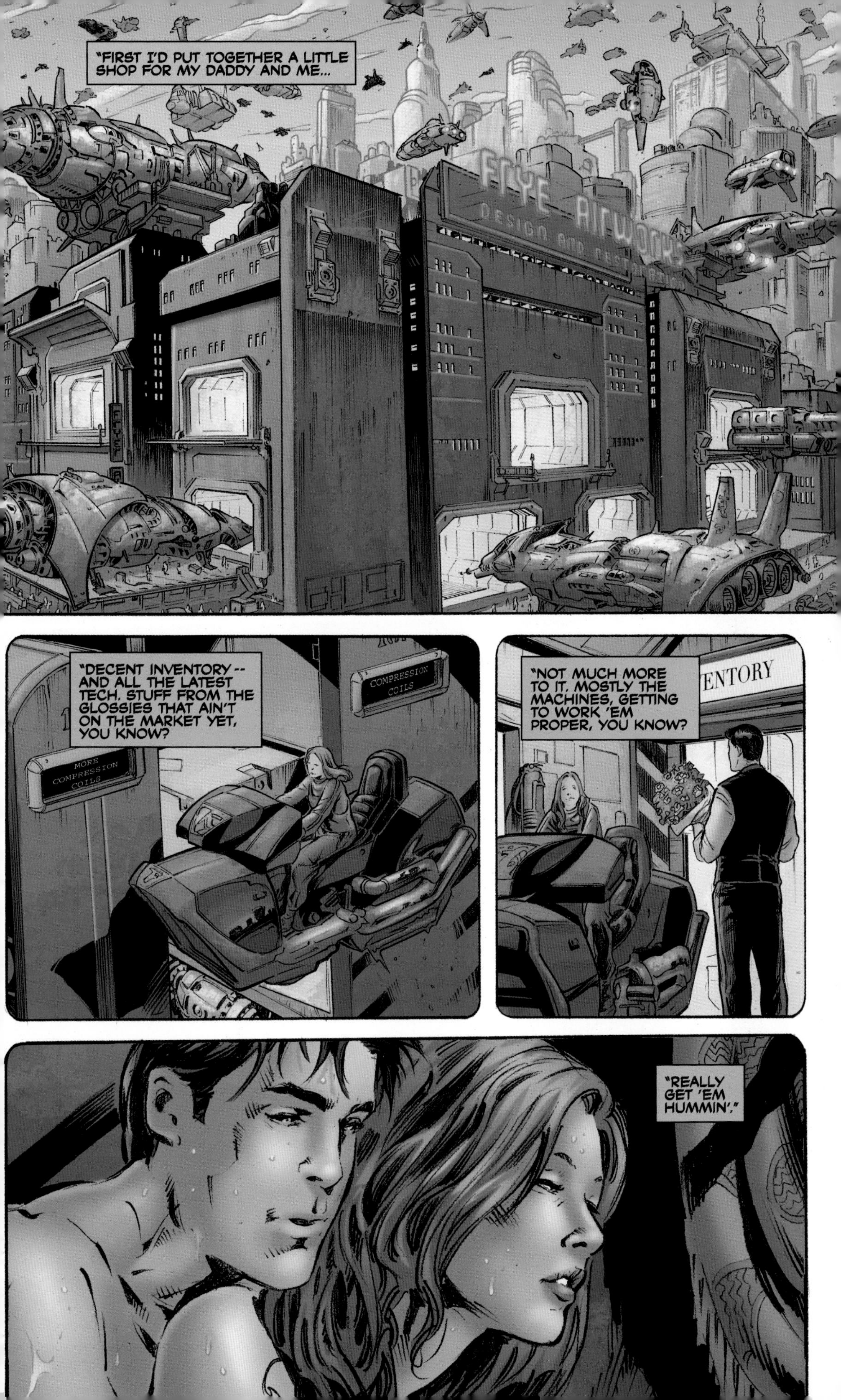
"FIRST I'D PUT TOGETHER A LITTLE SHOP FOR MY DADDY AND ME...
FLYE AIRWORKS
"DECENT INVENTORY -- AND ALL THE LATEST TECH. STUFF FROM THE GLOSSIES THAT AIN'T ON THE MARKET YET, YOU KNOW?
COMPRESSION COILS
MORE COMPRESSION COILS
"NOT MUCH MORE TO IT, MOSTLY THE MACHINES, GETTING TO WORK 'EM PROPER, YOU KNOW?
ENTORY
"REALLY GET 'EM HUMMIN'."

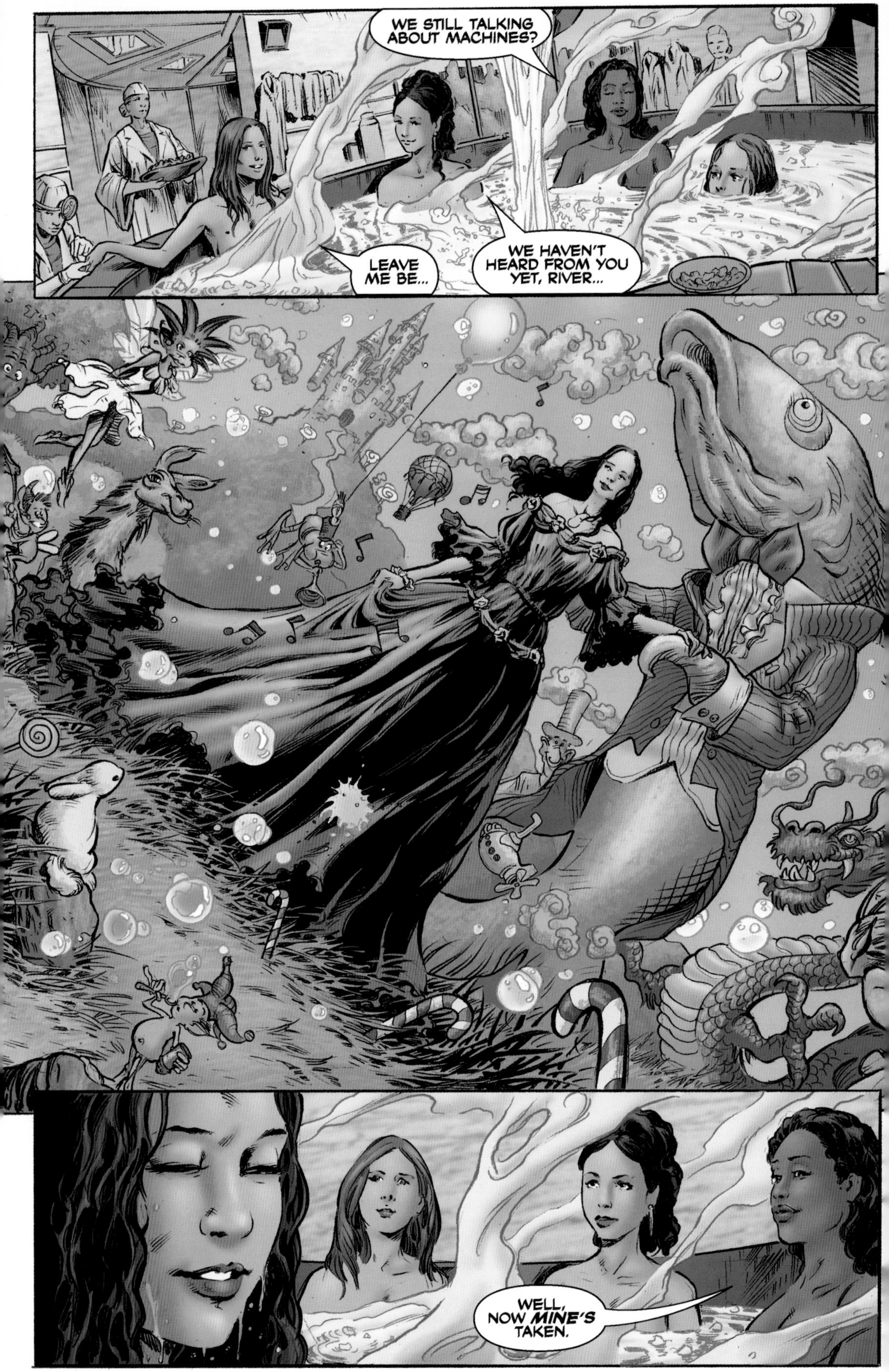
WE STILL TALKING ABOUT MACHINES?
LEAVE ME BE...
WE HAVEN'T HEARD FROM YOU YET, RIVER...
WELL, NOW *MINE'S* TAKEN.

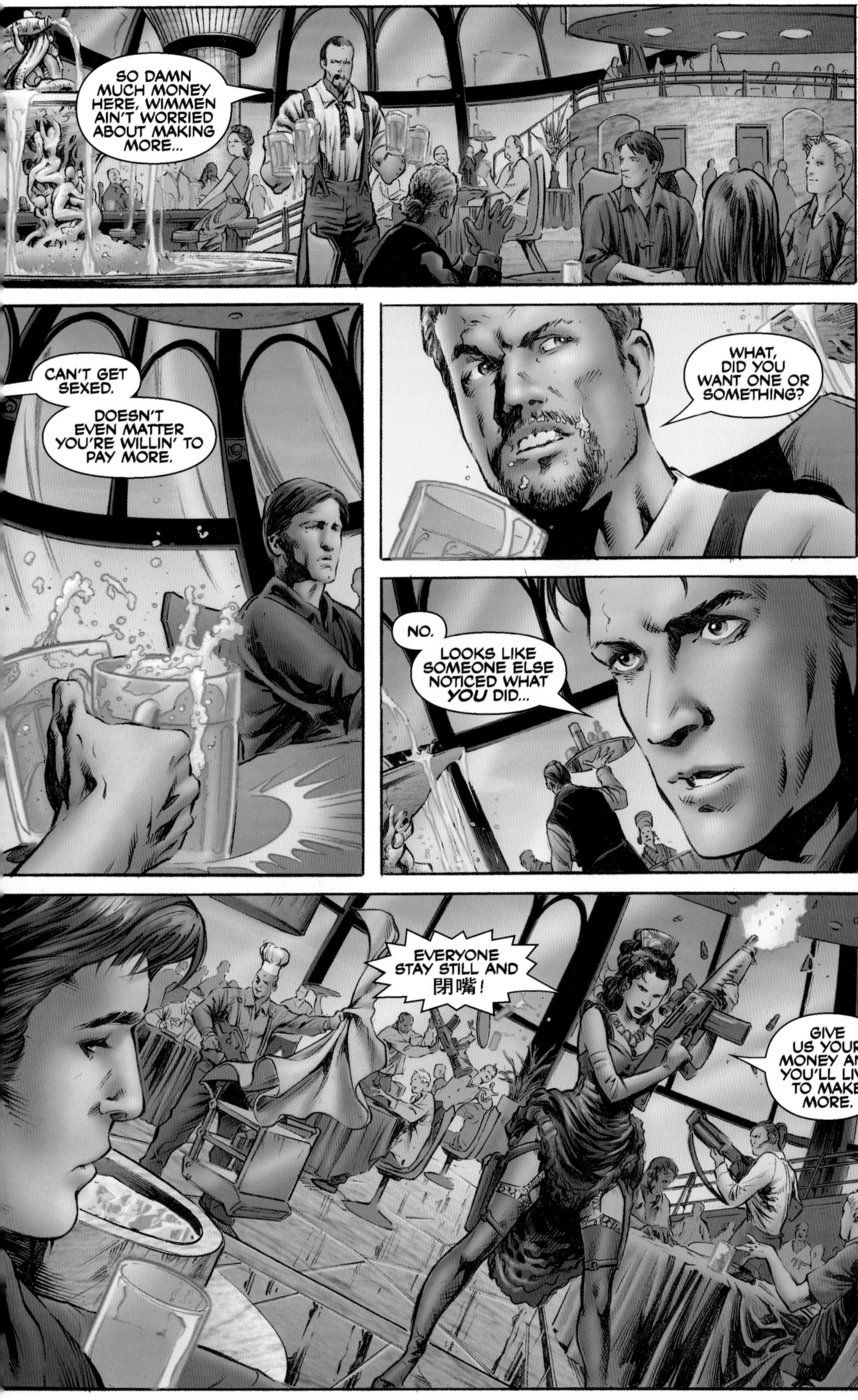

SO DAMN MUCH MONEY HERE, WIMMEN AIN'T WORRIED ABOUT MAKING MORE...
CAN'T GET SEXED.
DOESN'T EVEN MATTER YOU'RE WILLIN' TO PAY MORE.
WHAT, DID YOU WANT ONE OR SOMETHING?
NO.
LOOKS LIKE SOMEONE ELSE NOTICED WHAT *YOU* DID...
EVERYONE STAY STILL AND 閉嘴!
GIVE US YOUR MONEY AND YOU'LL LIVE TO MAKE MORE.

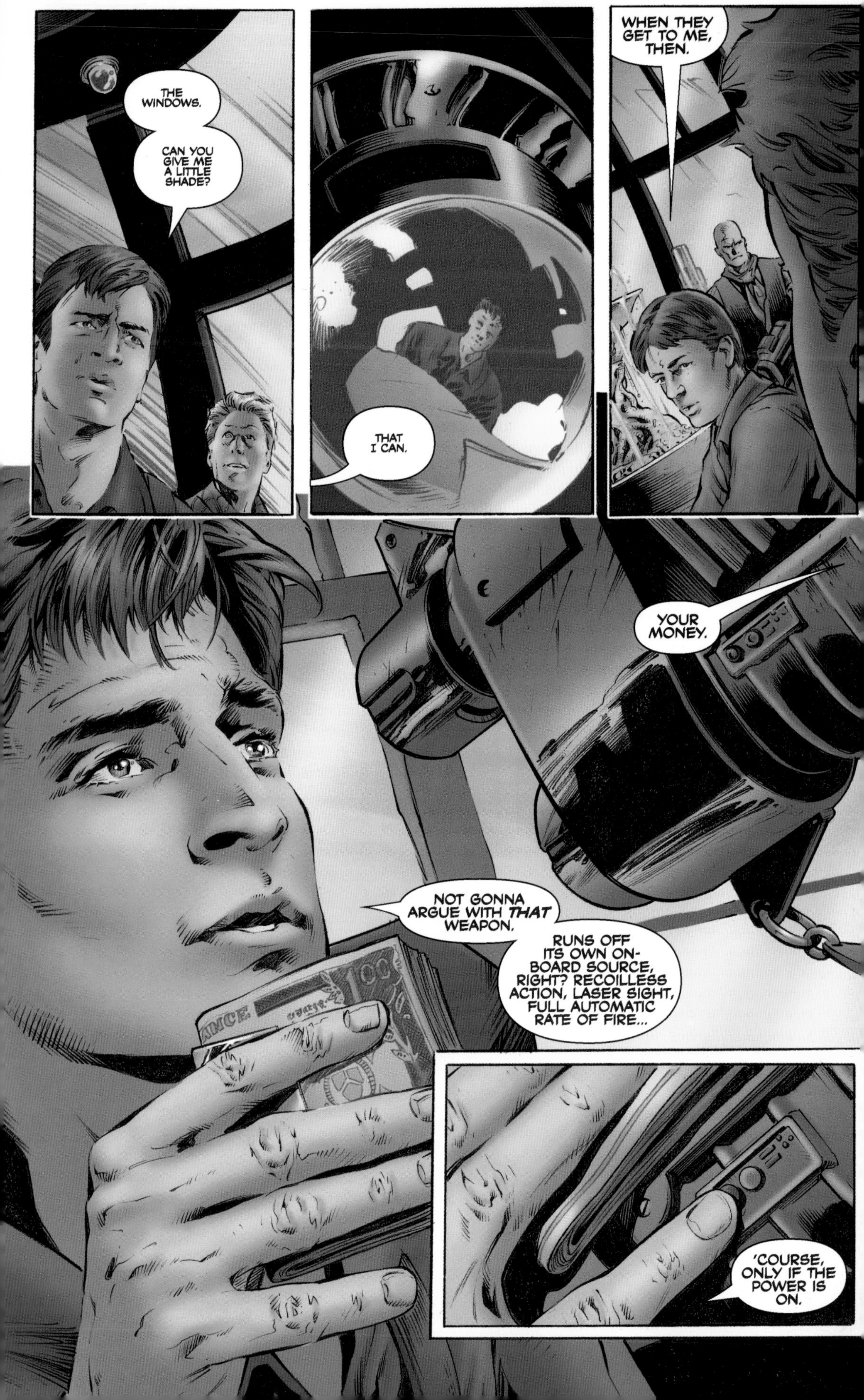
THE WINDOWS.
CAN YOU GIVE ME A LITTLE SHADE?
THAT I CAN.
WHEN THEY GET TO ME, THEN.
YOUR MONEY.
NOT GONNA ARGUE WITH *THAT* WEAPON.
RUNS OFF ITS OWN ON-BOARD SOURCE, RIGHT? RECOILLESS ACTION, LASER SIGHT, FULL AUTOMATIC RATE OF FIRE...
'COURSE, ONLY IF THE POWER IS ON.

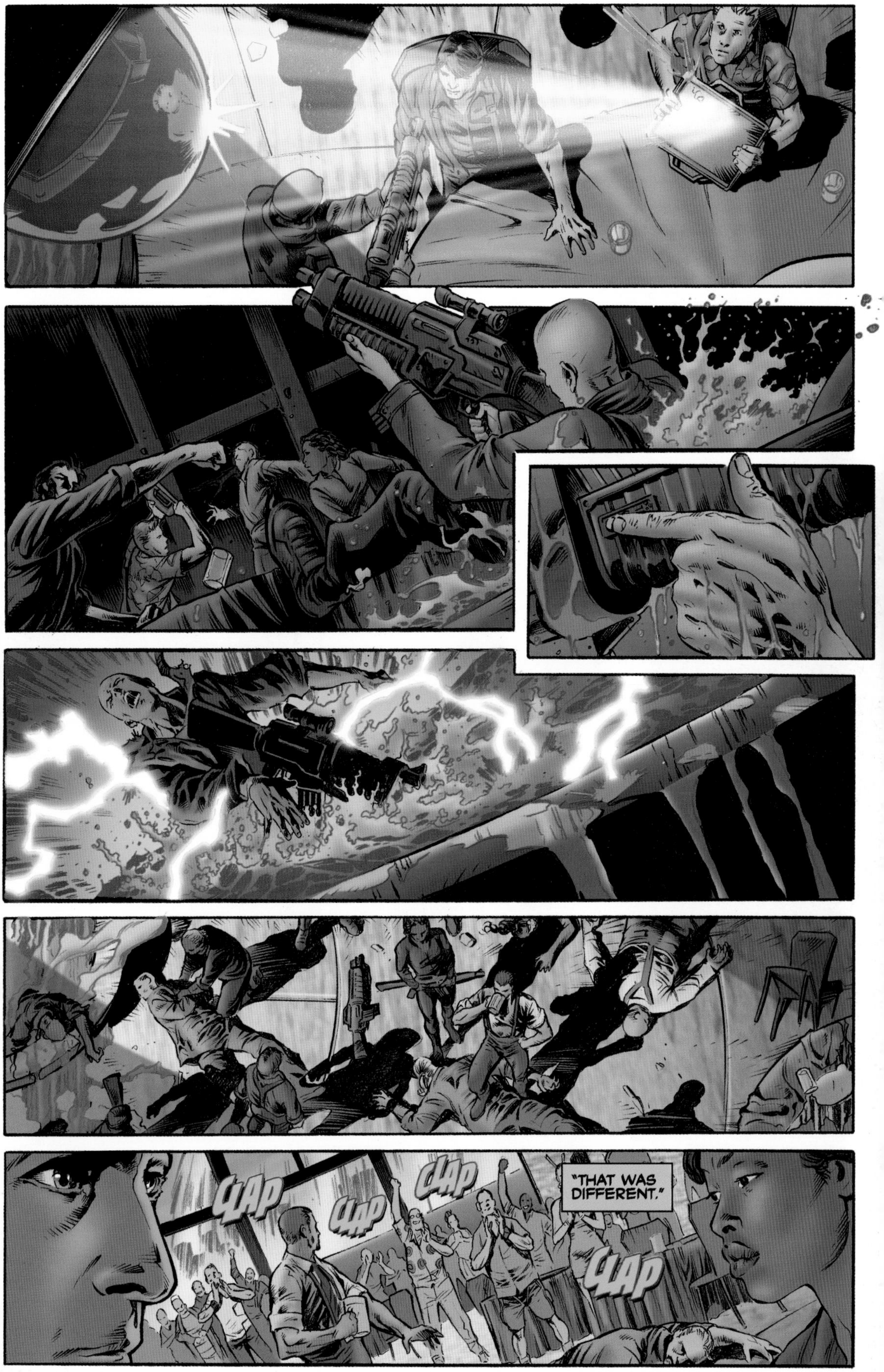
CLAP
CLAP
CLAP
"THAT WAS DIFFERENT."
CLAP

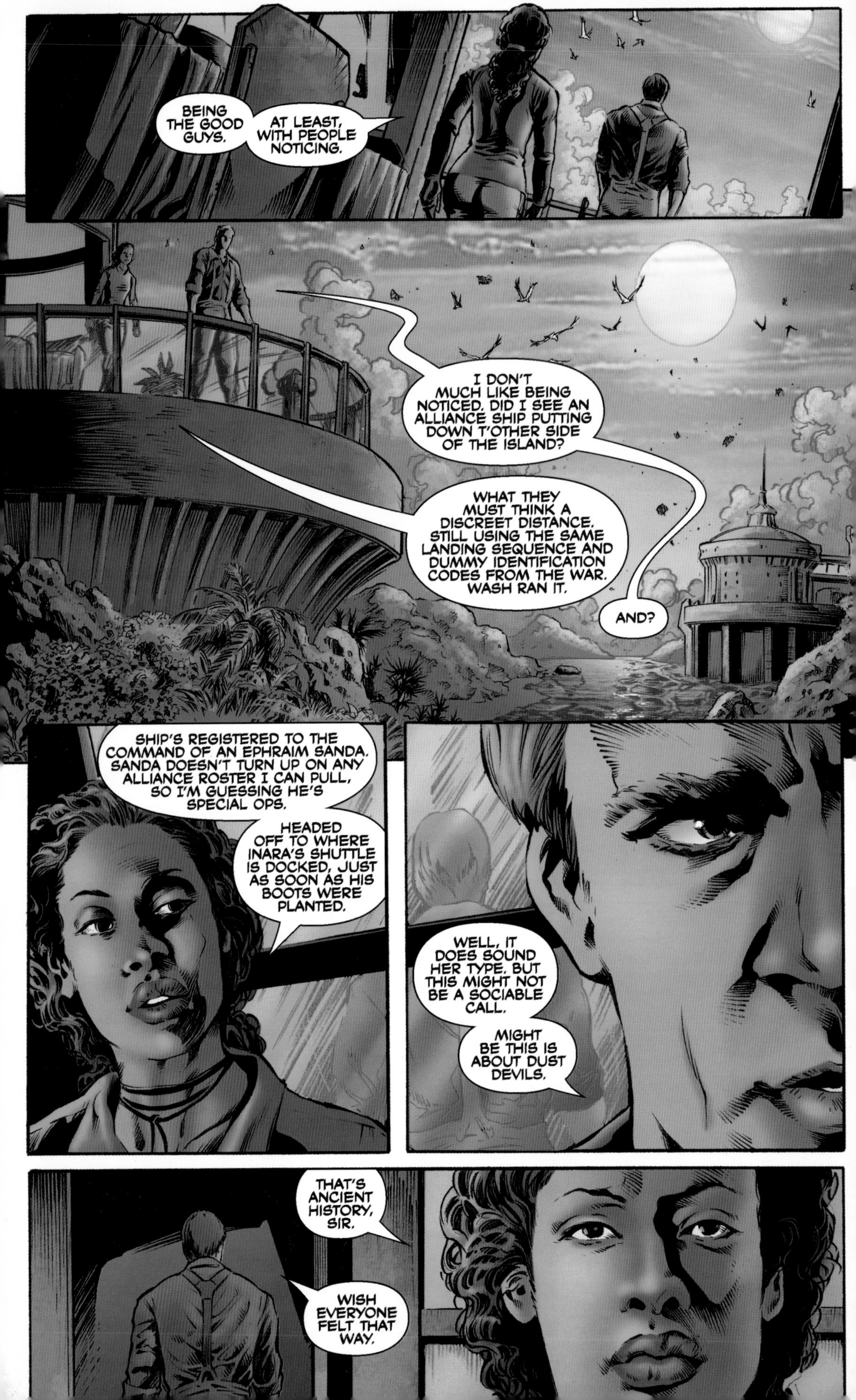
BEING THE GOOD GUYS.
AT LEAST, WITH PEOPLE NOTICING.
I DON'T MUCH LIKE BEING NOTICED. DID I SEE AN ALLIANCE SHIP PUTTING DOWN T'OTHER SIDE OF THE ISLAND?
WHAT THEY MUST THINK A DISCREET DISTANCE. STILL USING THE SAME LANDING SEQUENCE AND DUMMY IDENTIFICATION CODES FROM THE WAR. WASH RAN IT.
AND?
SHIP'S REGISTERED TO THE COMMAND OF AN EPHRAIM SANDA. SANDA DOESN'T TURN UP ON ANY ALLIANCE ROSTER I CAN PULL, SO I'M GUESSING HE'S SPECIAL OPS.
HEADED OFF TO WHERE INARA'S SHUTTLE IS DOCKED, JUST AS SOON AS HIS BOOTS WERE PLANTED.
WELL, IT DOES SOUND HER TYPE. BUT THIS MIGHT NOT BE A SOCIABLE CALL.
MIGHT BE THIS IS ABOUT DUST DEVILS.
THAT'S ANCIENT HISTORY, SIR.
WISH EVERYONE FELT THAT WAY.

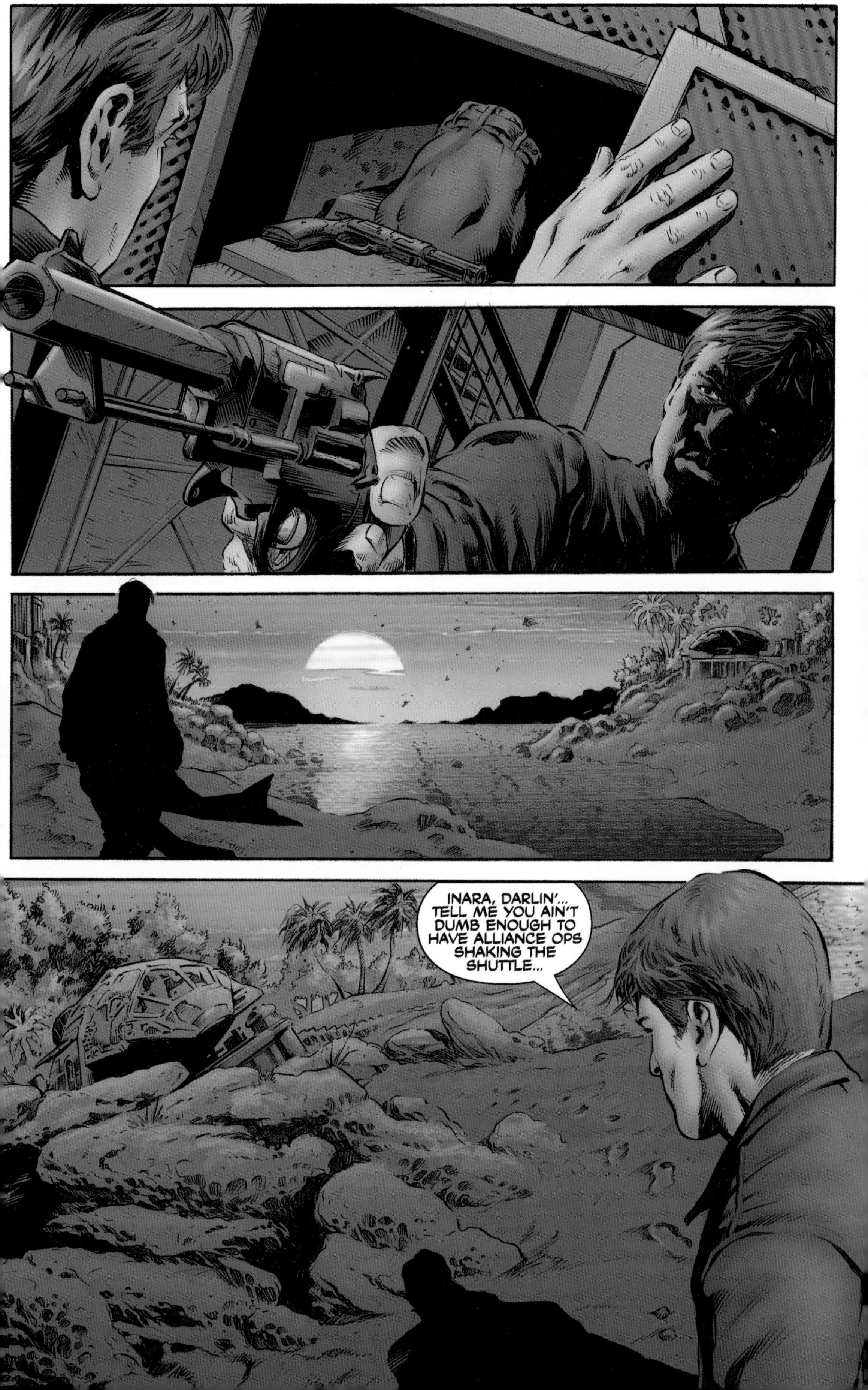
INARA, DARLIN'...
TELL ME YOU AIN'T DUMB ENOUGH TO HAVE ALLIANCE OPS SHAKING THE SHUTTLE...

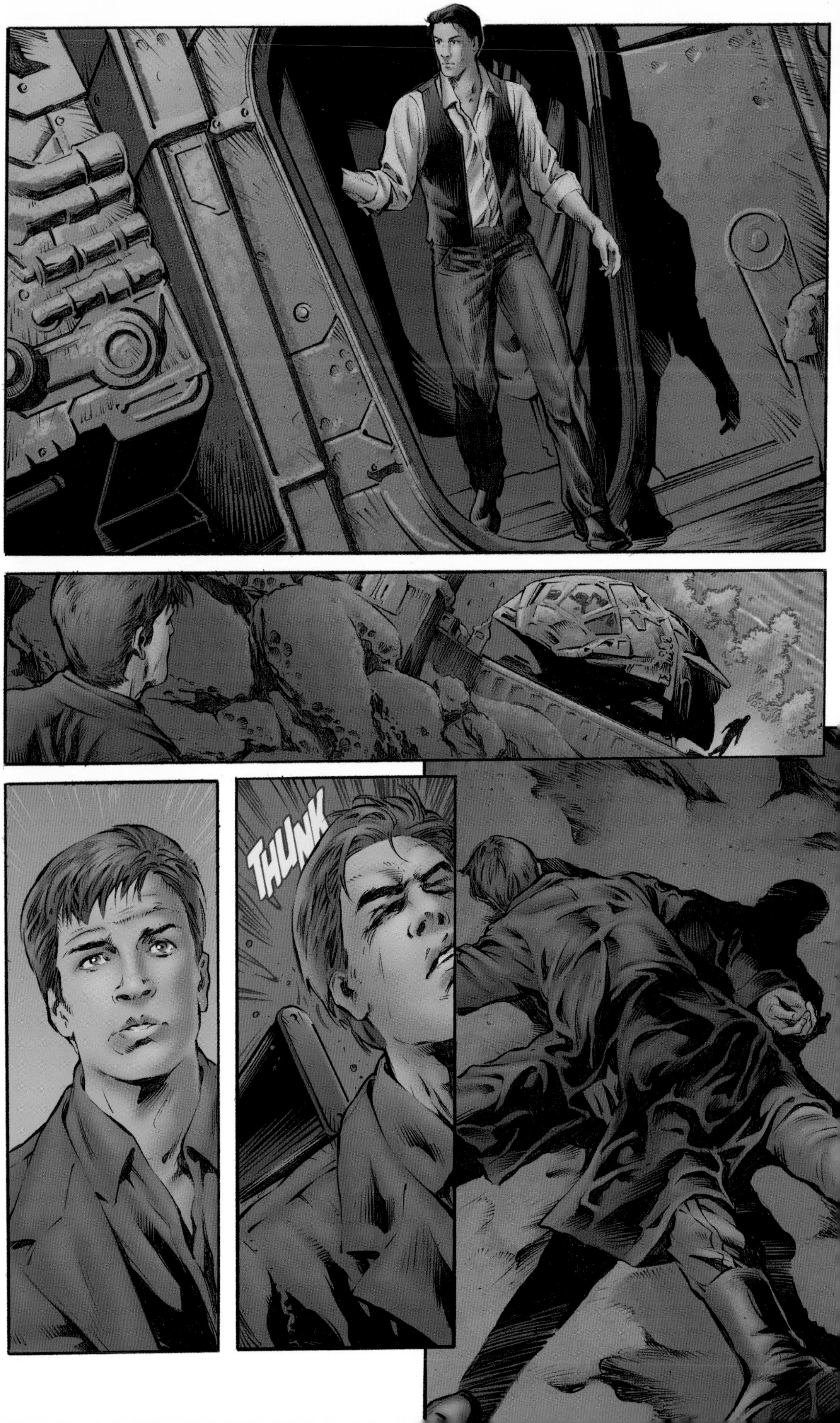
THUNK

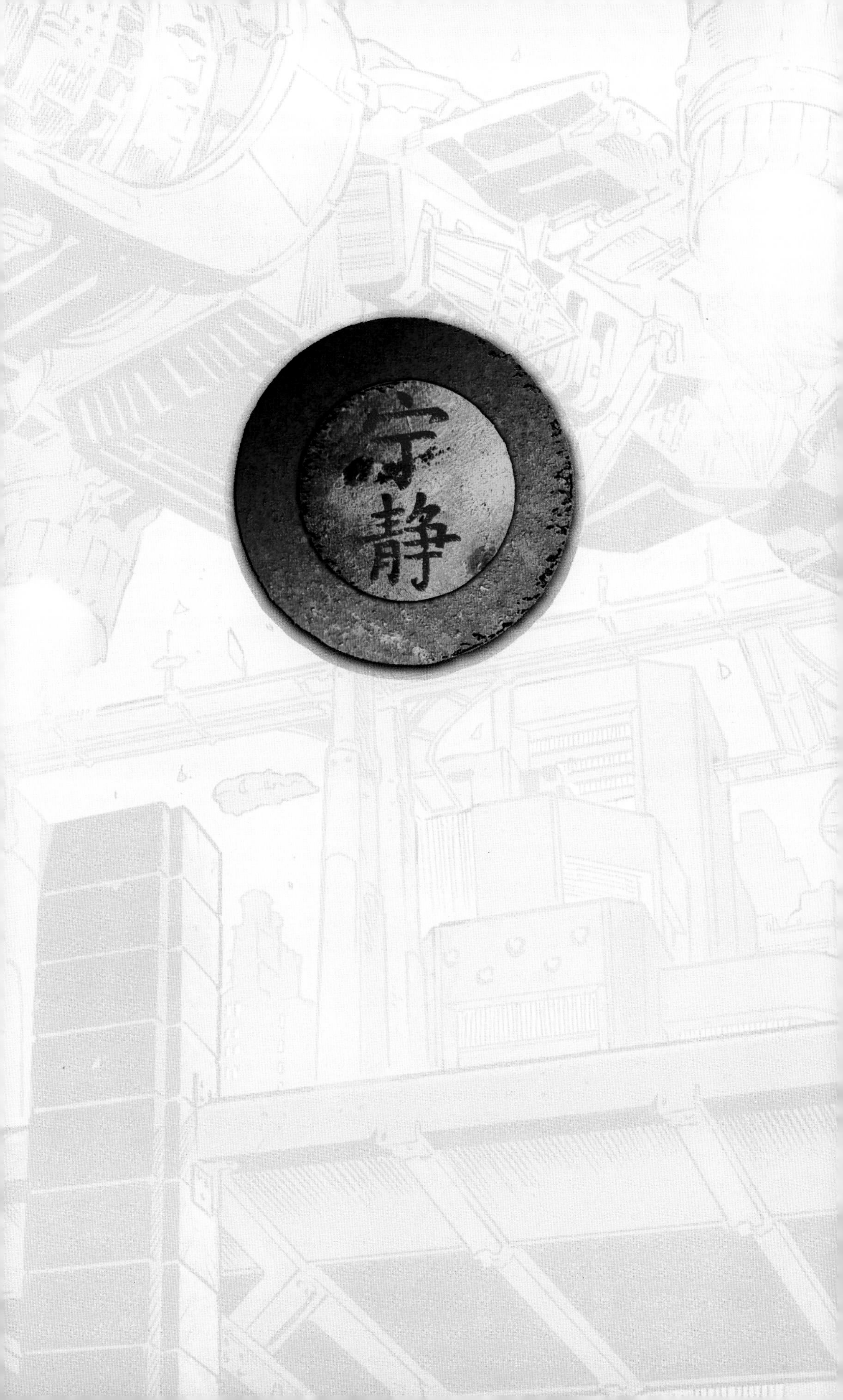
守静

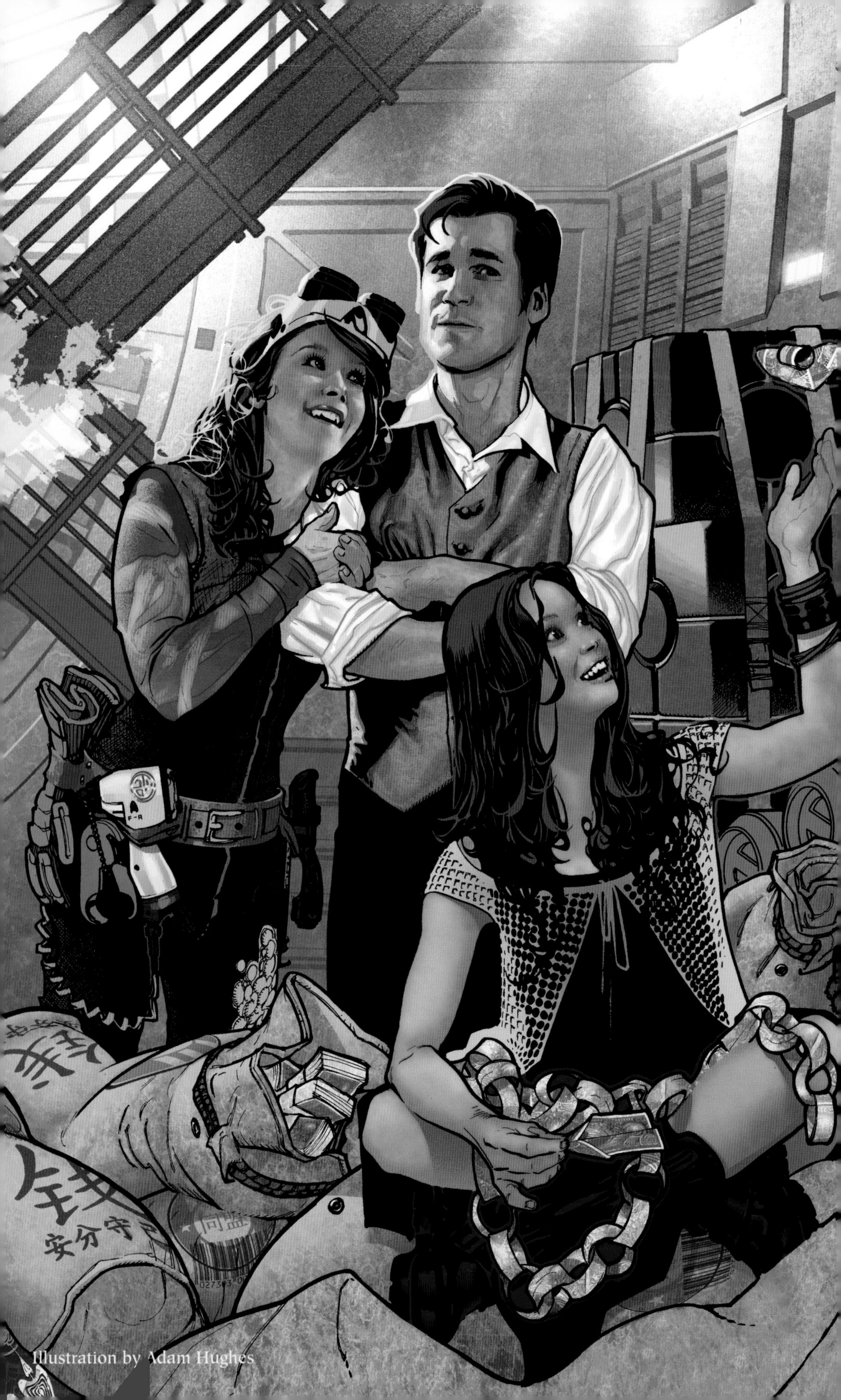
钱
安分守

Illustration by Adam Hughes

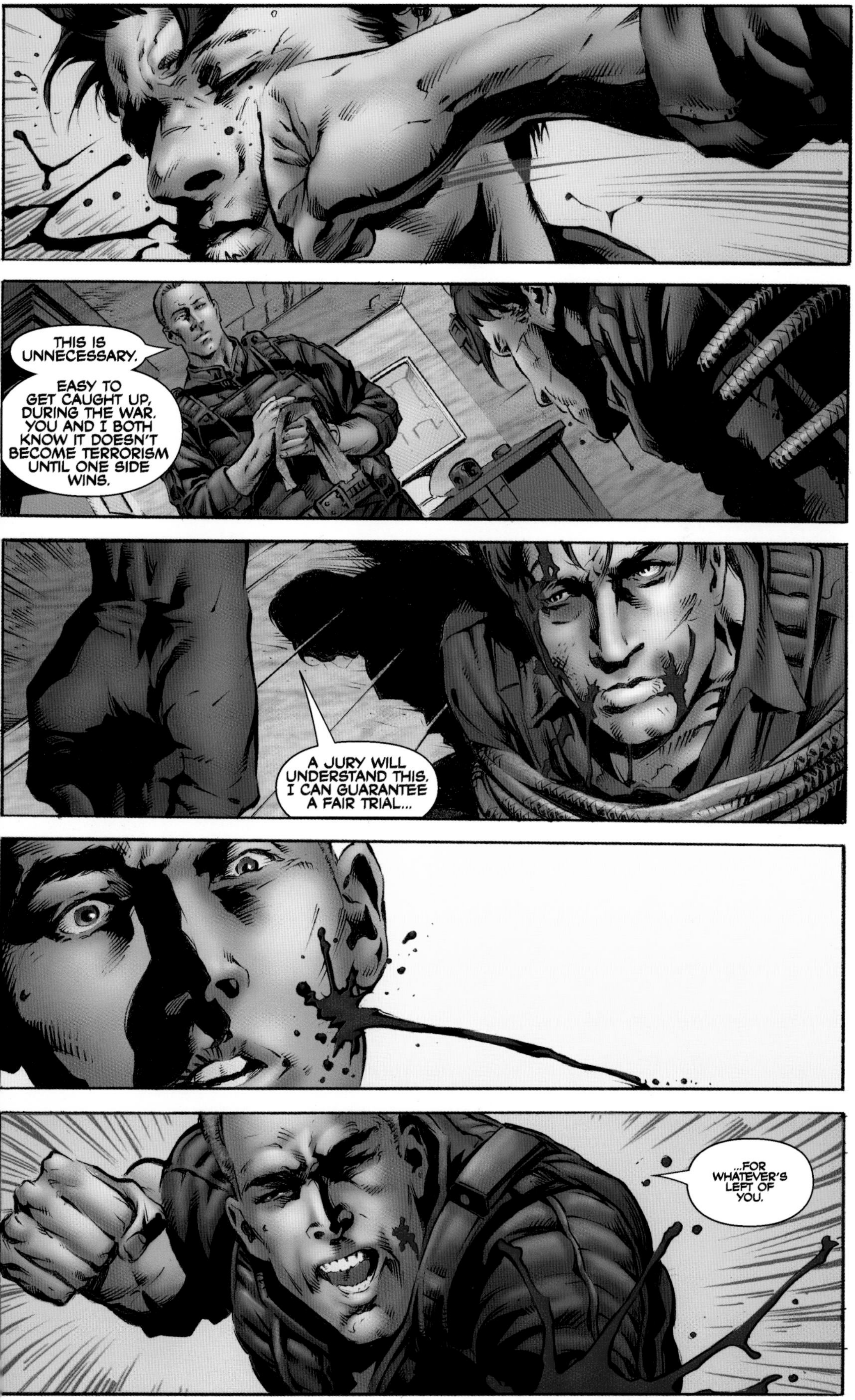
THIS IS UNNECESSARY.
EASY TO GET CAUGHT UP, DURING THE WAR. YOU AND I BOTH KNOW IT DOESN'T BECOME TERRORISM UNTIL ONE SIDE WINS.
A JURY WILL UNDERSTAND THIS. I CAN GUARANTEE A FAIR TRIAL...
...FOR WHATEVER'S LEFT OF YOU.

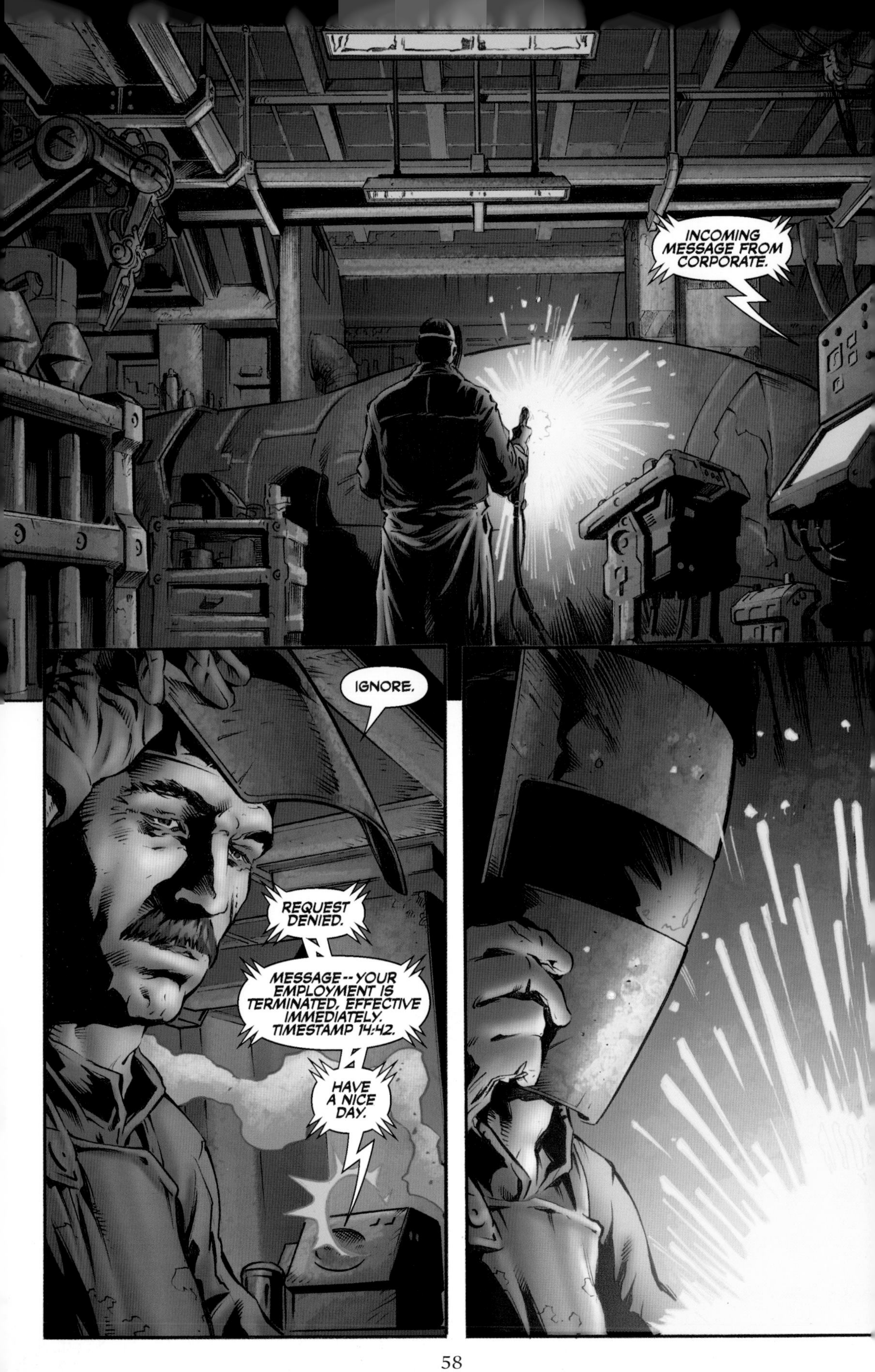
INCOMING MESSAGE FROM CORPORATE.
IGNORE.
REQUEST DENIED.
MESSAGE -- YOUR EMPLOYMENT IS TERMINATED, EFFECTIVE IMMEDIATELY. TIMESTAMP 14:42.
HAVE A NICE DAY.

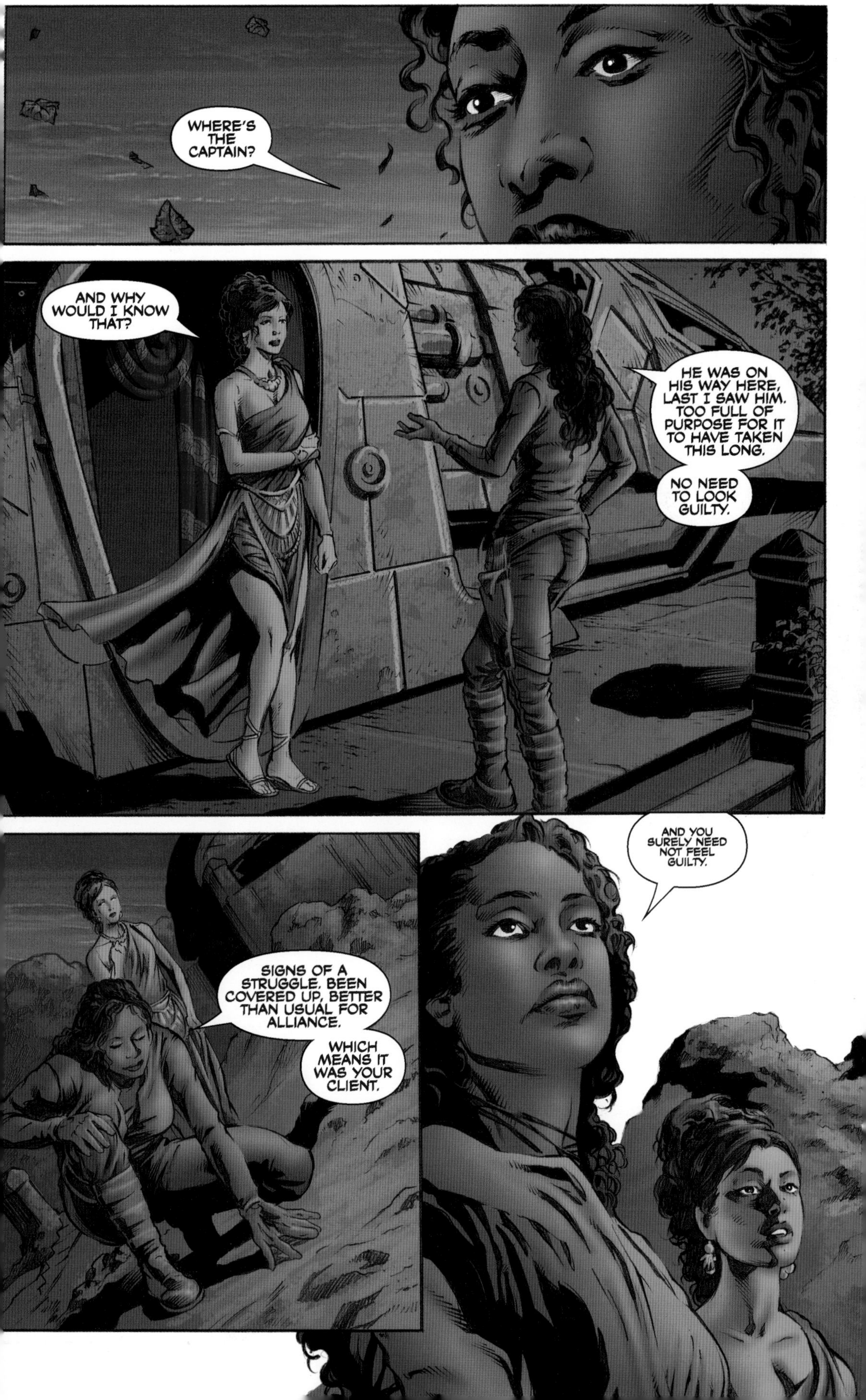
WHERE'S THE CAPTAIN?
AND WHY WOULD I KNOW THAT?
HE WAS ON HIS WAY HERE, LAST I SAW HIM. TOO FULL OF PURPOSE FOR IT TO HAVE TAKEN THIS LONG.
NO NEED TO LOOK GUILTY.
SIGNS OF A STRUGGLE. BEEN COVERED UP, BETTER THAN USUAL FOR ALLIANCE.
WHICH MEANS IT WAS YOUR CLIENT.
AND YOU SURELY NEED NOT FEEL GUILTY.

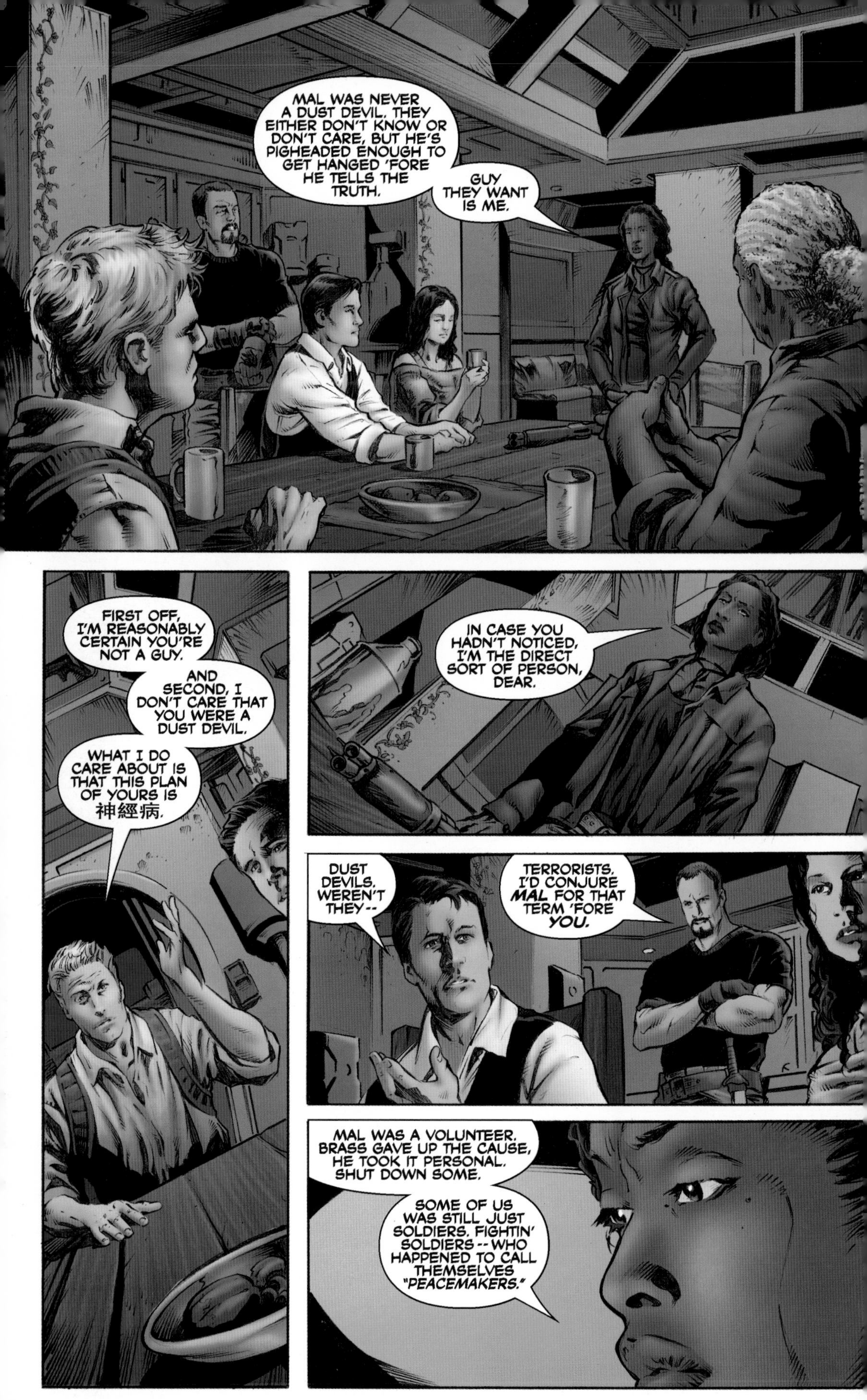
MAL WAS NEVER A DUST DEVIL. THEY EITHER DON'T KNOW OR DON'T CARE, BUT HE'S PIGHEADED ENOUGH TO GET HANGED 'FORE HE TELLS THE TRUTH.
GUY THEY WANT IS ME.
FIRST OFF, I'M REASONABLY CERTAIN YOU'RE NOT A GUY.
AND SECOND, I DON'T CARE THAT YOU WERE A DUST DEVIL.
WHAT I DO CARE ABOUT IS THAT THIS PLAN OF YOURS IS 神經病.
IN CASE YOU HADN'T NOTICED, I'M THE DIRECT SORT OF PERSON, DEAR.
DUST DEVILS. WEREN'T THEY--
TERRORISTS. I'D CONJURE *MAL* FOR THAT TERM 'FORE *YOU.*
MAL WAS A VOLUNTEER. BRASS GAVE UP THE CAUSE, HE TOOK IT PERSONAL. SHUT DOWN SOME.
SOME OF US WAS STILL JUST SOLDIERS. FIGHTIN' SOLDIERS -- WHO HAPPENED TO CALL THEMSELVES *"PEACEMAKERS."*

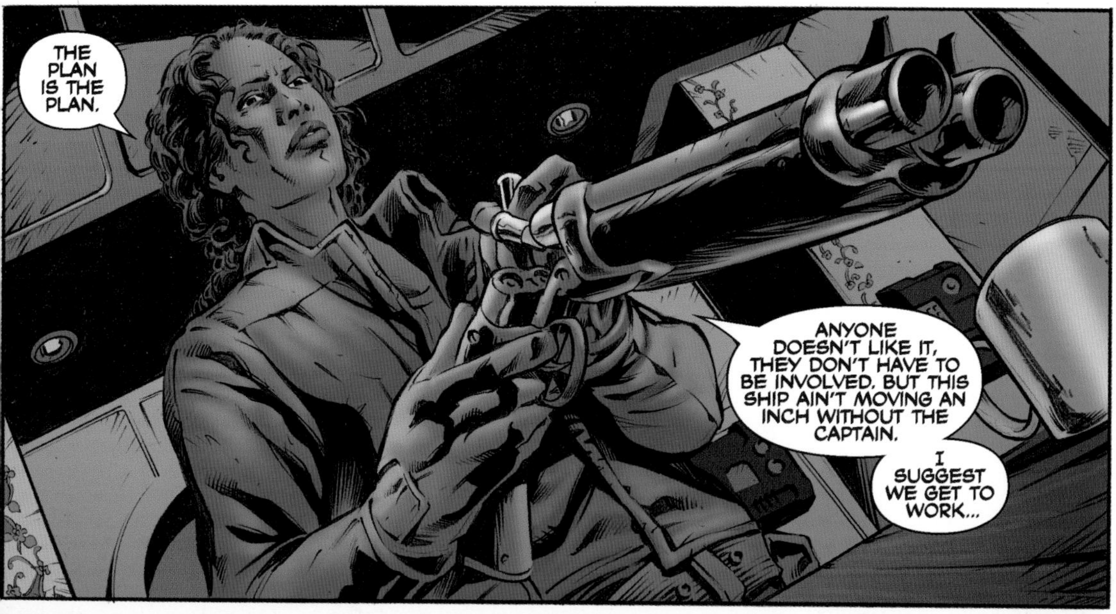
THE PLAN IS THE PLAN.
ANYONE DOESN'T LIKE IT, THEY DON'T HAVE TO BE INVOLVED. BUT THIS SHIP AIN'T MOVING AN INCH WITHOUT THE CAPTAIN.
I SUGGEST WE GET TO WORK...
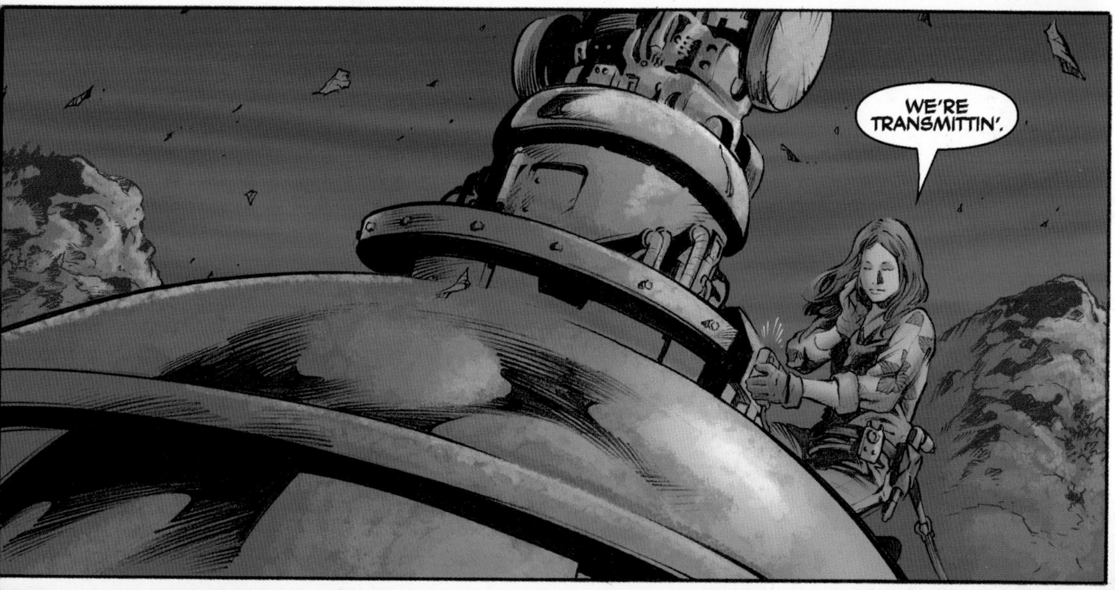
WE'RE TRANSMITTIN'.
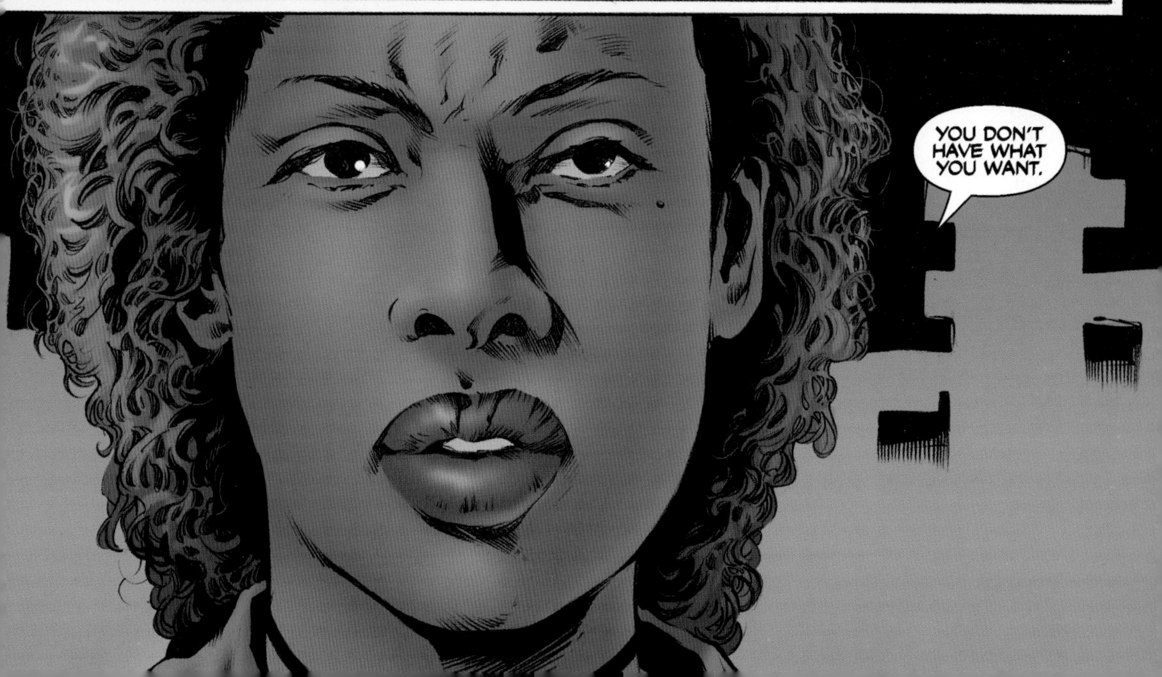
YOU DON'T HAVE WHAT YOU WANT.

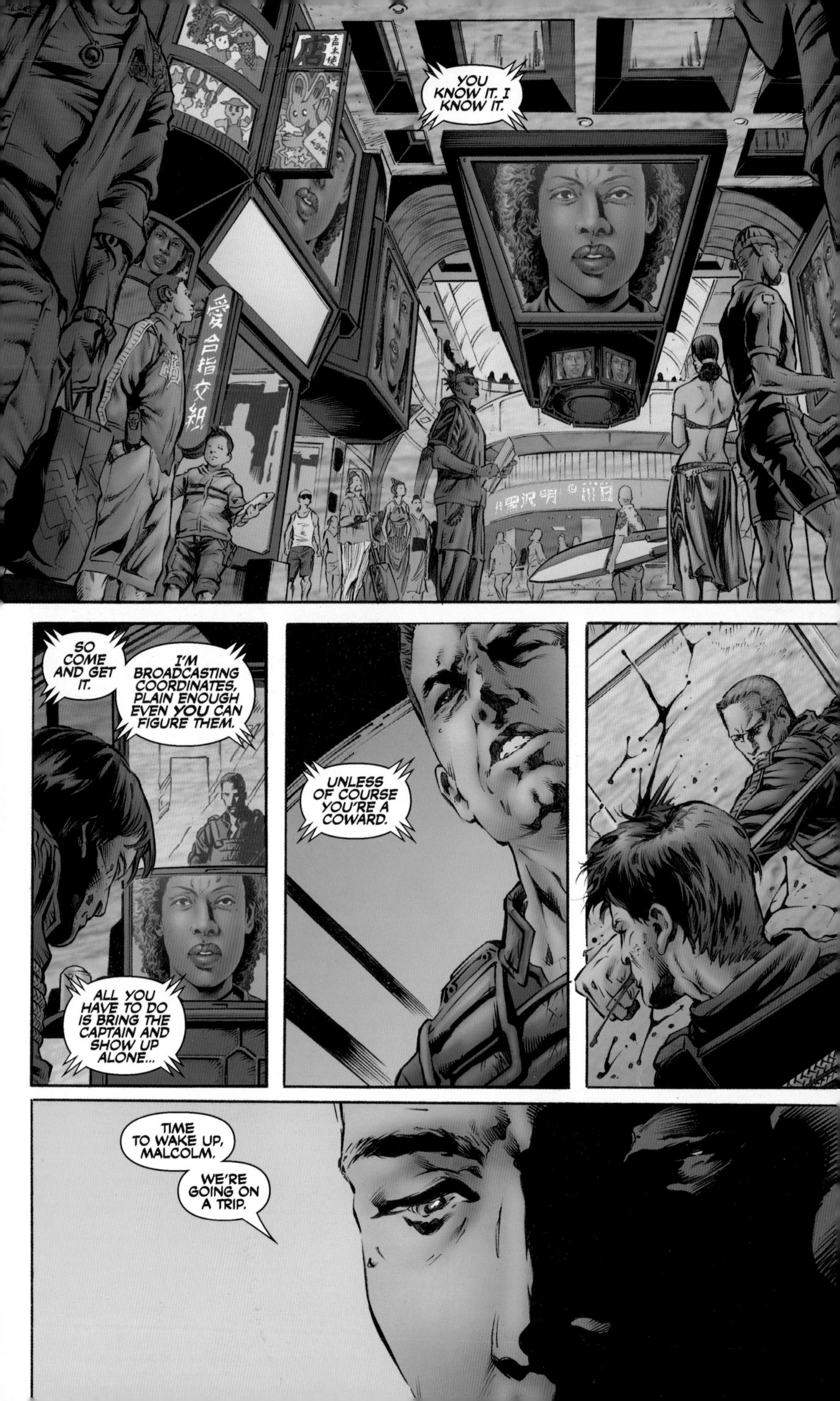
YOU KNOW IT. I KNOW IT.
SO COME AND GET IT.
I'M BROADCASTING COORDINATES, PLAIN ENOUGH EVEN YOU CAN FIGURE THEM.
ALL YOU HAVE TO DO IS BRING THE CAPTAIN AND SHOW UP ALONE...
UNLESS OF COURSE YOU'RE A COWARD.
TIME TO WAKE UP, MALCOLM.
WE'RE GOING ON A TRIP.

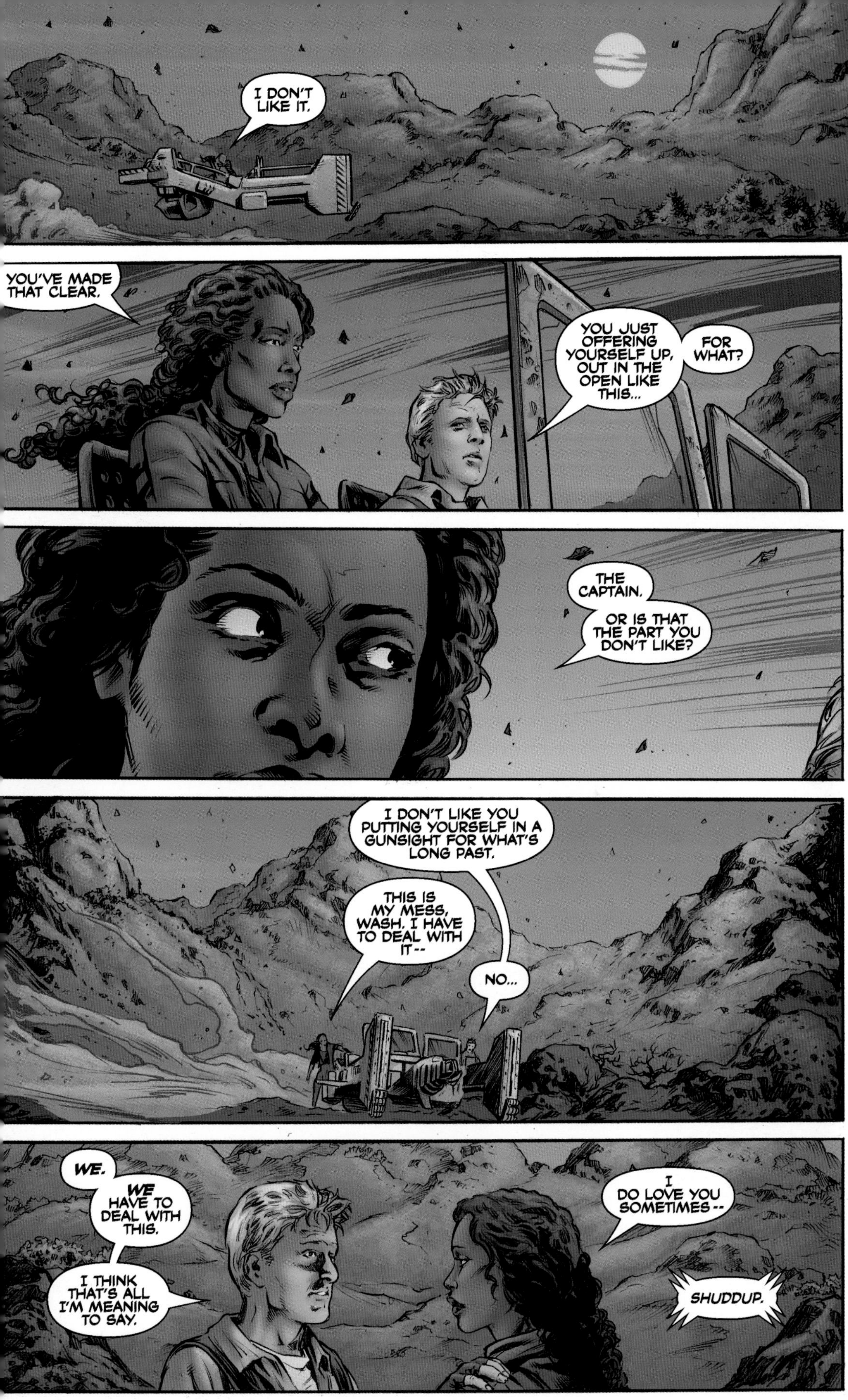

I DON'T LIKE IT.
YOU'VE MADE THAT CLEAR.
YOU JUST OFFERING YOURSELF UP, OUT IN THE OPEN LIKE THIS...
FOR WHAT?
THE CAPTAIN.
OR IS THAT THE PART YOU DON'T LIKE?
I DON'T LIKE YOU PUTTING YOURSELF IN A GUNSIGHT FOR WHAT'S LONG PAST.
THIS IS MY MESS, WASH. I HAVE TO DEAL WITH IT--
NO...
WE.
WE HAVE TO DEAL WITH THIS.
I THINK THAT'S ALL I'M MEANING TO SAY.
I DO LOVE YOU SOMETIMES--
SHUDDUP.

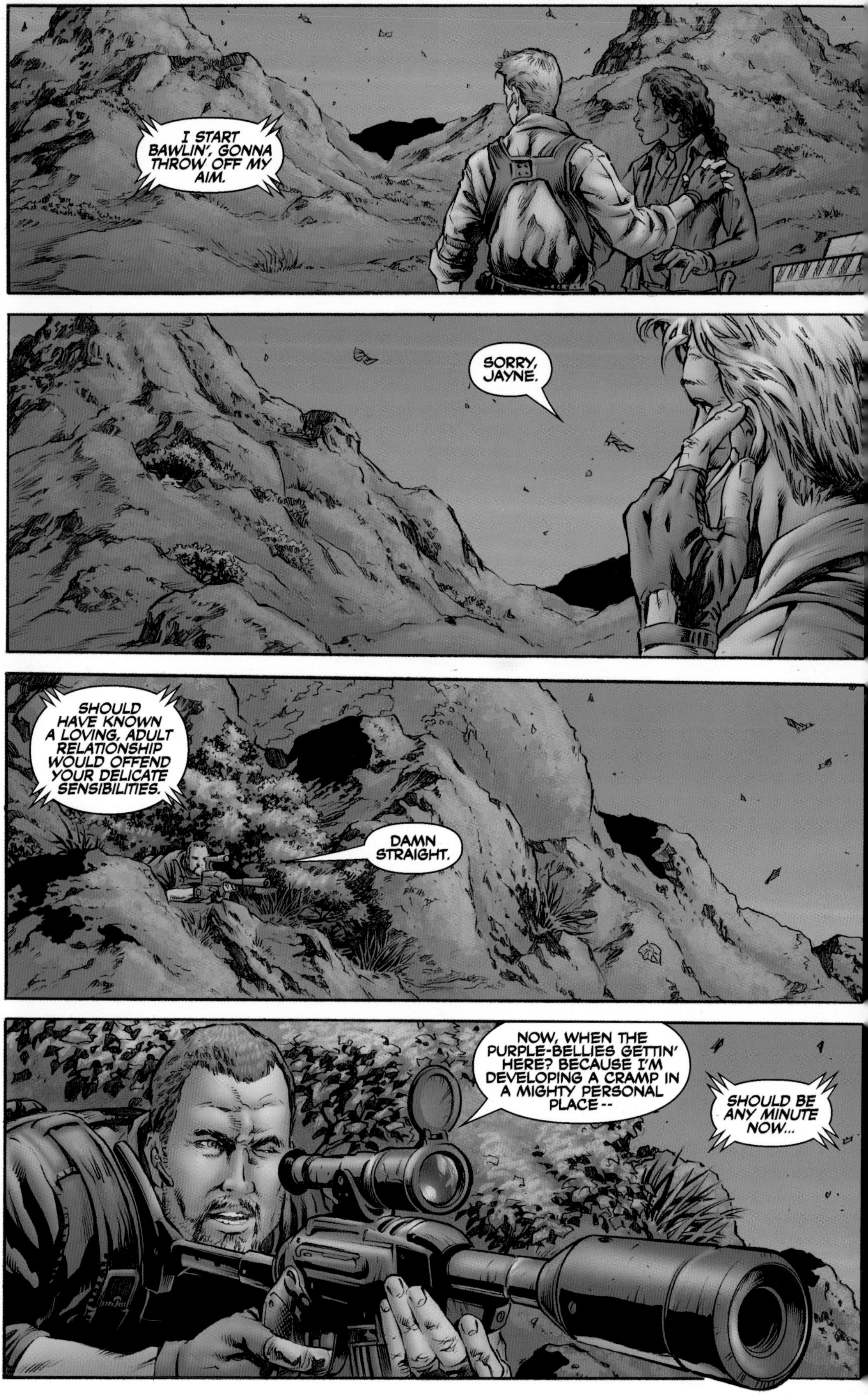

I START BAWLIN', GONNA THROW OFF MY AIM.
SORRY, JAYNE.
SHOULD HAVE KNOWN A LOVING, ADULT RELATIONSHIP WOULD OFFEND YOUR DELICATE SENSIBILITIES.
DAMN STRAIGHT.
NOW, WHEN THE PURPLE-BELLIES GETTIN' HERE? BECAUSE I'M DEVELOPING A CRAMP IN A MIGHTY PERSONAL PLACE --
SHOULD BE ANY MINUTE NOW...

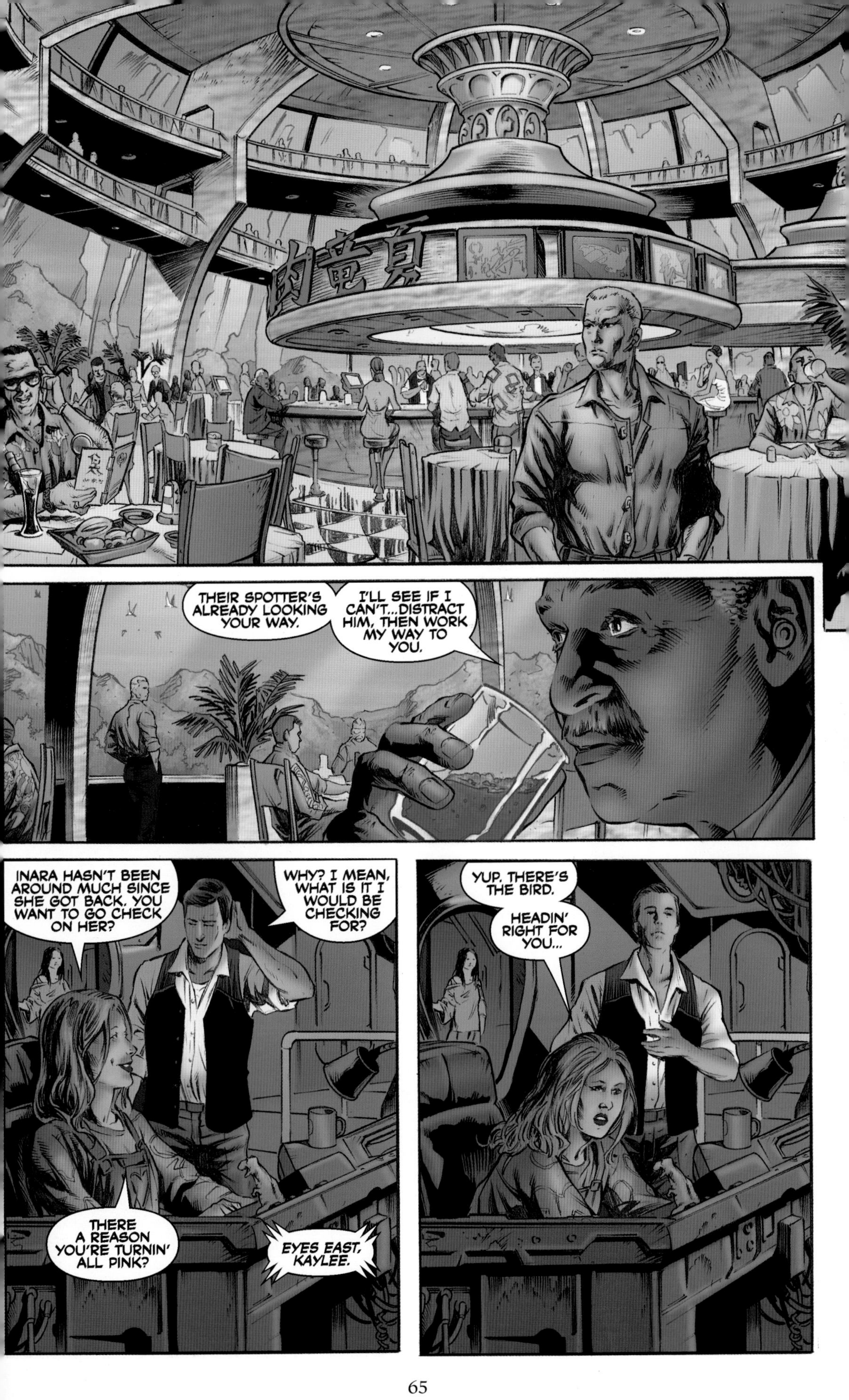
THEIR SPOTTER'S ALREADY LOOKING YOUR WAY.
I'LL SEE IF I CAN'T...DISTRACT HIM, THEN WORK MY WAY TO YOU.
INARA HASN'T BEEN AROUND MUCH SINCE SHE GOT BACK. YOU WANT TO GO CHECK ON HER?
WHY? I MEAN, WHAT IS IT I WOULD BE CHECKING FOR?
THERE A REASON YOU'RE TURNIN' ALL PINK?
EYES EAST, KAYLEE.
YUP, THERE'S THE BIRD.
HEADIN' RIGHT FOR YOU...

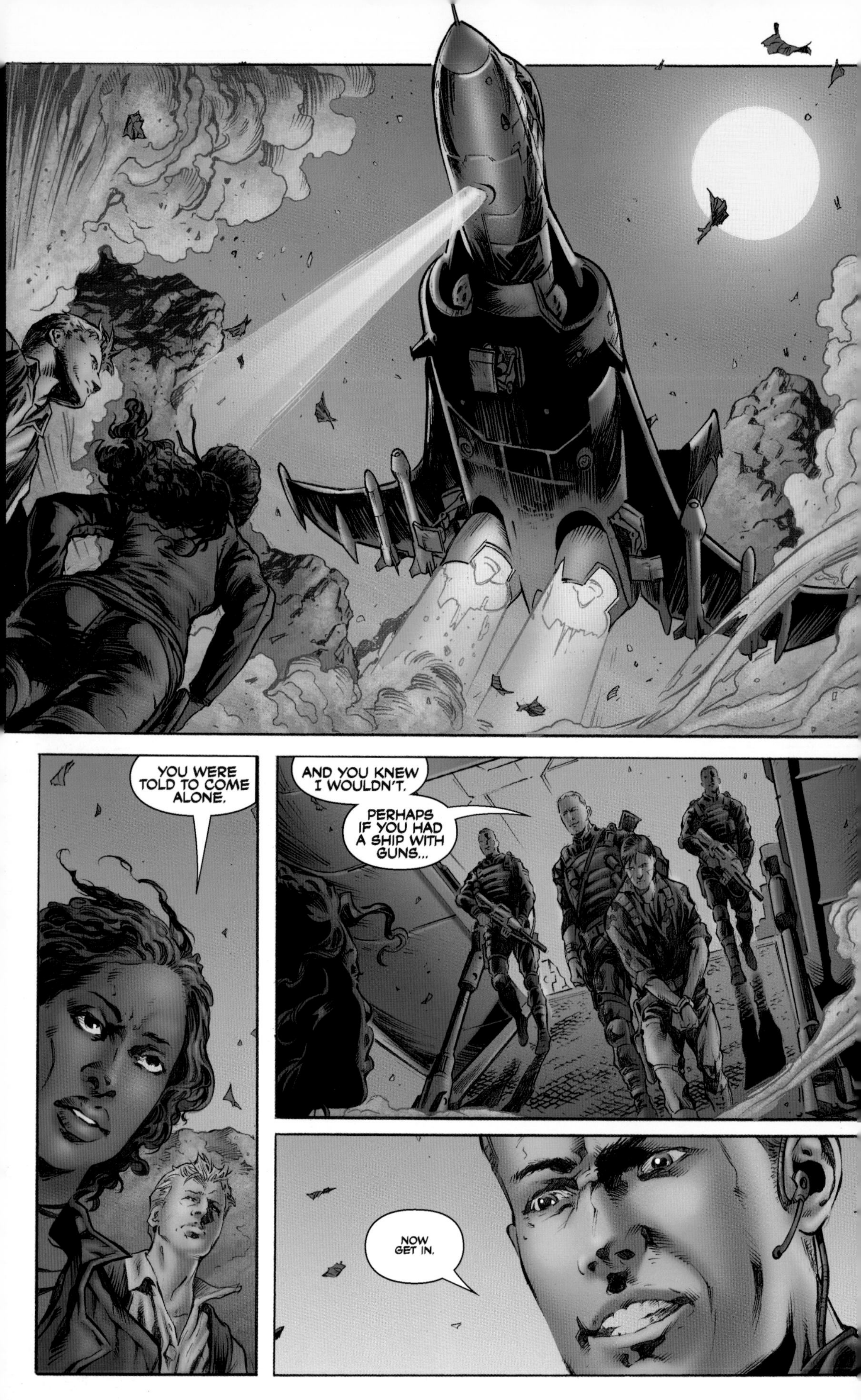
YOU WERE TOLD TO COME ALONE.
AND YOU KNEW I WOULDN'T.
PERHAPS IF YOU HAD A SHIP WITH GUNS...
NOW GET IN.

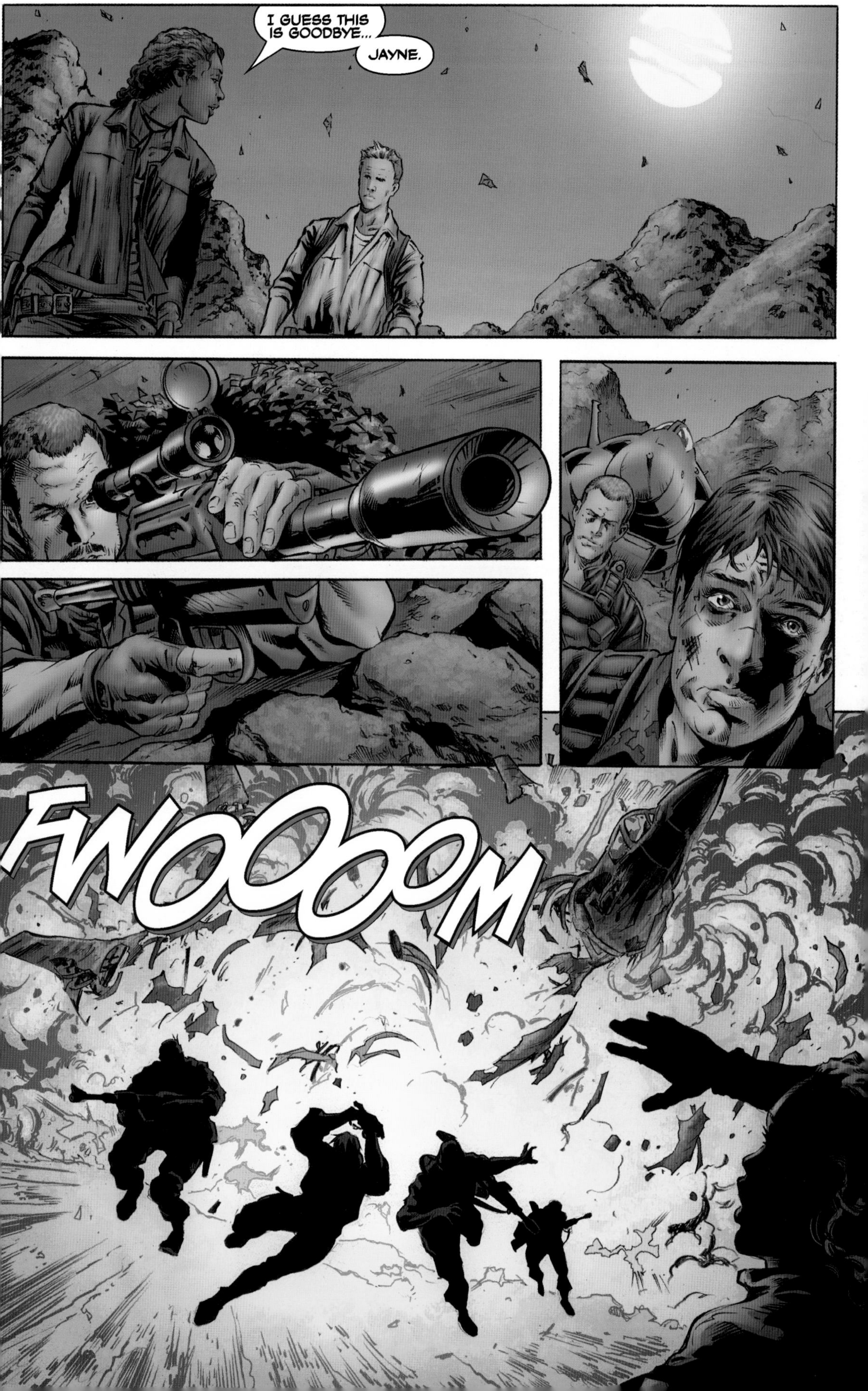

I GUESS THIS IS GOODBYE...
JAYNE.
FWOOOOM

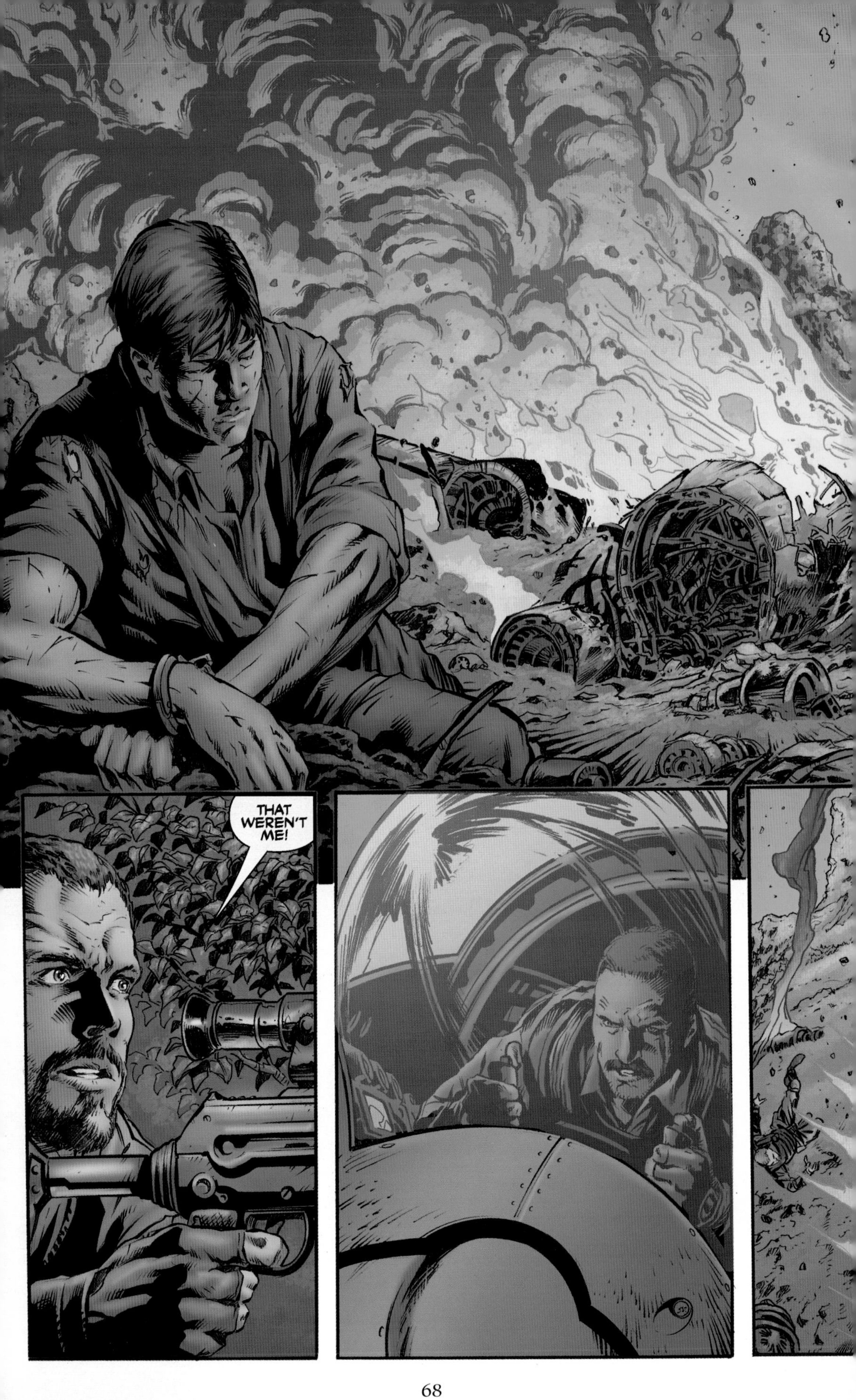
THAT WEREN'T ME!

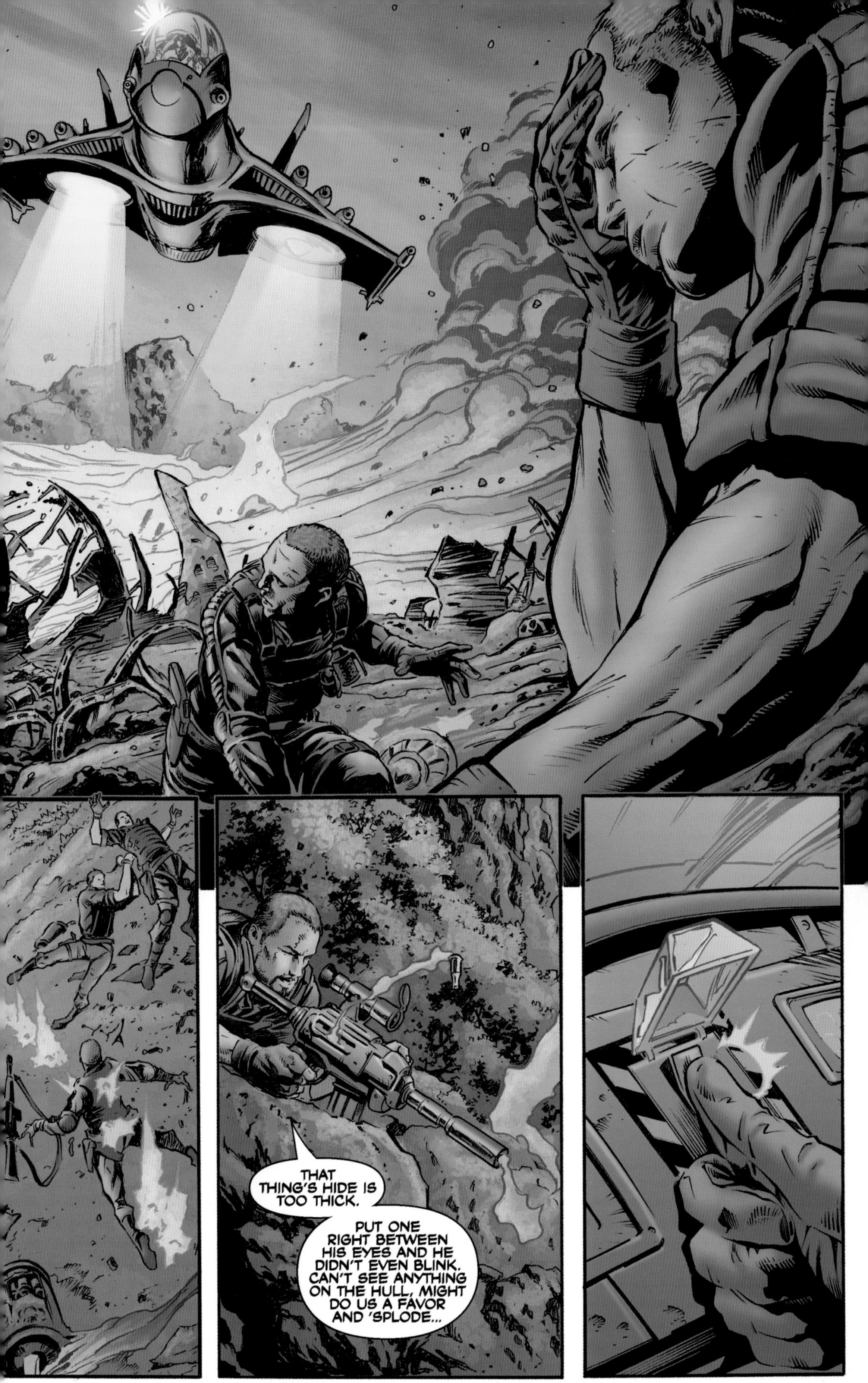
THAT THING'S HIDE IS TOO THICK.
PUT ONE RIGHT BETWEEN HIS EYES AND HE DIDN'T EVEN BLINK. CAN'T SEE ANYTHING ON THE HULL, MIGHT DO US A FAVOR AND 'SPLODE...

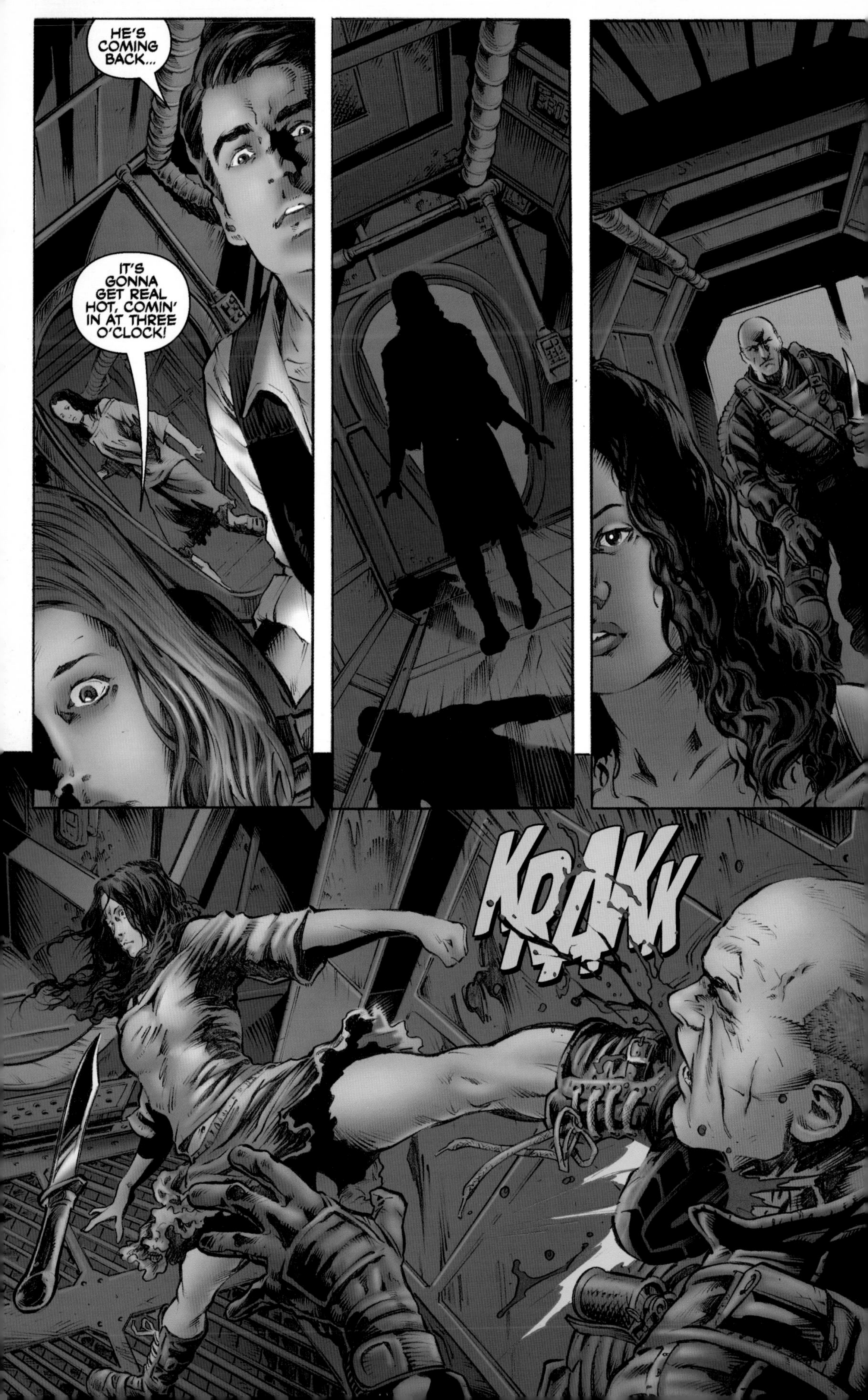
HE'S COMING BACK...
IT'S GONNA GET REAL HOT, COMIN' IN AT THREE O'CLOCK!
KRAKK

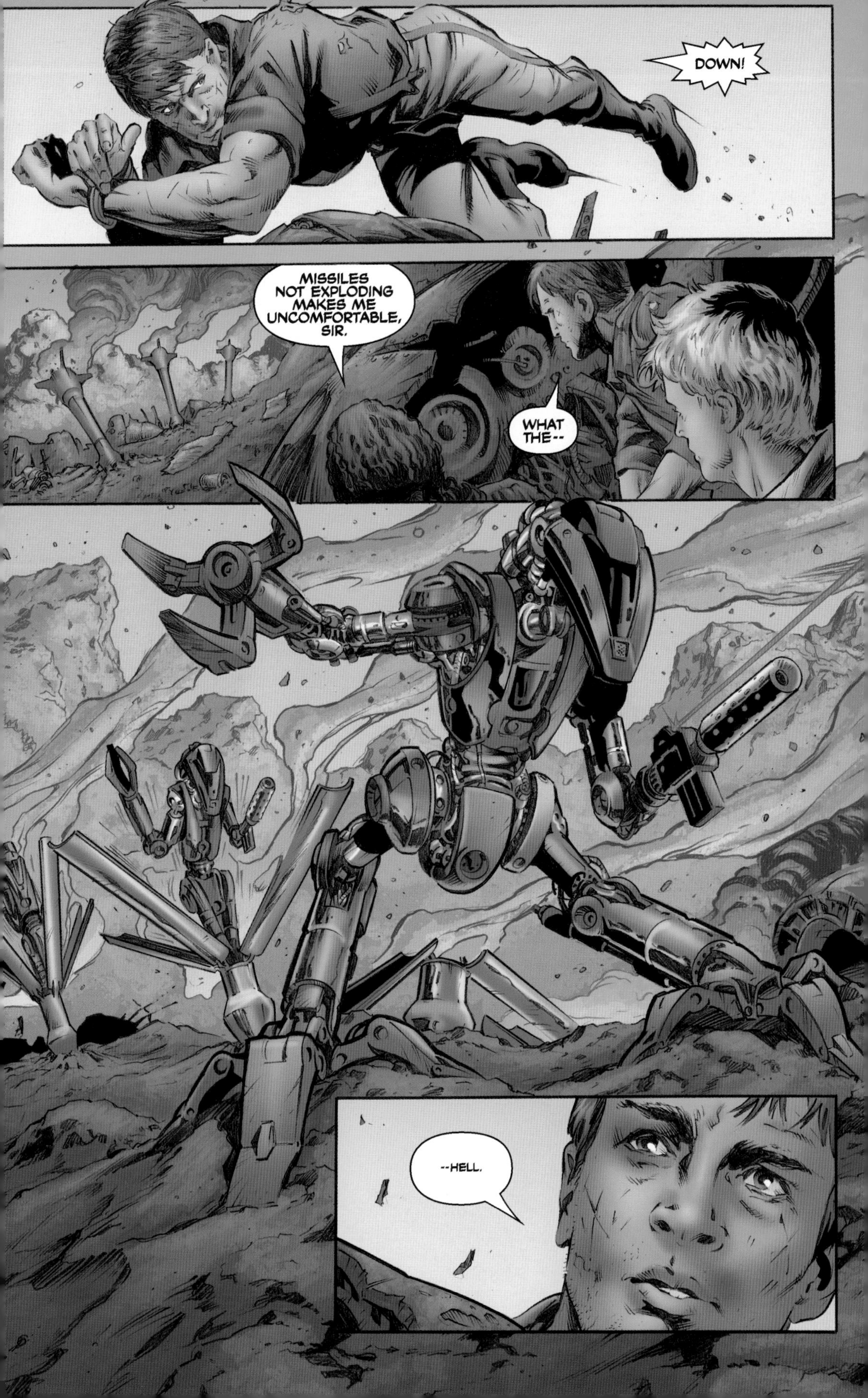
DOWN!
MISSILES NOT EXPLODING MAKES ME UNCOMFORTABLE, SIR.
WHAT THE--
--HELL.

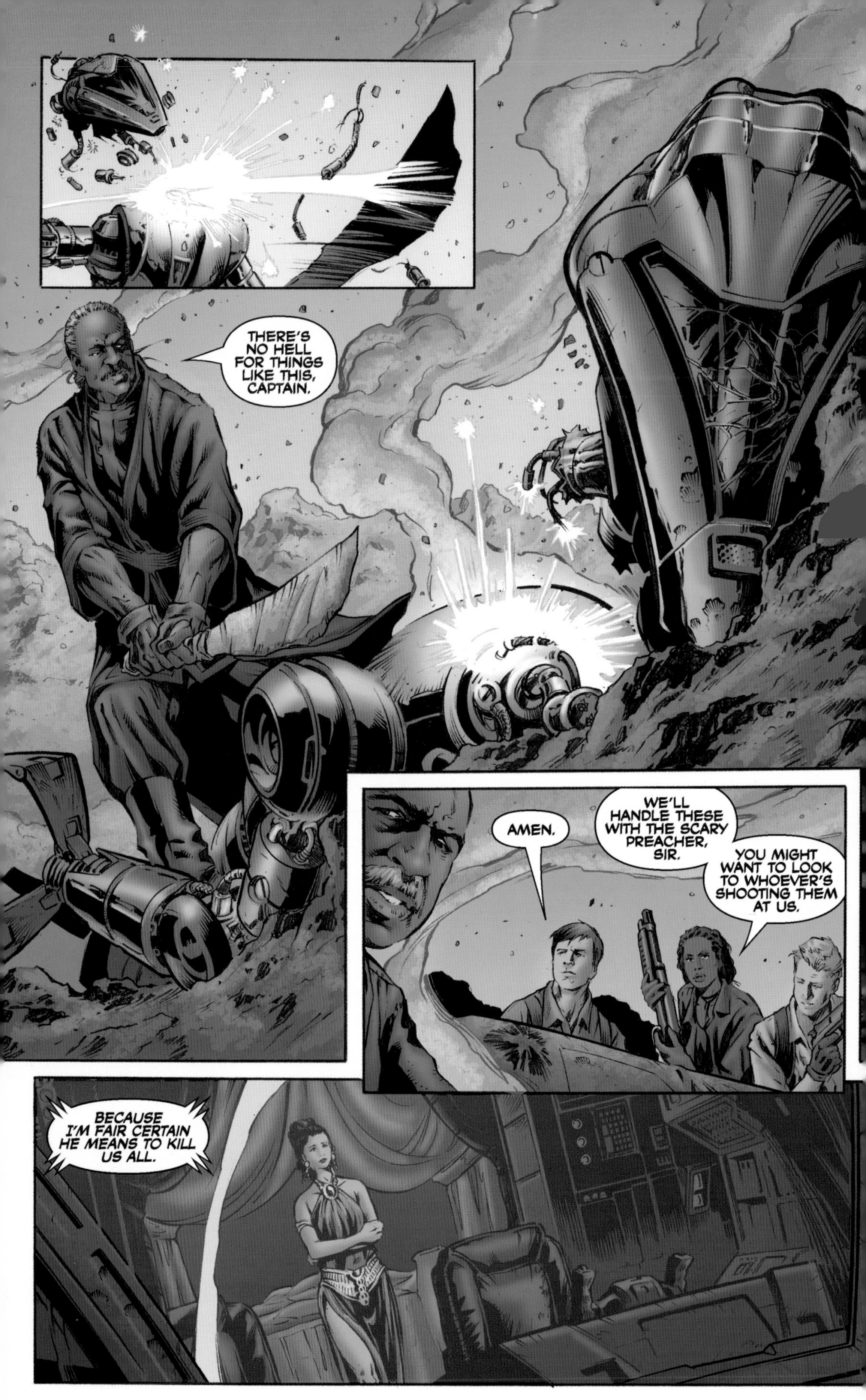
THERE'S NO HELL FOR THINGS LIKE THIS, CAPTAIN.
AMEN.
WE'LL HANDLE THESE WITH THE SCARY PREACHER, SIR.
YOU MIGHT WANT TO LOOK TO WHOEVER'S SHOOTING THEM AT US.
BECAUSE I'M FAIR CERTAIN HE MEANS TO KILL US ALL.

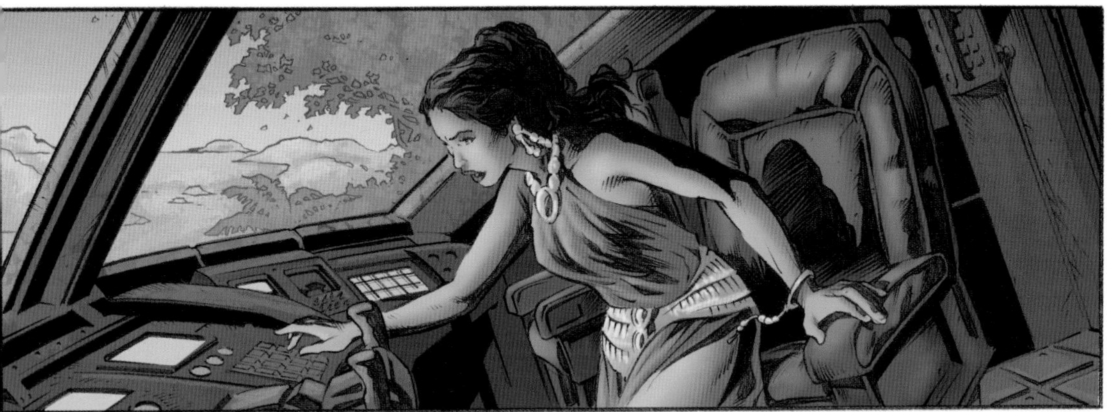

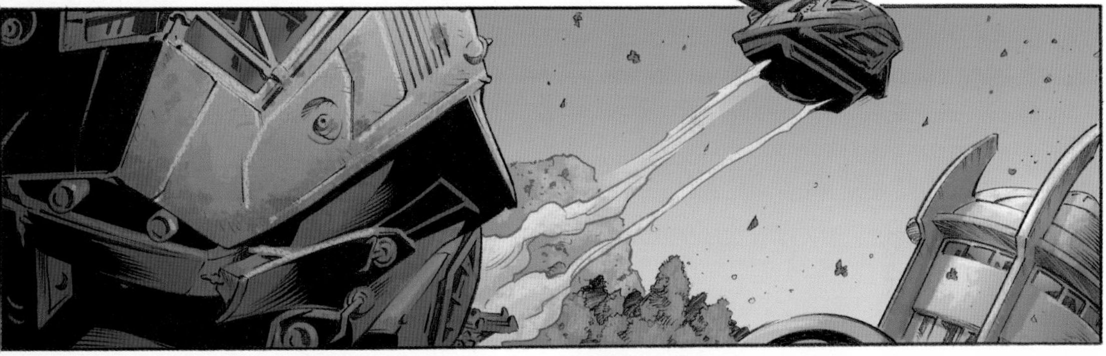

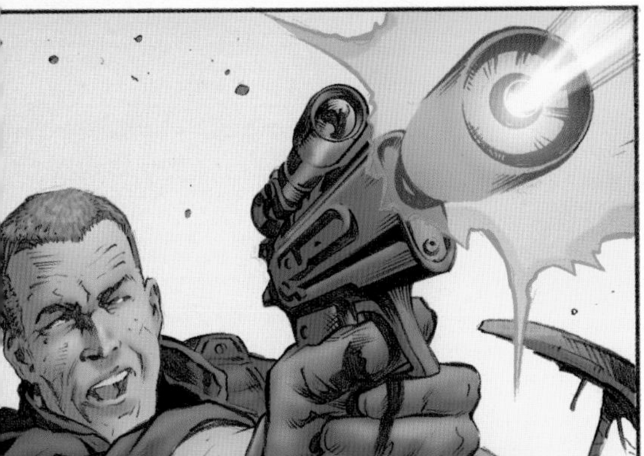

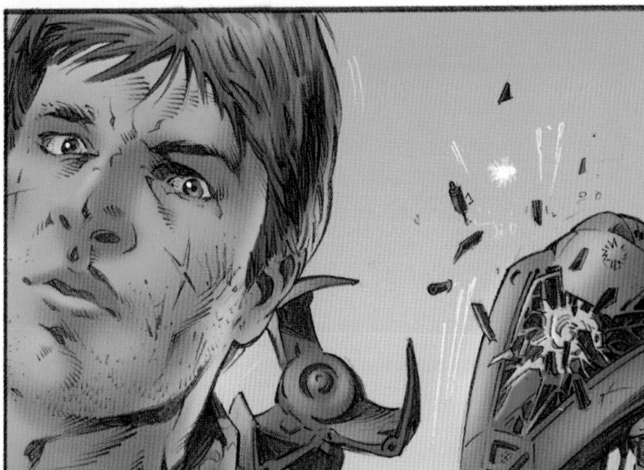

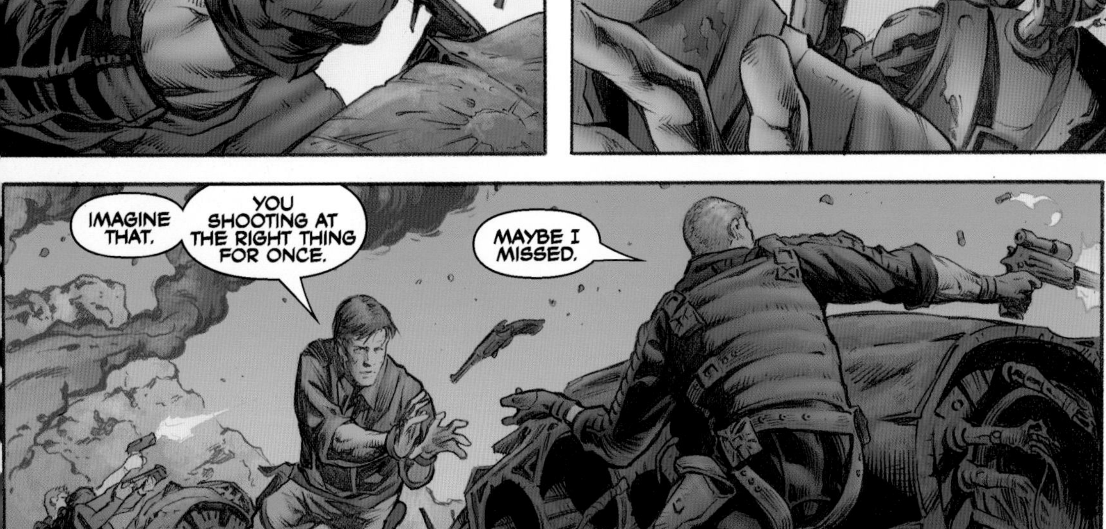
IMAGINE THAT.
YOU SHOOTING AT THE RIGHT THING FOR ONCE.
MAYBE I MISSED.

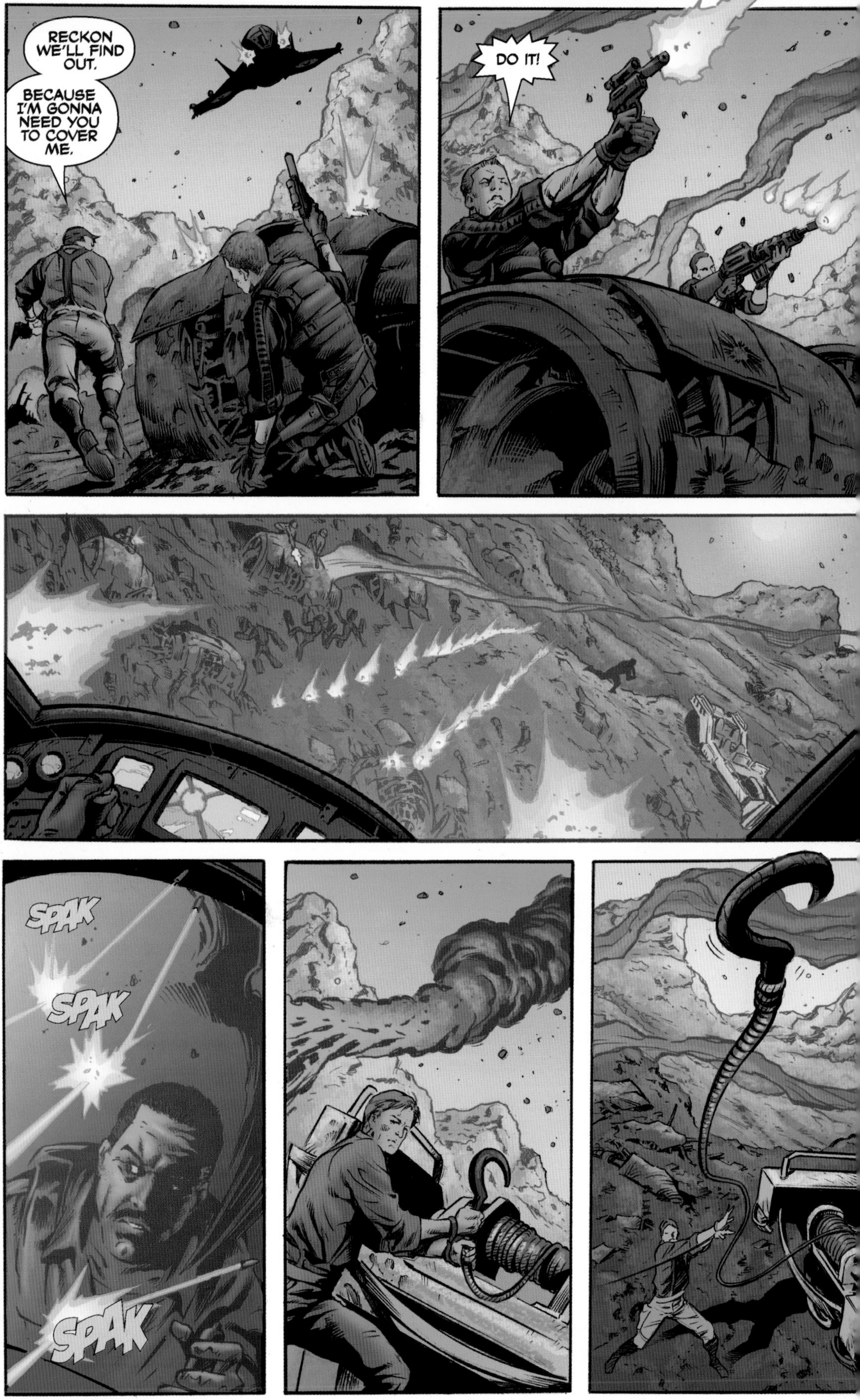
RECKON WE'LL FIND OUT.
BECAUSE I'M GONNA NEED YOU TO COVER ME.
DO IT!
SPAK
SPAK
SPAK

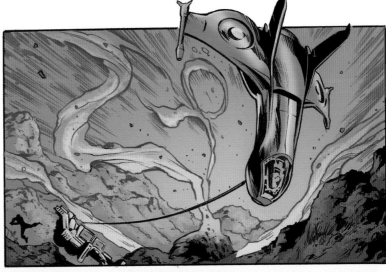

GUESS WE'LL NEVER KNOW WHAT HIS PROBLEM WAS...

WE GOOD HERE?

GOOD ENOUGH.

ACTUALLY, THERE'S THIS ONE THING...

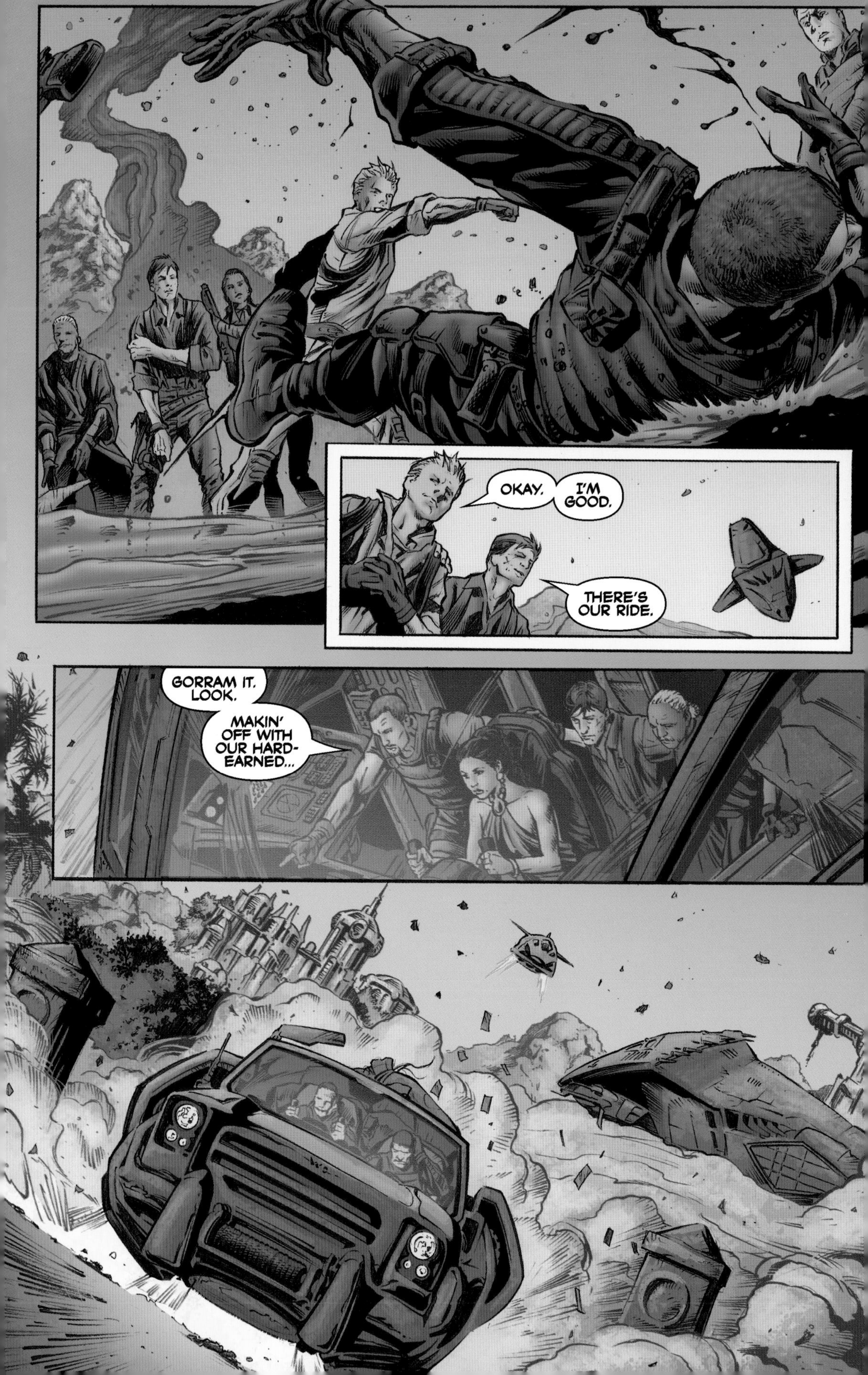
OKAY.
I'M GOOD.
THERE'S OUR RIDE.
GORRAM IT. LOOK.
MAKIN' OFF WITH OUR HARD-EARNED...

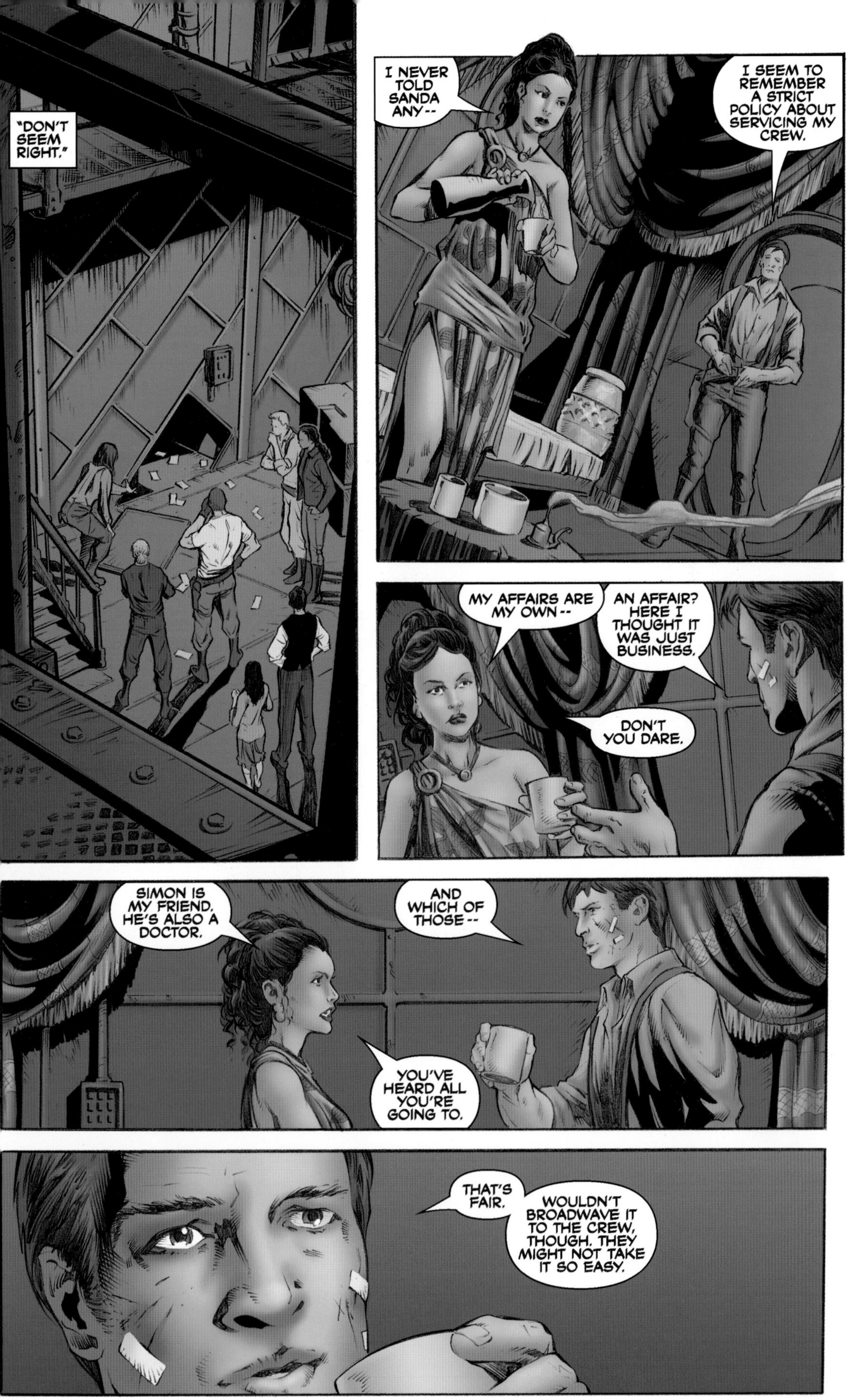
"DON'T SEEM RIGHT."
I NEVER TOLD SANDA ANY--
I SEEM TO REMEMBER A STRICT POLICY ABOUT SERVICING MY CREW.
MY AFFAIRS ARE MY OWN--
AN AFFAIR? HERE I THOUGHT IT WAS JUST BUSINESS.
DON'T YOU DARE.
SIMON IS MY FRIEND. HE'S ALSO A DOCTOR.
AND WHICH OF THOSE--
YOU'VE HEARD ALL YOU'RE GOING TO.
THAT'S FAIR.
WOULDN'T BROADWAVE IT TO THE CREW, THOUGH. THEY MIGHT NOT TAKE IT SO EASY.

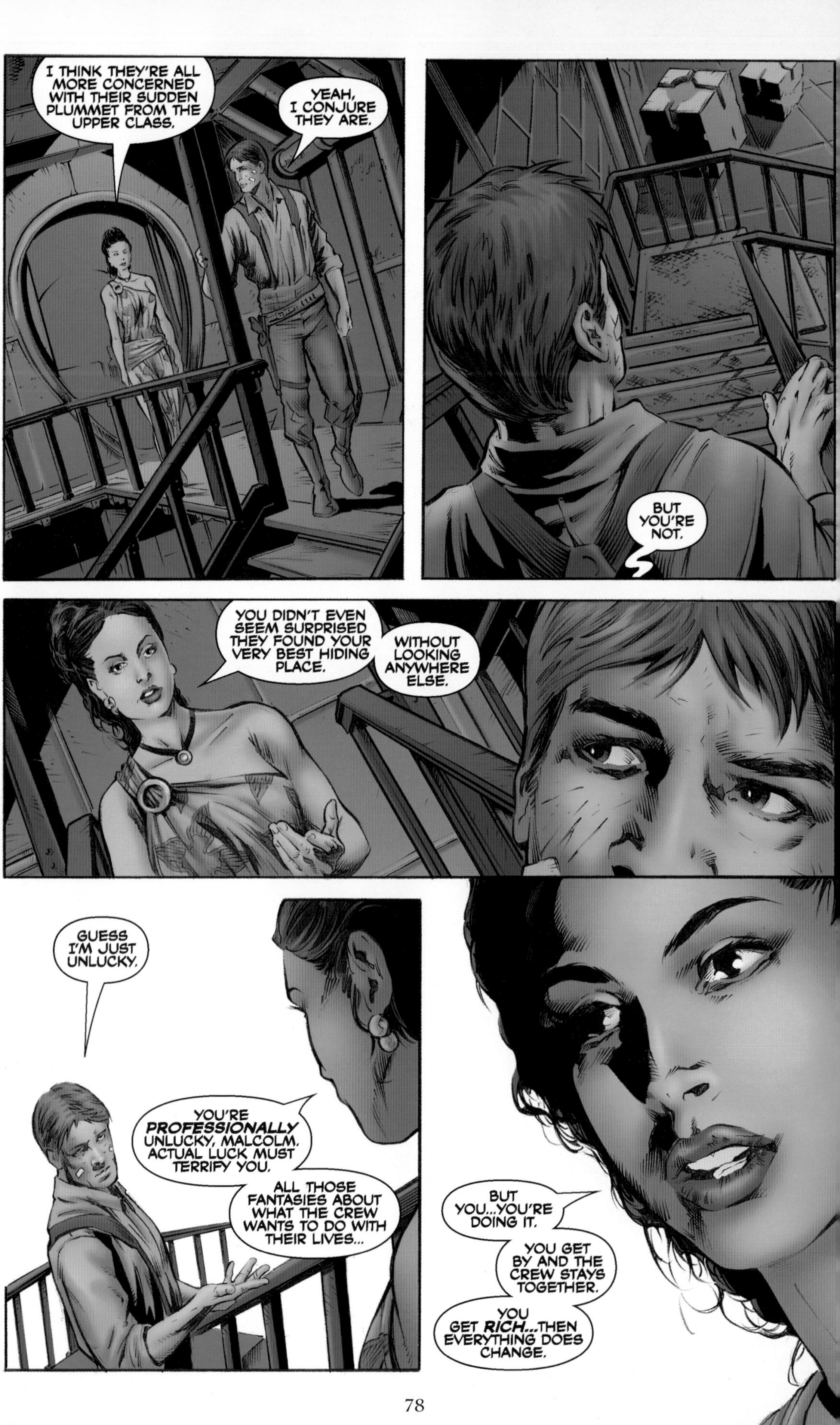
I THINK THEY'RE ALL MORE CONCERNED WITH THEIR SUDDEN PLUMMET FROM THE UPPER CLASS.
YEAH, I CONJURE THEY ARE.
BUT YOU'RE NOT.
YOU DIDN'T EVEN SEEM SURPRISED THEY FOUND YOUR VERY BEST HIDING PLACE.
WITHOUT LOOKING ANYWHERE ELSE.
GUESS I'M JUST UNLUCKY.
YOU'RE PROFESSIONALLY UNLUCKY, MALCOLM. ACTUAL LUCK MUST TERRIFY YOU.
ALL THOSE FANTASIES ABOUT WHAT THE CREW WANTS TO DO WITH THEIR LIVES...
BUT YOU...YOU'RE DOING IT.
YOU GET BY AND THE CREW STAYS TOGETHER.
YOU GET RICH...THEN EVERYTHING DOES CHANGE.

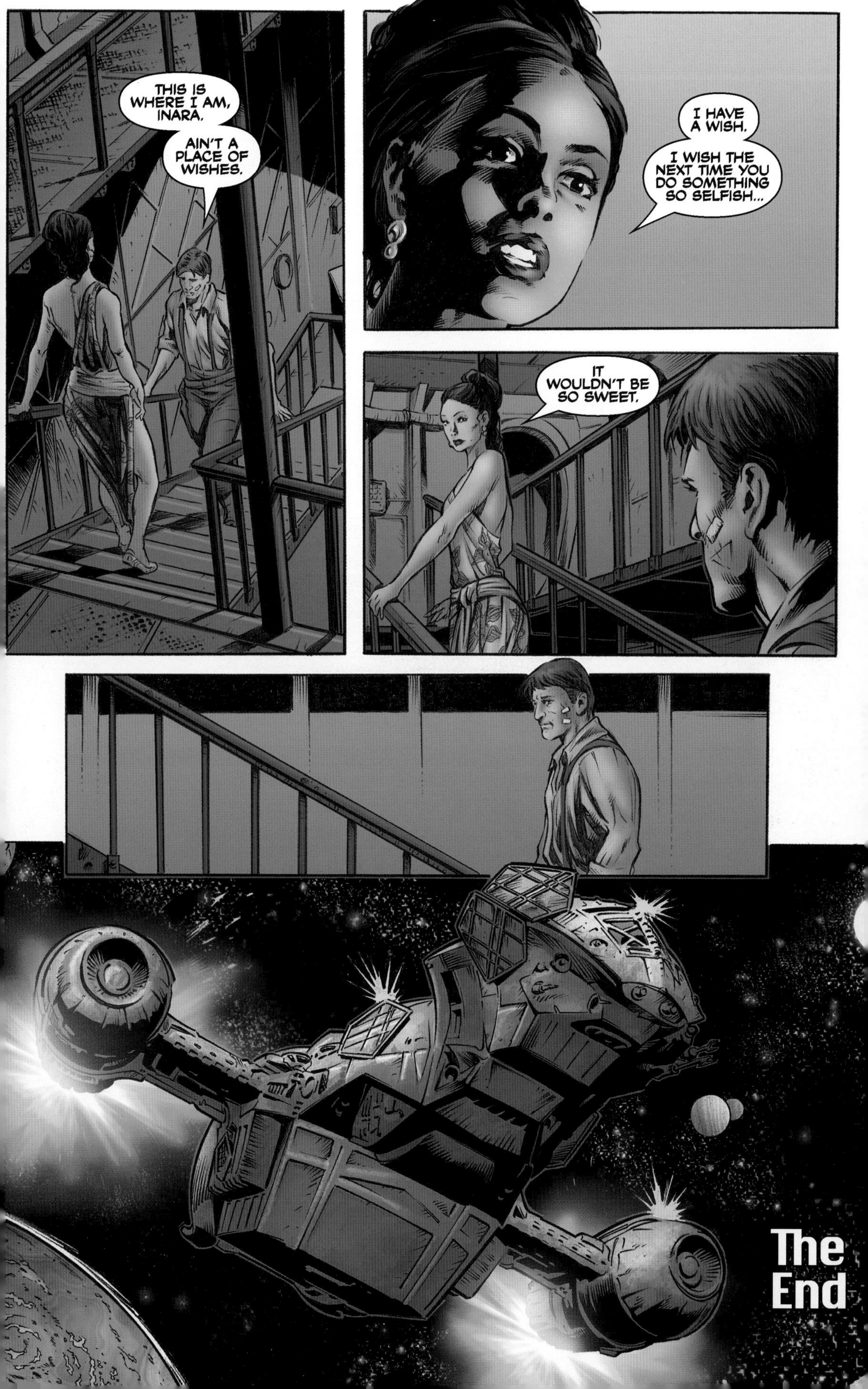

THIS IS WHERE I AM, INARA.
AIN'T A PLACE OF WISHES.
I HAVE A WISH.
I WISH THE NEXT TIME YOU DO SOMETHING SO SELFISH...
IT WOULDN'T BE SO SWEET.
The End

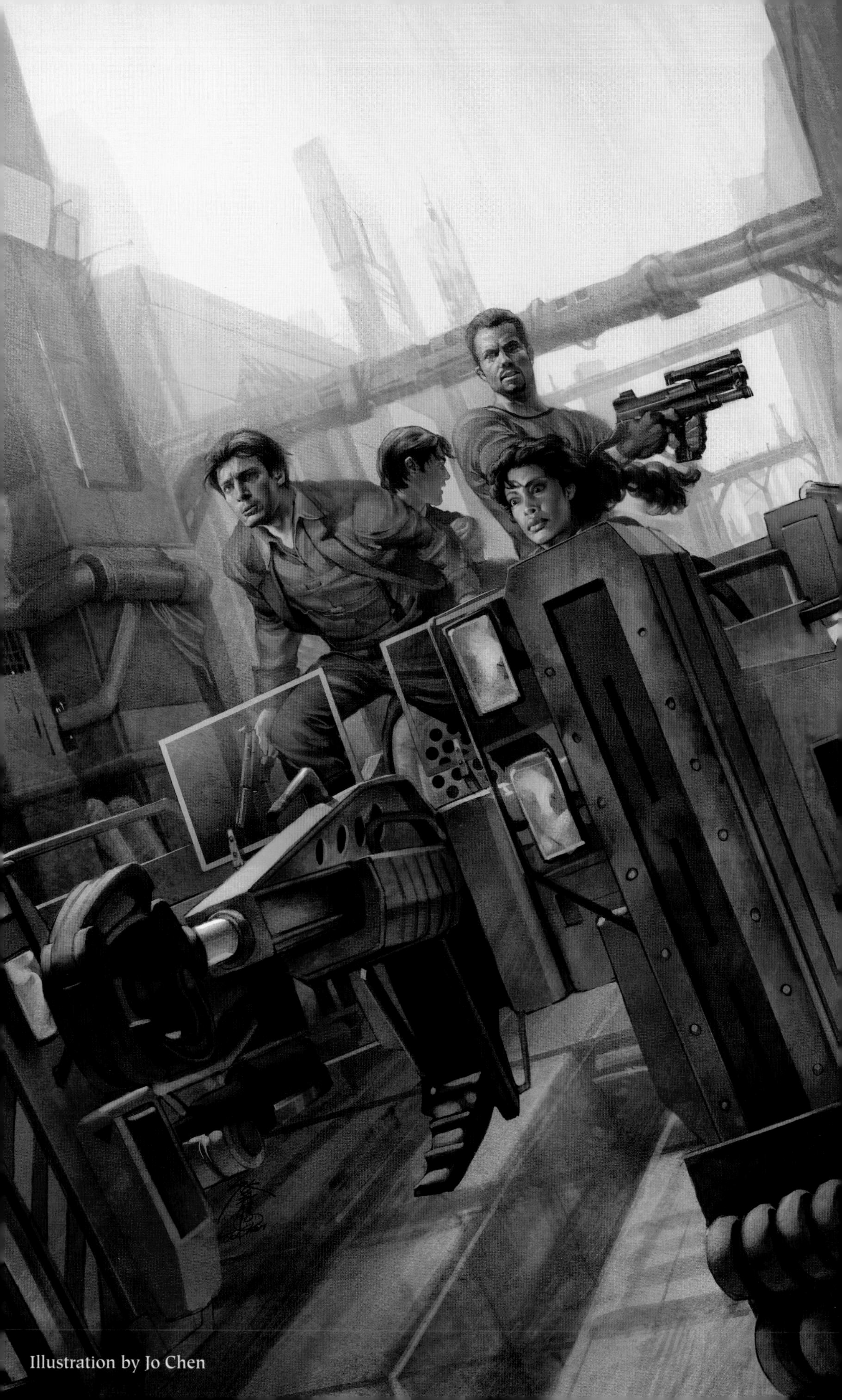

Illustration by Jo Chen

AFTERWORD

When Joss Whedon gave me the chance to play a man called Jayne, the "Hero of Canton," I couldn't believe my luck. I'd never been asked to play a girl before, so I knew I was going to have to summon my inner hero, Carol Burnett.

Joss's way with words provided me the opportunity to play a tough guy (girl's name) with comedic flair. In the past, I had been typically cast in roles that called on me to be tough, so to be tough and funny was a great adventure.

In 2002, the script for *Firefly* landed on my doorstep. This was the start of my days as a conduit for those mind-bending Whedonisms. The characters not only cussed in Chinese; they were also fluent in sarcasm. Not only did I fall in love with Jayne's sense of humor, but the show brought endless laughter, banter, practical jokes, and lifelong friendships as a bonus.

Fans' thoughtful and detailed examinations of all areas of *Firefly*, along with their kindness and encouragement, lifted our spirits and reinforced our dedication to delivering what we thought was the best danged show on television. *Firefly* had the most fun writing, hardest-working professional crew, and most dedicated support staff I'd ever seen. We were all honored and blessed to be a part of such an amazing team.

So, when it was announced to the cast and crew of *Firefly* on a cold December night that the network was pulling the plug, we all felt as if we were being disemboweled by Reavers. The show had been a blessing and a beacon of light in the lives of all involved, and we felt a great sense of loss that night.

Then came an unprecedented Hollywood story of redemption and renewal . . .

Joss called to tell us that he would find a way to keep *Serenity* flying, even if he had to erect the sets in his backyard (which isn't quite big enough for a spaceship . . . and construction permits are really complicated in his neighborhood). This is not something we soldiers of Hollywood ever hear. When Joss realized that he was producing a new project, I think he came to the conclusion that he was going to need his backyard for his kids, so off he went in search of another hangar for the ship and its crew.

Universal to the rescue!

Before we knew it, we got the shiniest news. We were going to be flying to the outer planets by summer, and not for television, but in a major motion-picture release by Universal Studios. Joss had done it. He was able to take an old, broken-down craft and a splintered crew, persuade the Hollywood powers that be to patch up the ship and crew, and get them back in the air. After many months of blogging with fans of undying passion, Joss was getting to bring his crew to the big screen. He had fought the toughest battle, and he had won.

Fearlessly led back out into the black by Joss, we shared in your hopes that *Serenity* would fly even higher than before.

It was summer of 2004 in Los Angeles, and we were at home again, this time on the Universal lot. The sets were bigger and badder than I could remember during the series: life was grand. Somewhere near the end of the shoot the cast boarded a more modern craft and took the short trek to Comic-Con in San Diego. As the trailer for the movie played to an unprecedented crowd of nearly six thousand fans, every hair on my neck was standing. Joss and the fans had gotten their well-deserved wish. They were going to get their movie. I was joyous for *Firefly*'s beloved fans, and even more so for Joss. He'd done the impossible.

What an incredible feat. *Dare to dream*, I thought at that moment. And then: *Wow, who is this Joss guy anyway? How does he create such magic? Where did these people come from? How lucky am I to have had the opportunity to live in this wonderful world of Whedon?*

Now with the Dark Horse comics series of *Serenity*, we all have more chances to devour the characters Joss brought to life when *Serenity* took its maiden voyage.

I have been very blessed to be forever known as "The Man They Call Jayne," gorrammit!

—ADAM BALDWIN
(not a girl's name)

THE OTHER HALF

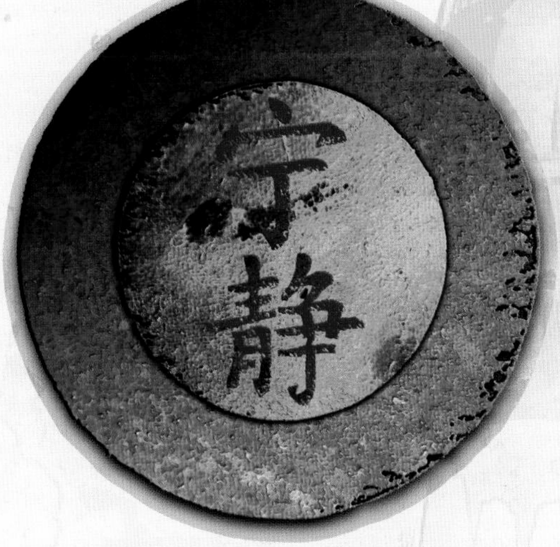
宁静

STORY
JIM KRUEGER

ART
WILL CONRAD

COLORS
JULIUS OHTA

LETTERS
MICHAEL HEISLER

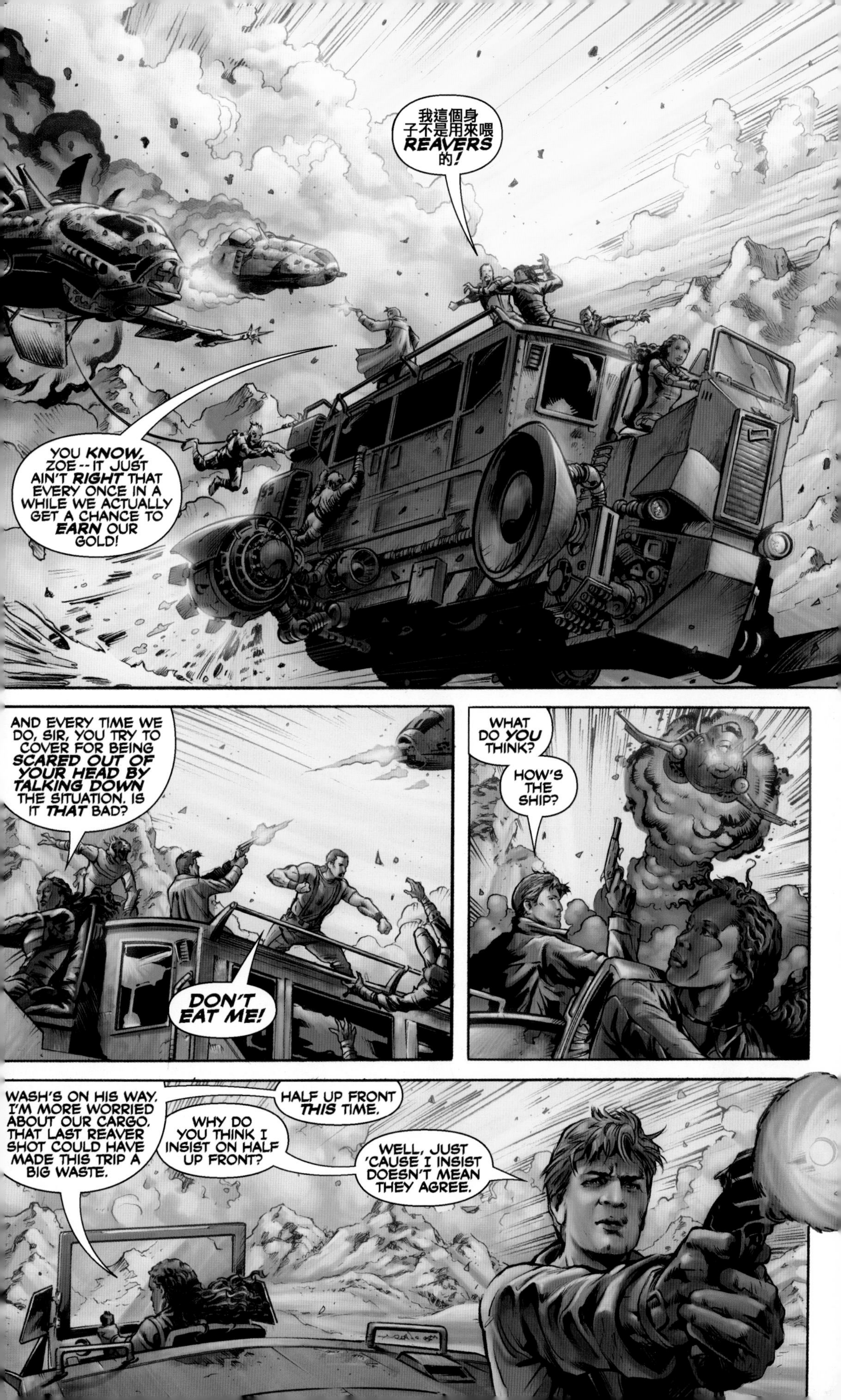

我這個身子不是用來喂REAVERS的!
YOU KNOW, ZOE -- IT JUST AIN'T RIGHT THAT EVERY ONCE IN A WHILE WE ACTUALLY GET A CHANCE TO EARN OUR GOLD!
AND EVERY TIME WE DO, SIR, YOU TRY TO COVER FOR BEING SCARED OUT OF YOUR HEAD BY TALKING DOWN THE SITUATION. IS IT THAT BAD?
DON'T EAT ME!
WHAT DO YOU THINK?
HOW'S THE SHIP?
WASH'S ON HIS WAY. I'M MORE WORRIED ABOUT OUR CARGO. THAT LAST REAVER SHOT COULD HAVE MADE THIS TRIP A BIG WASTE.
HALF UP FRONT THIS TIME.
WHY DO YOU THINK I INSIST ON HALF UP FRONT?
WELL, JUST 'CAUSE I INSIST DOESN'T MEAN THEY AGREE.

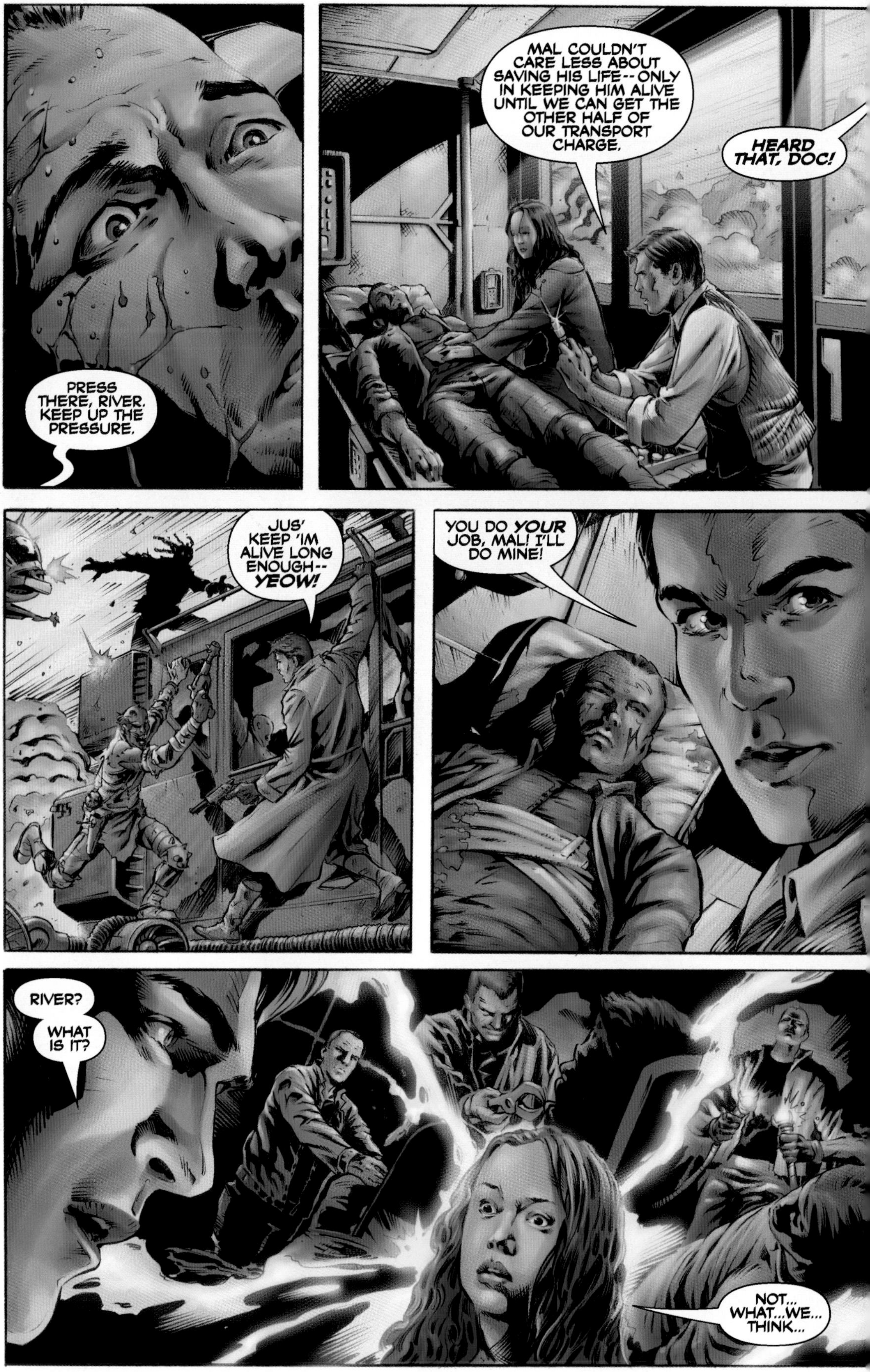

PRESS THERE, RIVER. KEEP UP THE PRESSURE.
MAL COULDN'T CARE LESS ABOUT SAVING HIS LIFE--ONLY IN KEEPING HIM ALIVE UNTIL WE CAN GET THE OTHER HALF OF OUR TRANSPORT CHARGE.
HEARD THAT, DOC!
JUS' KEEP 'IM ALIVE LONG ENOUGH--YEOW!
YOU DO YOUR JOB, MAL! I'LL DO MINE!
RIVER?
WHAT IS IT?
NOT... WHAT...WE... THINK...

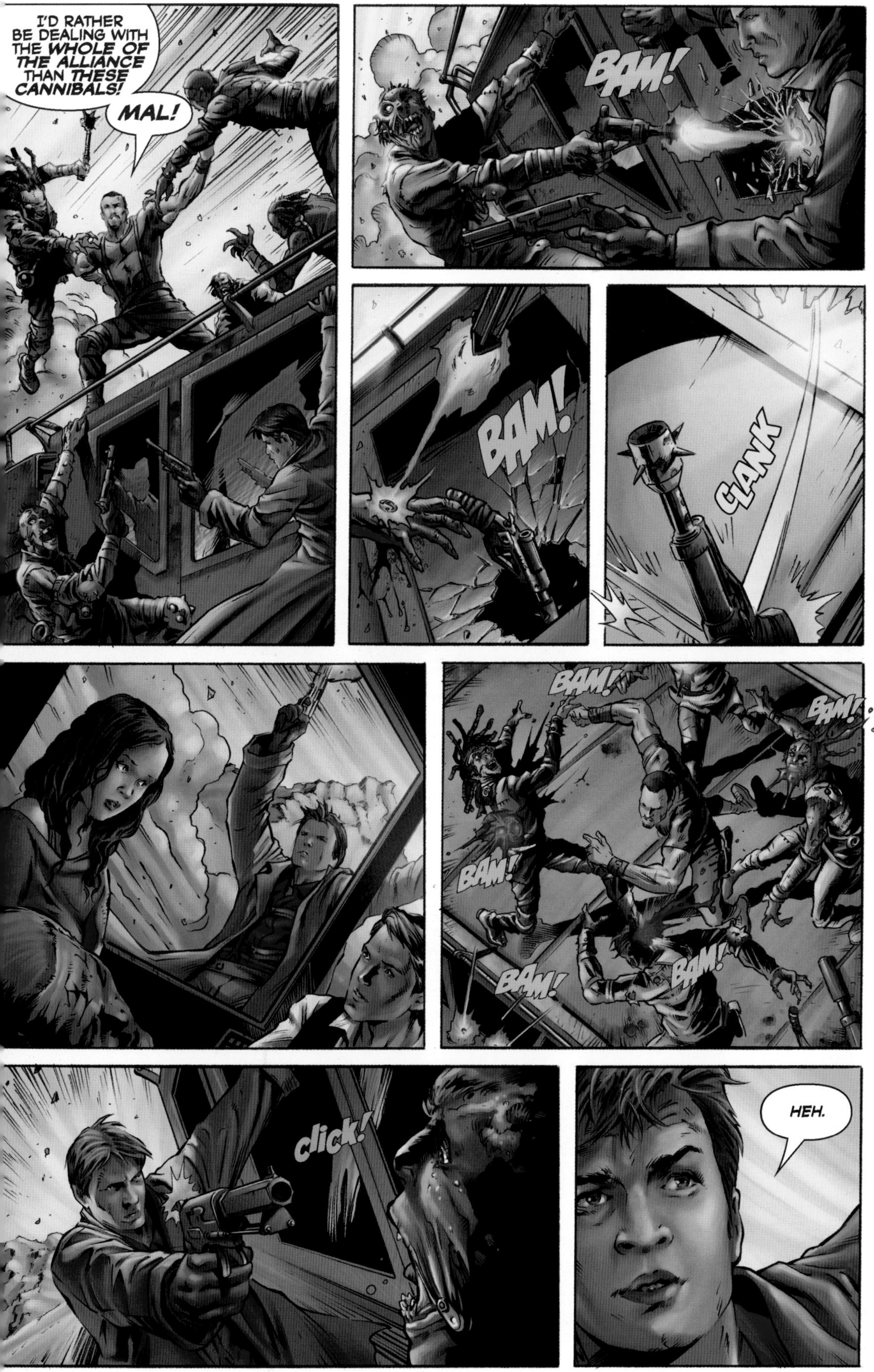

I'D RATHER BE DEALING WITH THE WHOLE OF THE ALLIANCE THAN THESE CANNIBALS!
MAL!
BAM!
BAM!
CLANK
BAM!
BAM!
BAM!
BAM!
BAM!
click!
HEH.

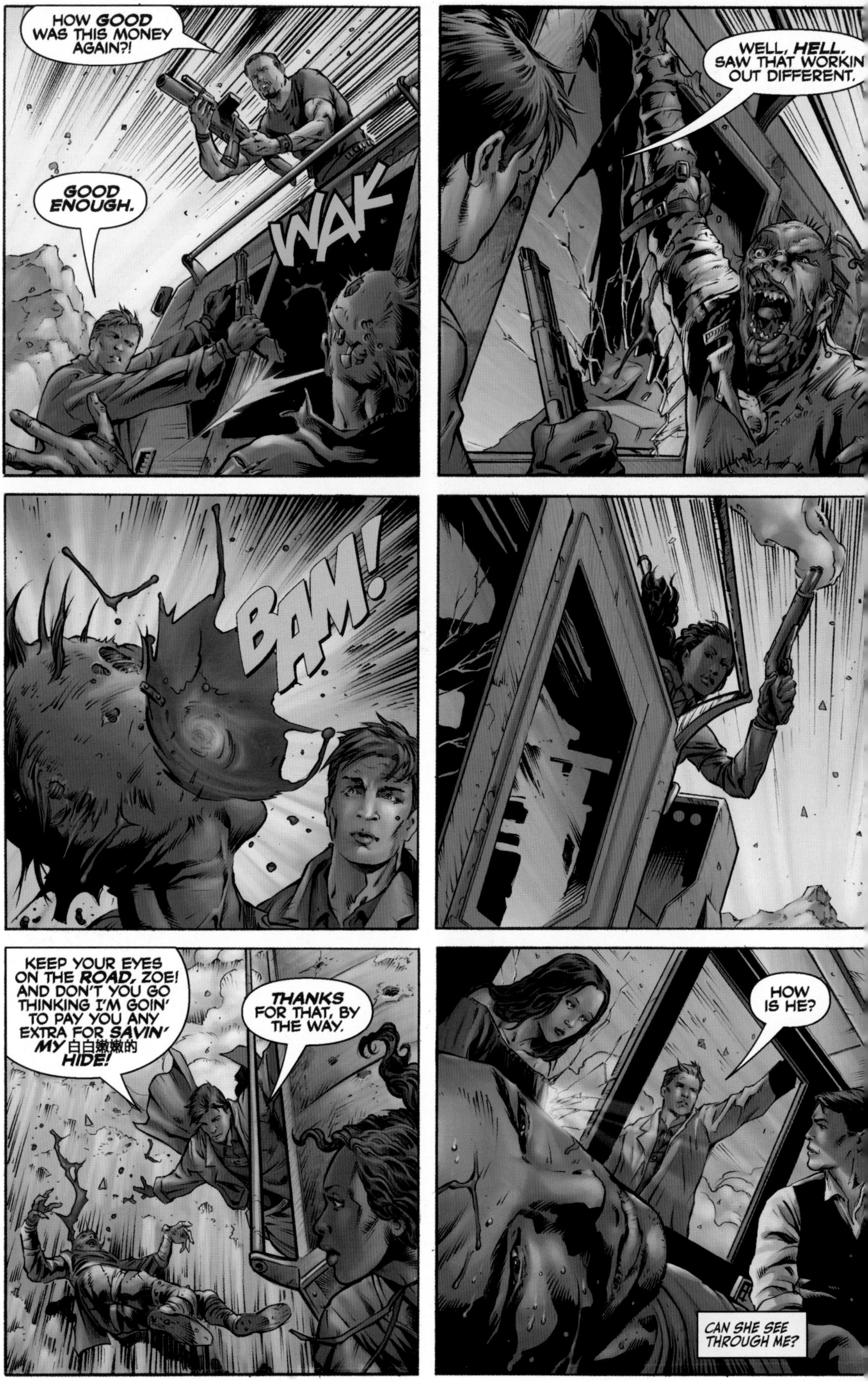

HOW GOOD WAS THIS MONEY AGAIN?!
GOOD ENOUGH.
WAK
WELL, HELL. SAW THAT WORKIN OUT DIFFERENT.
BAM!
KEEP YOUR EYES ON THE ROAD, ZOE! AND DON'T YOU GO THINKING I'M GOIN' TO PAY YOU ANY EXTRA FOR SAVIN' MY 白白嫩嫩的 HIDE!
THANKS FOR THAT, BY THE WAY.
HOW IS HE?
CAN SHE SEE THROUGH ME?

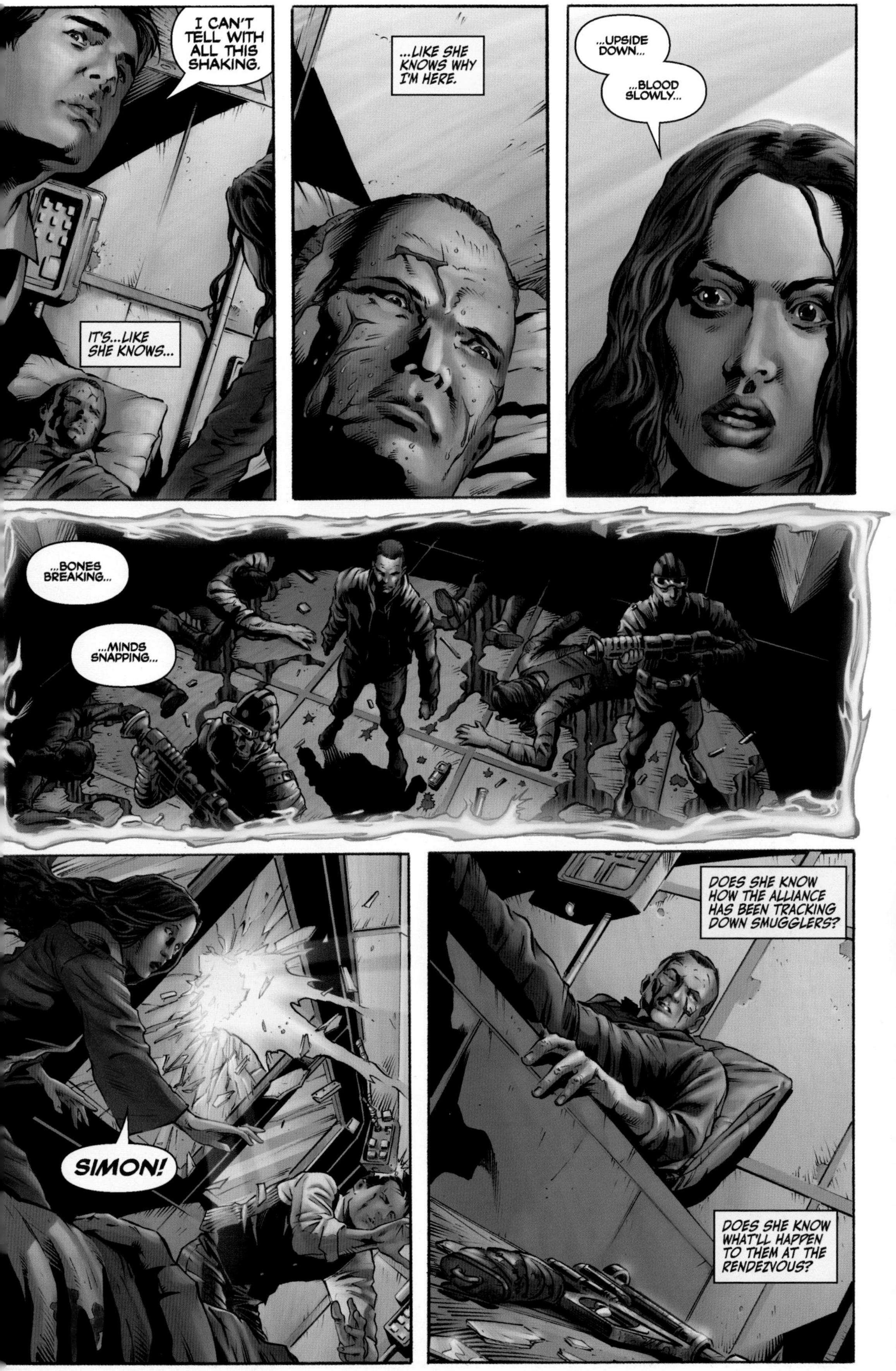
I CAN'T TELL WITH ALL THIS SHAKING.
IT'S...LIKE SHE KNOWS...
...LIKE SHE KNOWS WHY I'M HERE.
...UPSIDE DOWN...
...BLOOD SLOWLY...
...BONES BREAKING...
...MINDS SNAPPING...
SIMON!
DOES SHE KNOW HOW THE ALLIANCE HAS BEEN TRACKING DOWN SMUGGLERS?
DOES SHE KNOW WHAT'LL HAPPEN TO THEM AT THE RENDEZVOUS?

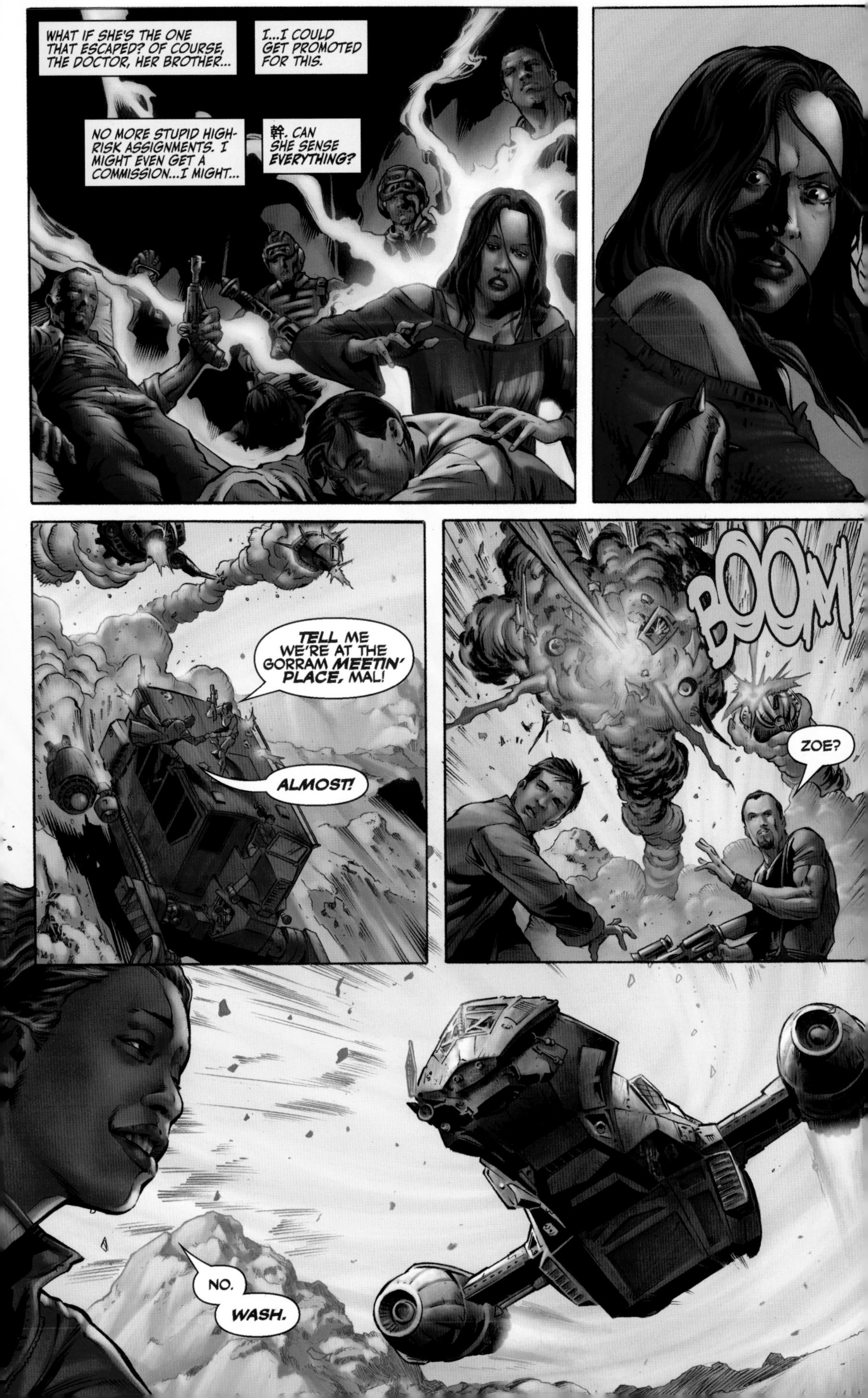
WHAT IF SHE'S THE ONE THAT ESCAPED? OF COURSE, THE DOCTOR, HER BROTHER...
I...I COULD GET PROMOTED FOR THIS.
NO MORE STUPID HIGH-RISK ASSIGNMENTS. I MIGHT EVEN GET A COMMISSION...I MIGHT...
幹. CAN SHE SENSE EVERYTHING?
TELL ME WE'RE AT THE GORRAM MEETIN' PLACE, MAL!
ALMOST!
BOOM
ZOE?
NO.
WASH.

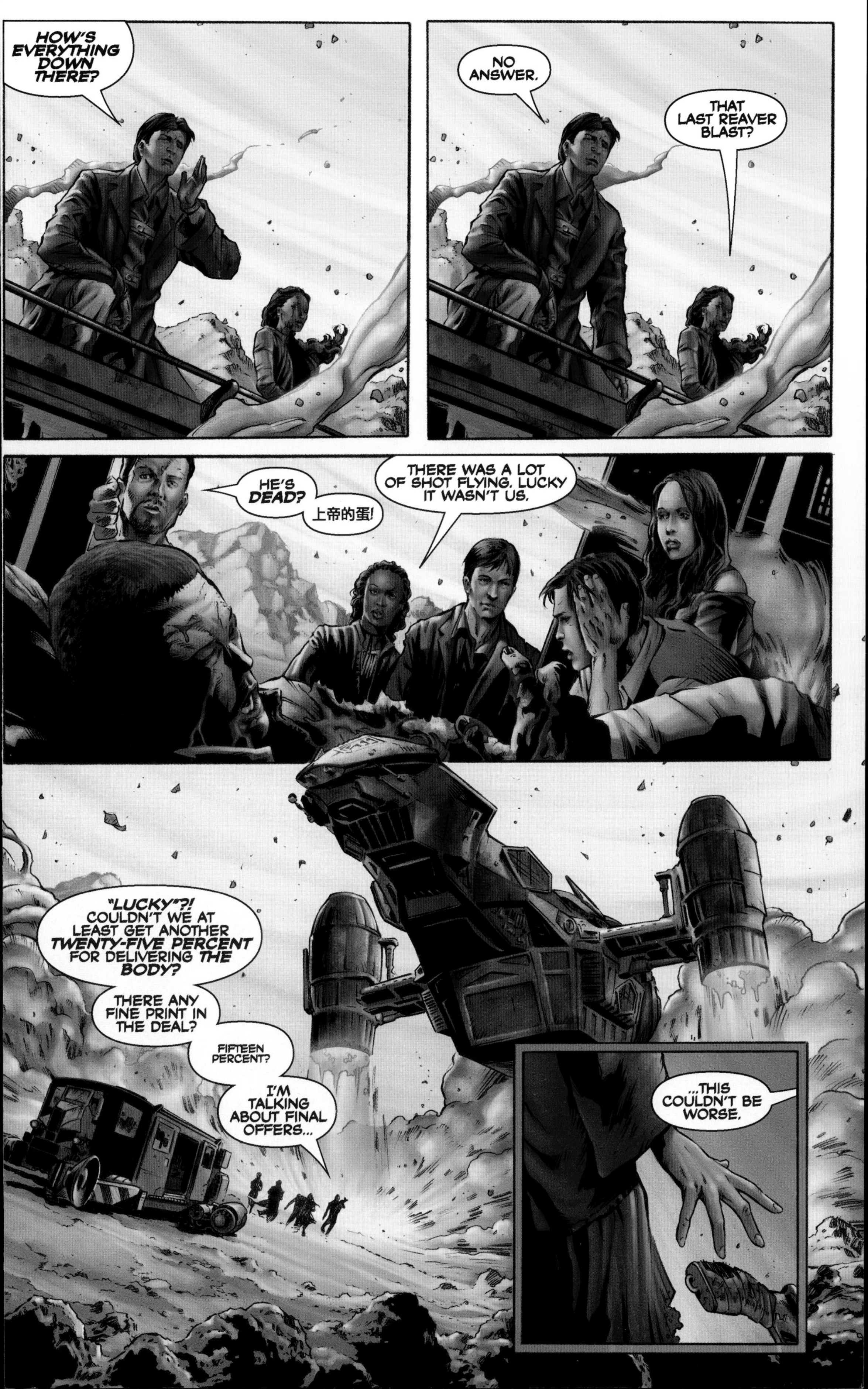
HOW'S EVERYTHING DOWN THERE?
NO ANSWER.
THAT LAST REAVER BLAST?
HE'S DEAD?
上帝的蛋!
THERE WAS A LOT OF SHOT FLYING. LUCKY IT WASN'T US.
"LUCKY"?! COULDN'T WE AT LEAST GET ANOTHER TWENTY-FIVE PERCENT FOR DELIVERING THE BODY?
THERE ANY FINE PRINT IN THE DEAL?
FIFTEEN PERCENT?
I'M TALKING ABOUT FINAL OFFERS...
...THIS COULDN'T BE WORSE.

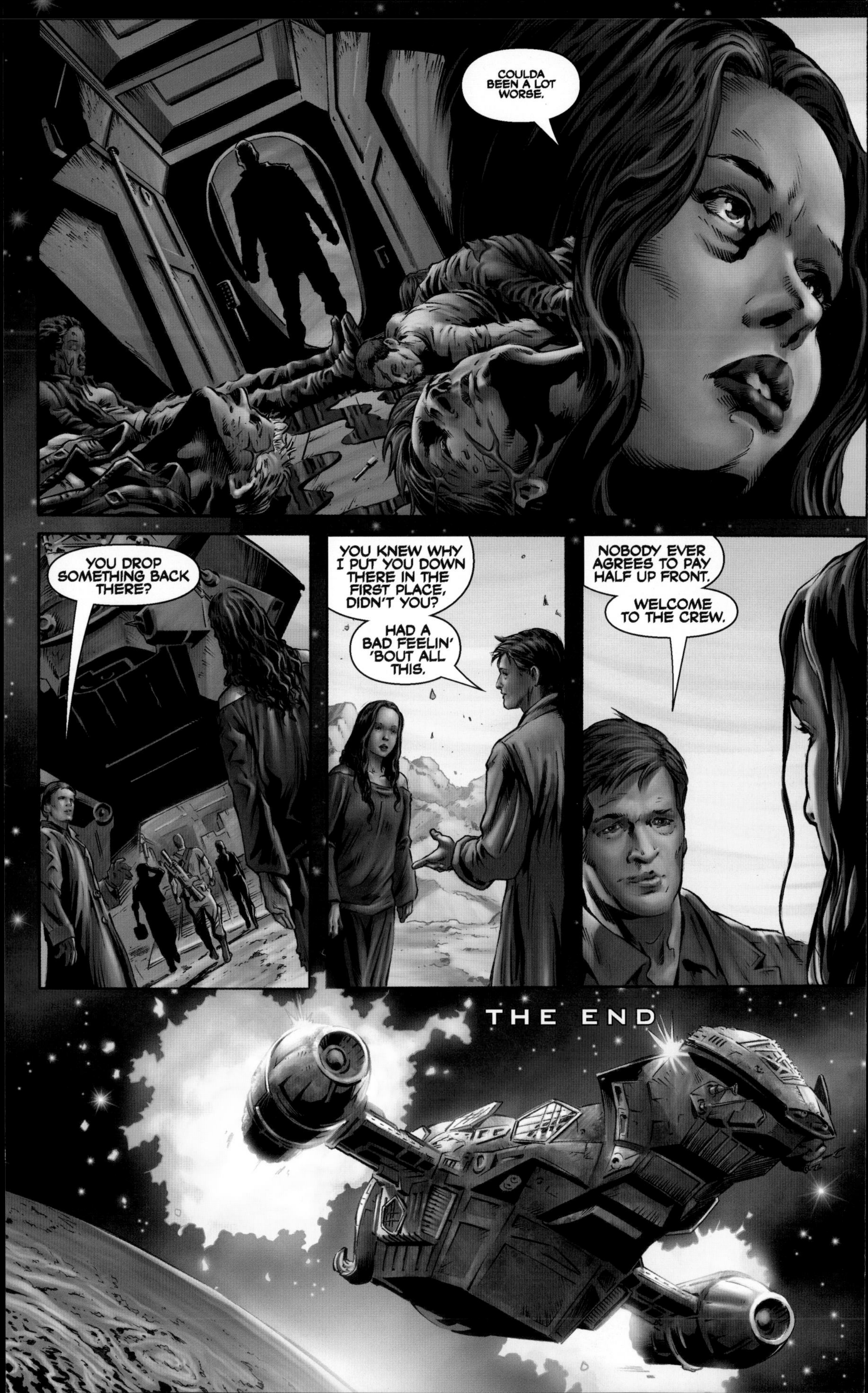
COULDA BEEN A LOT WORSE.
YOU DROP SOMETHING BACK THERE?
YOU KNEW WHY I PUT YOU DOWN THERE IN THE FIRST PLACE, DIDN'T YOU?
HAD A BAD FEELIN' 'BOUT ALL THIS.
NOBODY EVER AGREES TO PAY HALF UP FRONT.
WELCOME TO THE CREW.
THE END

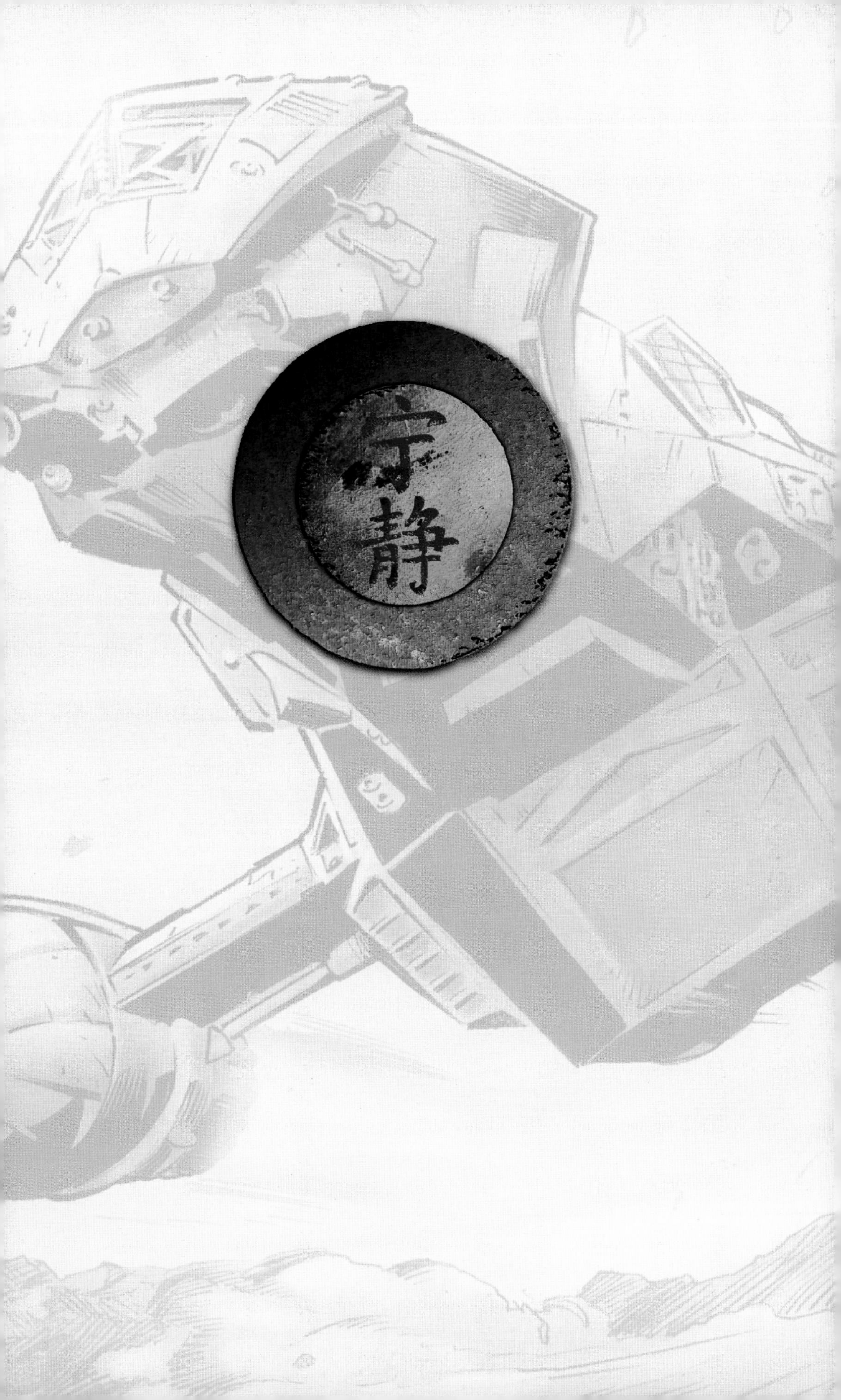
守静

DOWNTIME

STORY
ZACK WHEDON

ART
CHRIS SAMNEE

COLORS
DAVE STEWART

LETTERS
MICHAEL HEISLER

KAYLEE?

HEY, CAP'N!

WHY AIN'T WE FLYING?

AIN'T ON MY ACCOUNT. SHIP'S HUMMIN', MAL.

WASH!

MAL! MALCOLM! MY DEAR OLD PAL, MALCOLM.

WHY AIN'T WE FLYING?

WERE WE SUPPOSED TO BE GOING SOMEWHERE?

I AIN'T IN THE MOOD FOR ANY HILARITY, WASH. TELL ME WHY WE'RE STILL ON THE GROUND.

SNOW.

COMING DOWN HARD. CAN'T SEE A THING.

SNOW?

I'D TRY TO FLY THROUGH IT BUT THEN THERE'S THE POSSIBLE MOUNTAIN AND US CRASHING INTO IT...BODY PARTS EVERYWHERE...SOME OF THEM MINE...

WHAT ABOUT THE PLAN?

YES, STEP TWO OF WHICH WAS RUN THE HELL AWAY.

THERE WAS A PLAN?

YOU COULD CALL THIS PLAN B.

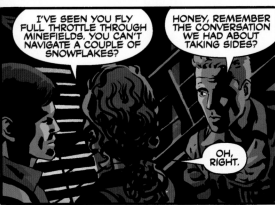

I'VE SEEN YOU FLY FULL THROTTLE THROUGH MINEFIELDS, YOU CAN'T NAVIGATE A COUPLE OF SNOWFLAKES?

HONEY, REMEMBER THE CONVERSATION WE HAD ABOUT TAKING SIDES?

OH, RIGHT.

WHAT HE SAID...ABOUT THE MOUNTAIN AND THE BODY PARTS.

HOME RUN, MY DEAR.

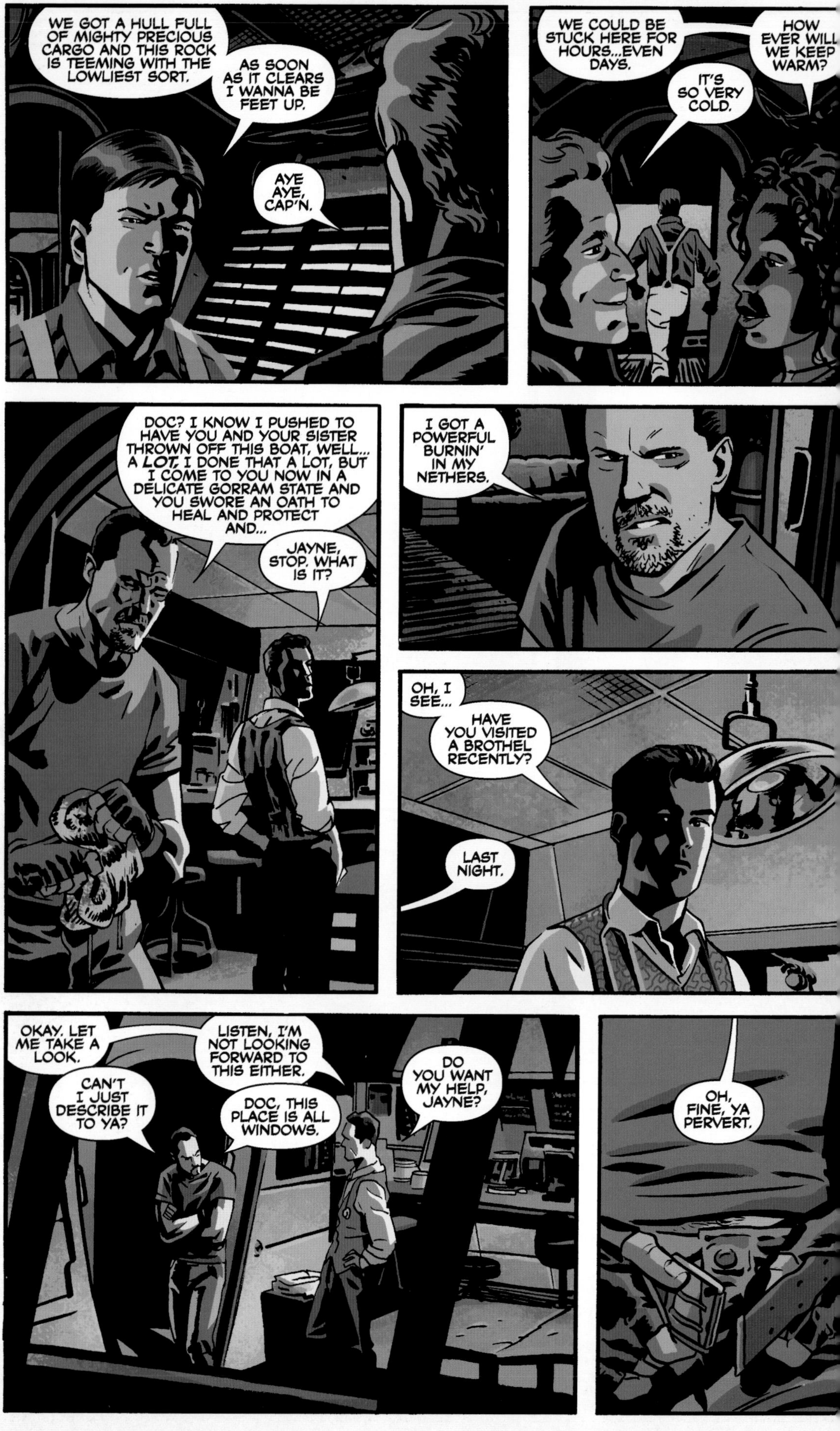
WE GOT A HULL FULL OF MIGHTY PRECIOUS CARGO AND THIS ROCK IS TEEMING WITH THE LOWLIEST SORT.
AS SOON AS IT CLEARS I WANNA BE FEET UP.
AYE AYE, CAP'N.
WE COULD BE STUCK HERE FOR HOURS...EVEN DAYS.
HOW EVER WILL WE KEEP WARM?
IT'S SO VERY COLD.
DOC? I KNOW I PUSHED TO HAVE YOU AND YOUR SISTER THROWN OFF THIS BOAT, WELL... A *LOT*, I DONE THAT A LOT, BUT I COME TO YOU NOW IN A DELICATE GORRAM STATE AND YOU SWORE AN OATH TO HEAL AND PROTECT AND...
JAYNE, STOP. WHAT IS IT?
I GOT A POWERFUL BURNIN' IN MY NETHERS.
OH, I SEE...
HAVE YOU VISITED A BROTHEL RECENTLY?
LAST NIGHT.
OKAY. LET ME TAKE A LOOK.
CAN'T I JUST DESCRIBE IT TO YA?
LISTEN, I'M NOT LOOKING FORWARD TO THIS EITHER.
DOC, THIS PLACE IS ALL WINDOWS.
DO YOU WANT MY HELP, JAYNE?
OH, FINE, YA PERVERT.

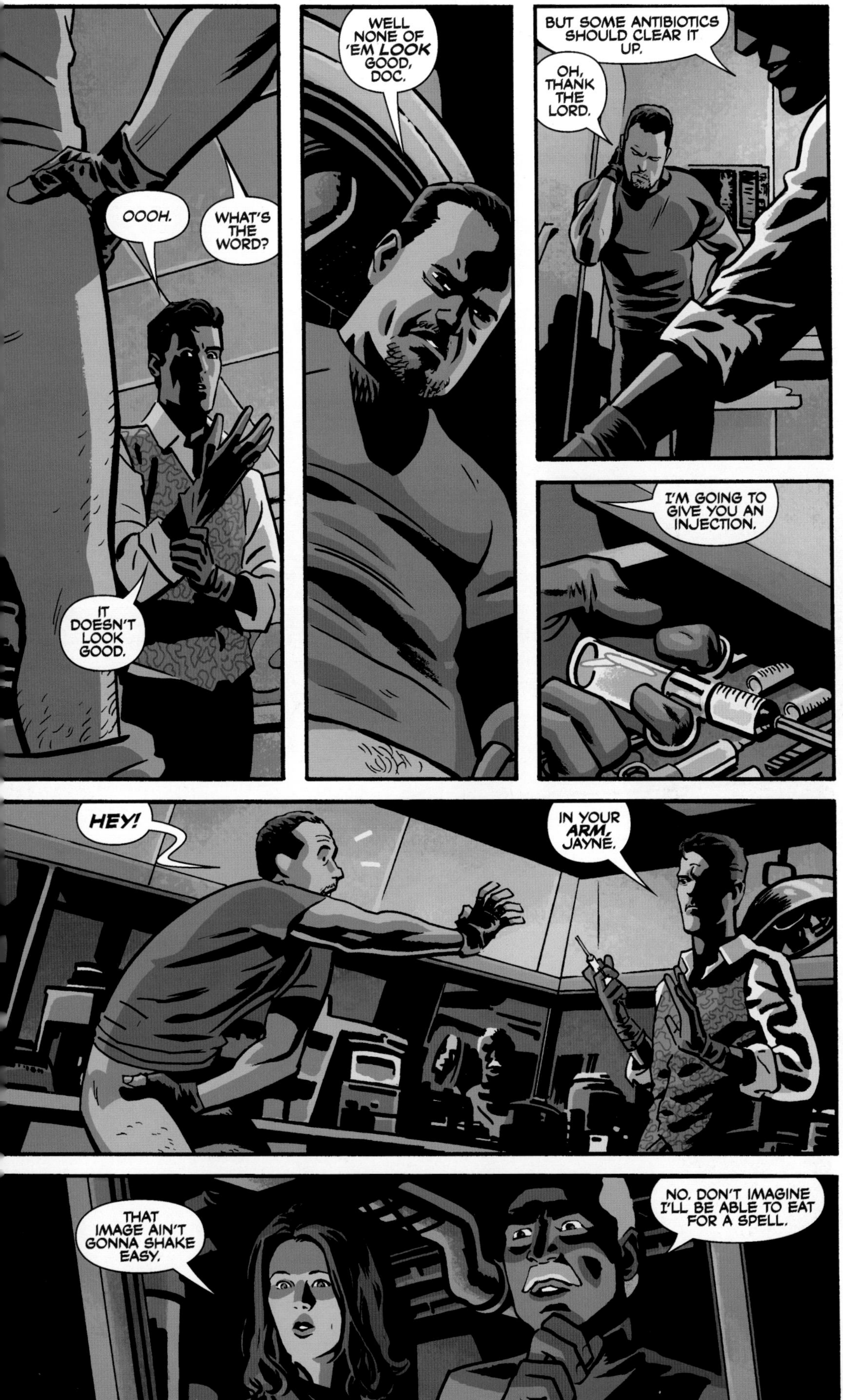
OOOH.
WHAT'S THE WORD?
IT DOESN'T LOOK GOOD.
WELL NONE OF 'EM LOOK GOOD, DOC.
BUT SOME ANTIBIOTICS SHOULD CLEAR IT UP.
OH, THANK THE LORD.
I'M GOING TO GIVE YOU AN INJECTION.
HEY!
IN YOUR ARM, JAYNE.
THAT IMAGE AIN'T GONNA SHAKE EASY.
NO, DON'T IMAGINE I'LL BE ABLE TO EAT FOR A SPELL.

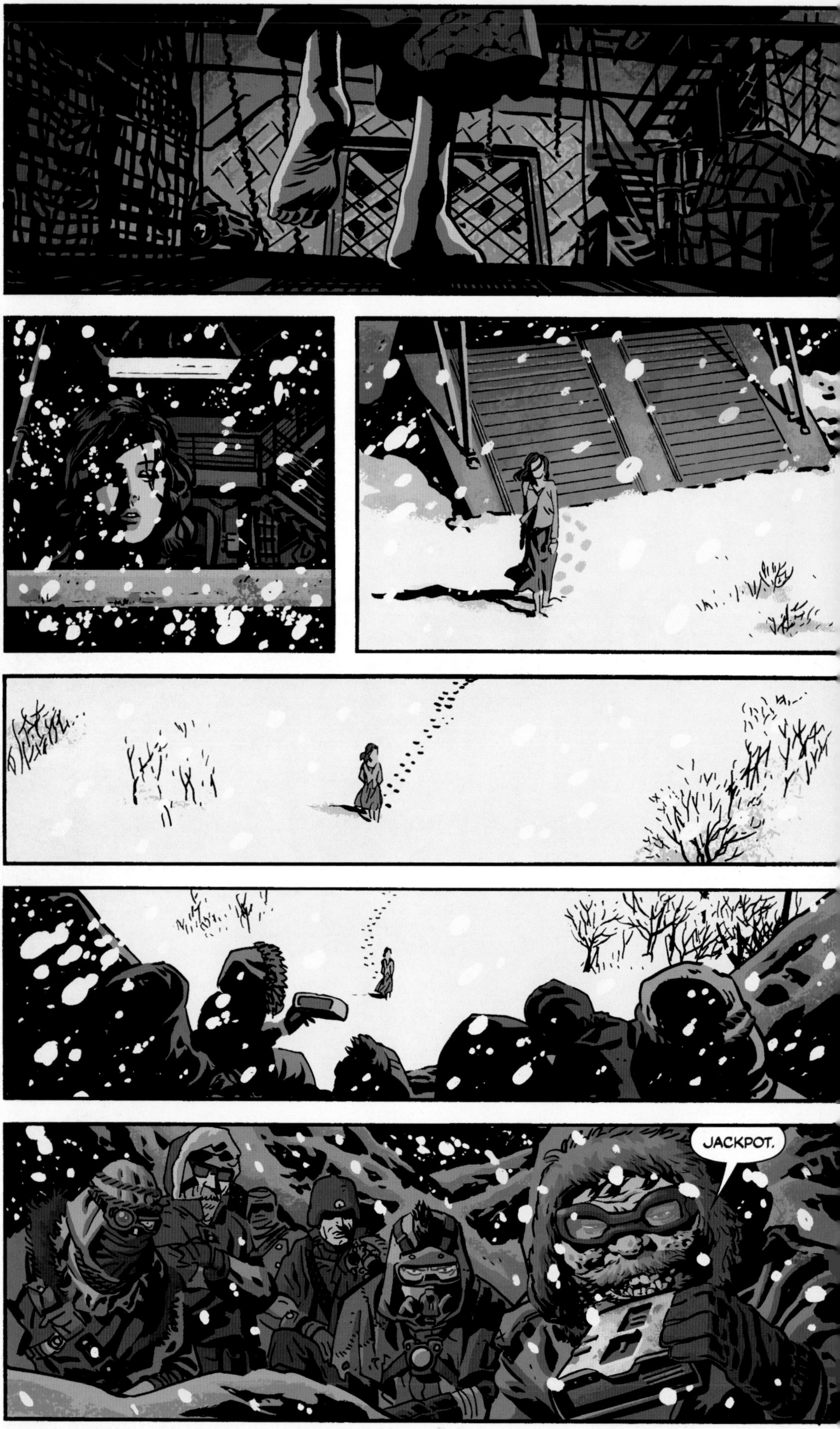
JACKPOT.

WHAT'S FOR DINNER?

OUR FINEST SLOP.

I THOUGHT WE WERE GETTIN' STOCKED IN TOWN.

ME TOO.

YEAH, DIDN'T WORK OUT THAT WAY, AND I GOT NO INTENTION OF HEADIN' BACK TO THAT OUTPOST.

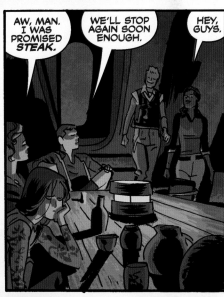

AW, MAN, I WAS PROMISED STEAK.

WE'LL STOP AGAIN SOON ENOUGH.

HEY, GUYS.

QUIT IT.

QUIT WHAT?

QUIT LOOKIN' LIKE THAT. BOTH OF YOUSE GOT A LOOK ON YOUR FACE.

WHAT LOOK?

SOME KIND OF STRANGE... HAPPY LOOK.

THERE'S NO LOOK.

I SEE IT.

ME TOO.

IT'S A SEX LOOK.

THERE IT GOES...

HEY.

NOTHING MUCH.

HEY, SIMON! WHAT'S DOIN'?

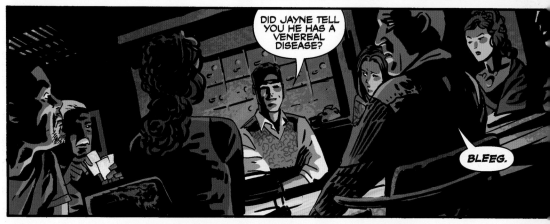
DID JAYNE TELL YOU HE HAS A VENEREAL DISEASE?

BLEEG.

DOC! AIN'T THERE A DOCTOR'S OATH OF SECRECY? A SACRED PACT OF SILENCE?!

SOMETHING LIKE THAT BUT... I JUST THINK IT'S KIND OF FUNNY.

HEY, HAS ANYONE SEEN RIVER?

HMM.

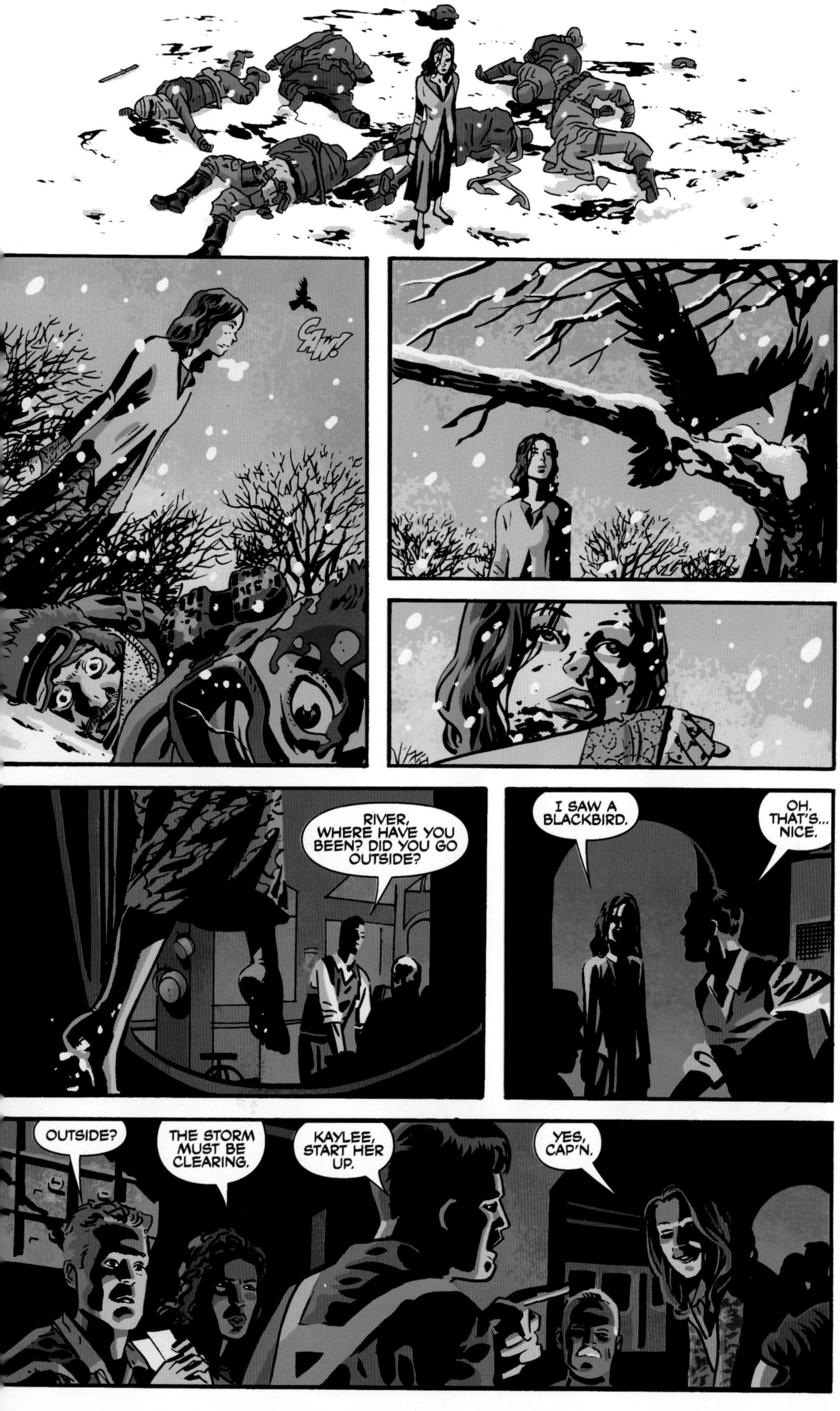
CAW!
RIVER, WHERE HAVE YOU BEEN? DID YOU GO OUTSIDE?
I SAW A BLACKBIRD.
OH. THAT'S... NICE.
OUTSIDE?
THE STORM MUST BE CLEARING.
KAYLEE, START HER UP.
YES, CAP'N.

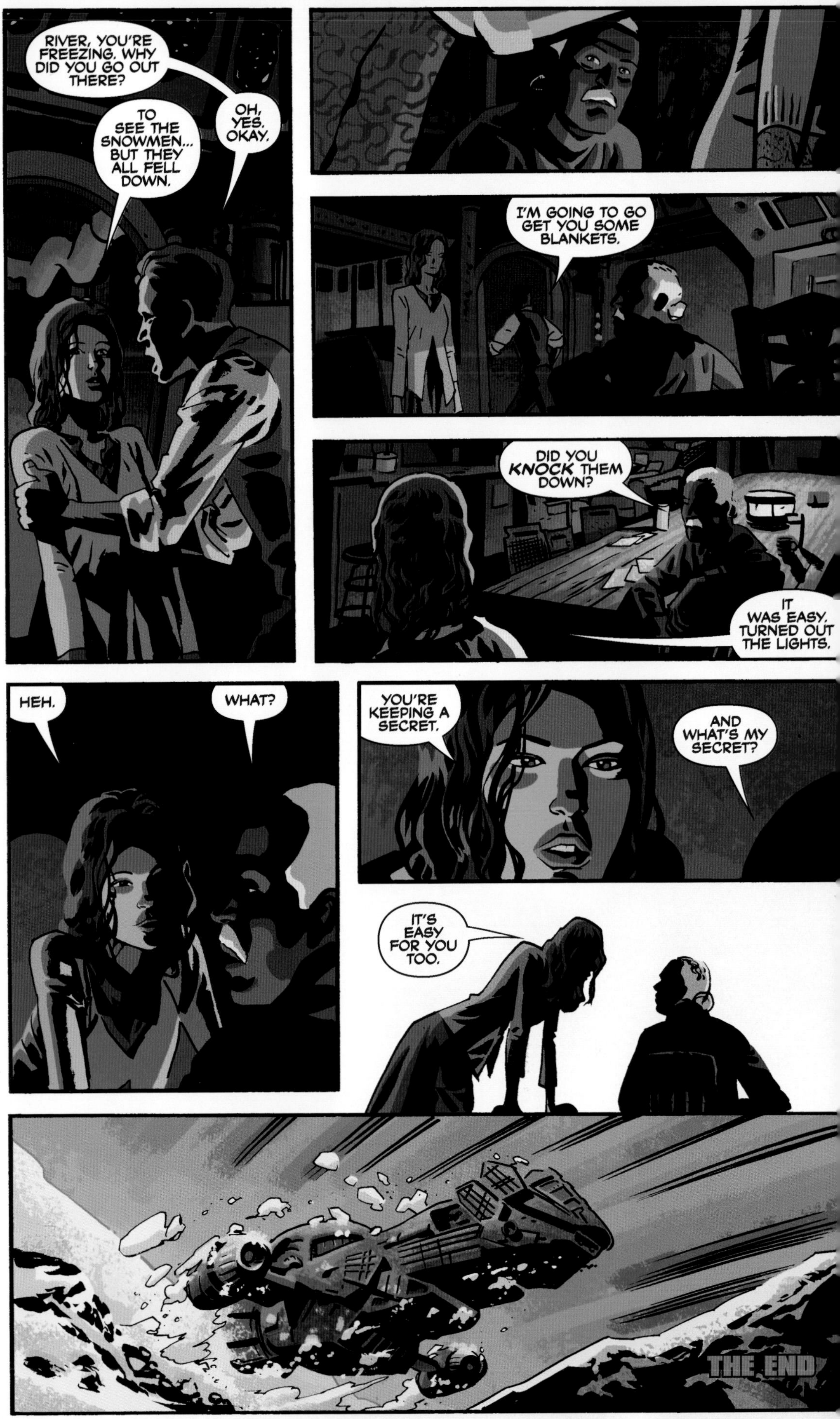
RIVER, YOU'RE FREEZING. WHY DID YOU GO OUT THERE?
TO SEE THE SNOWMEN... BUT THEY ALL FELL DOWN.
OH, YES. OKAY.
I'M GOING TO GO GET YOU SOME BLANKETS.
DID YOU KNOCK THEM DOWN?
IT WAS EASY. TURNED OUT THE LIGHTS.
HEH.
WHAT?
YOU'RE KEEPING A SECRET.
AND WHAT'S MY SECRET?
IT'S EASY FOR YOU TOO.
THE END

FLOAT OUT

STORY
PATTON OSWALT

ART
PATRIC REYNOLDS

COLORS
DAVE STEWART

LETTERS
MICHAEL HEISLER

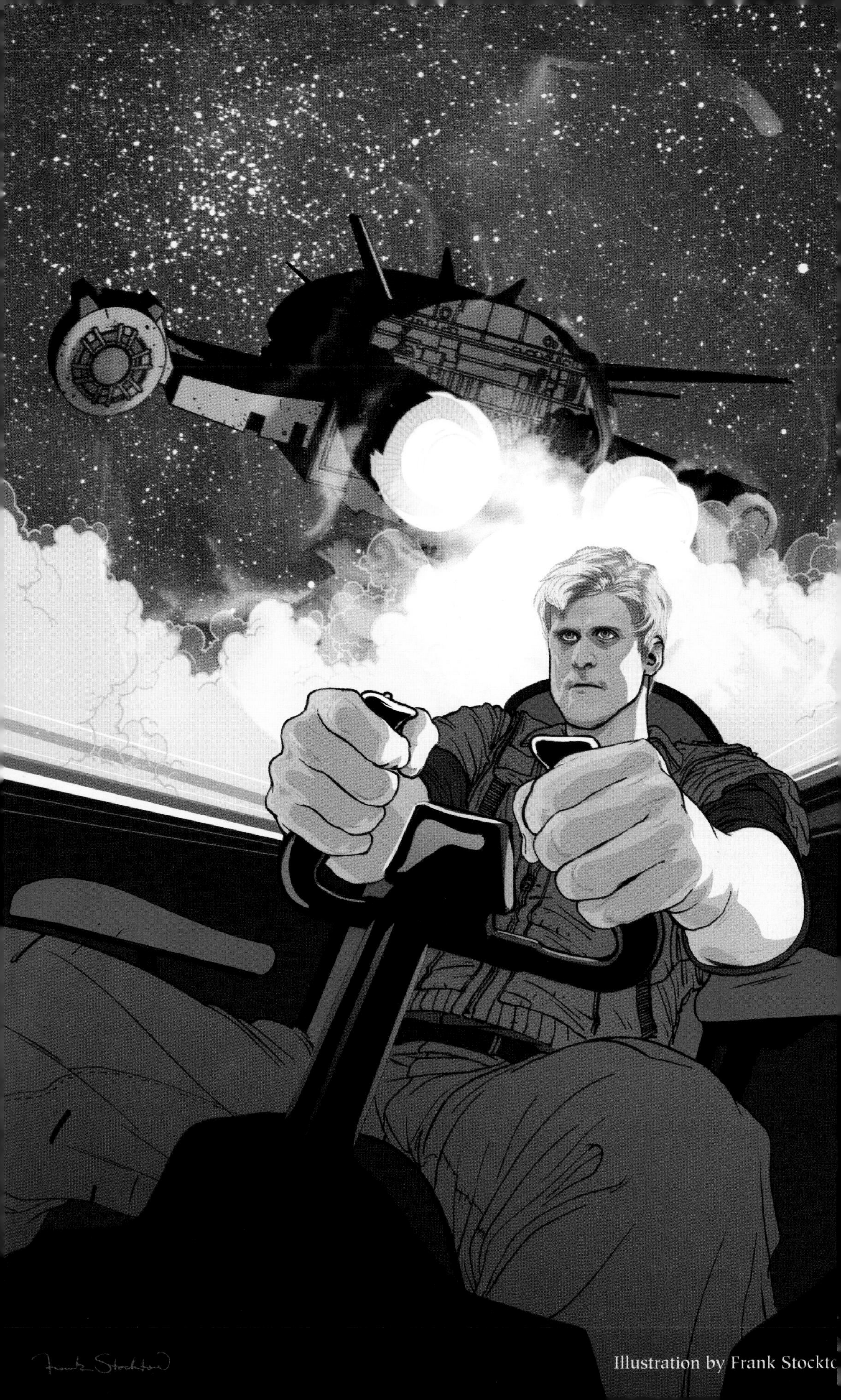

Illustration by Frank Stockto

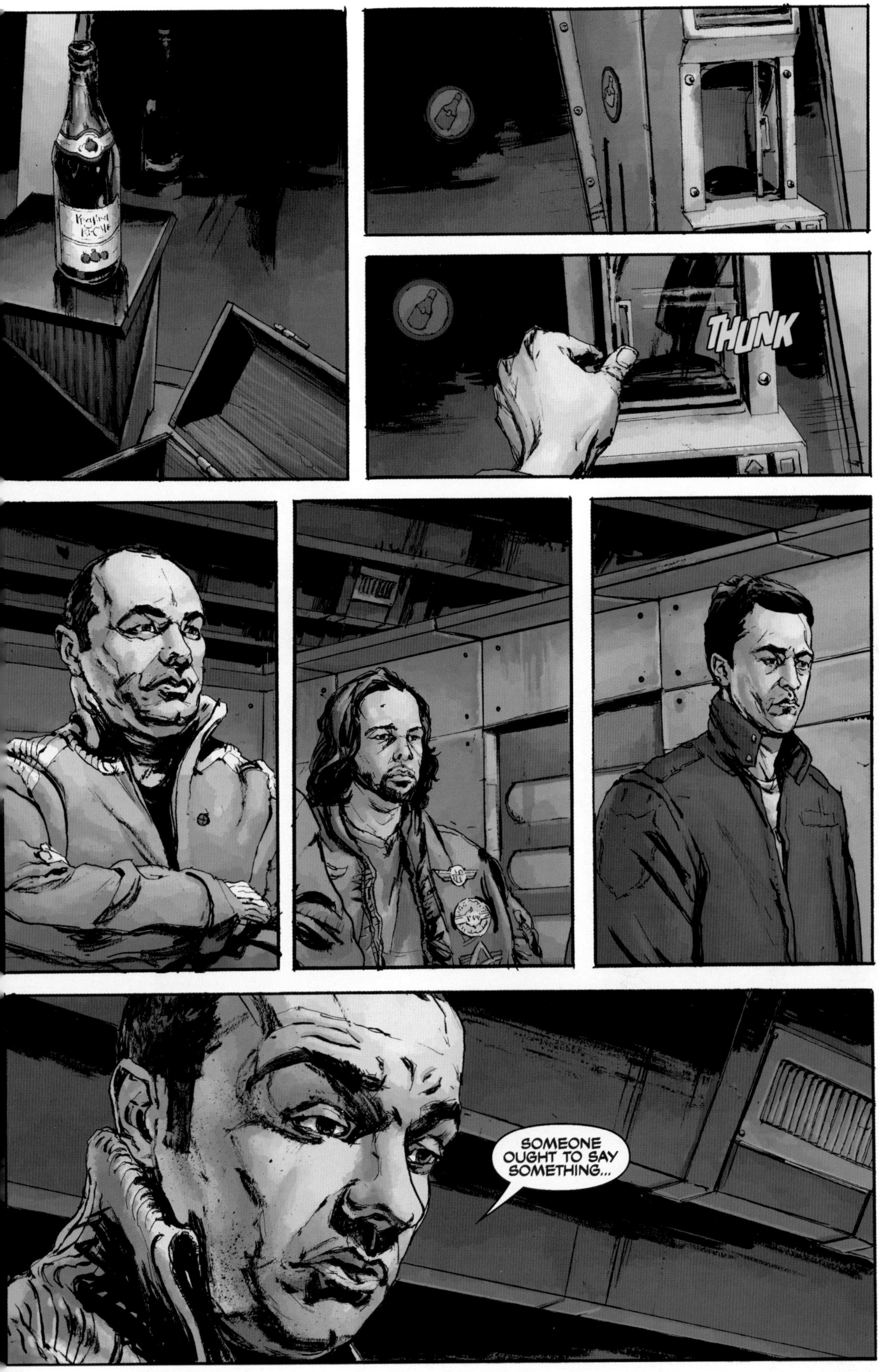
THUNK
SOMEONE OUGHT TO SAY SOMETHING...

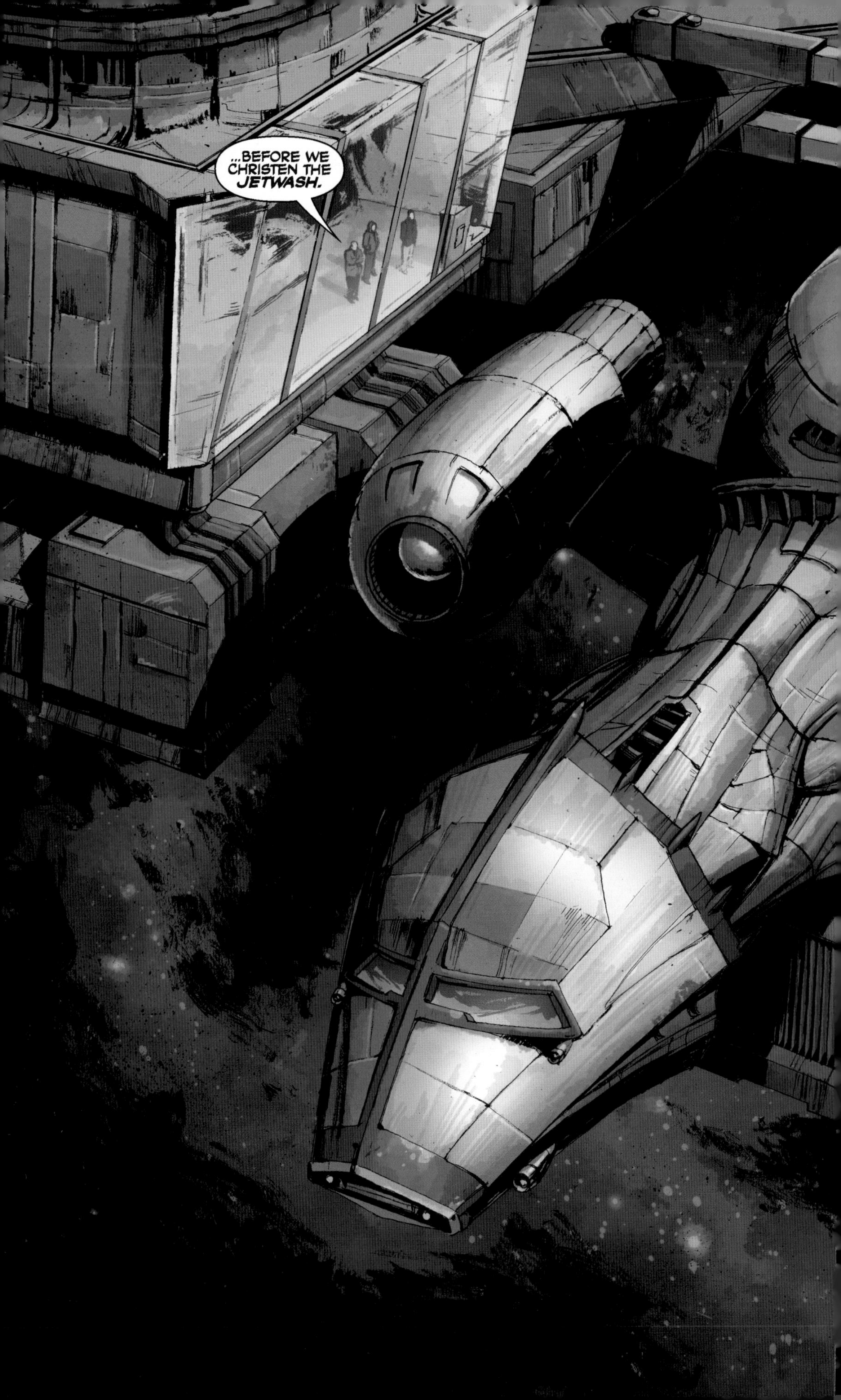
...BEFORE WE CHRISTEN THE JETWASH.

BOTH OF YOU? I'M NOT SPLITTIN' DUTIES AS CAPTAIN AND PILOT OF THIS SHIP WITH YOU TWO WEASEL-BAGGING EVERY FIVE MINUTES.

WOULDN'T WASH MAKE SOME SORT OF JOKE RIGHT ABOUT NOW?

HE'D MAKE EIGHT AND ONE'D BE FUNNY.

AS COMPARED TO YOUR SINGLE, PISSY REMARK FOR EVERY OCCASION, TREY?

DID I SAY I HAD AN ISSUE WITH LELAND?

WAIT, I THOUGHT WE WERE GETTING A PILOT. YOU'RE PUTTING OUR SHIP IN THE HANDS OF THE "ALMOST GHOST"?

THIRD OF IT'S MINE.

AND UNLESS WE SCARE UP A CHARTER, WE'VE GOT NO RATIONS, NO SICKBAY--

I KNEW WE SHOULD'VE GONE WITH AN OH-THREE-CLASS FIREFLY.

RELICS.

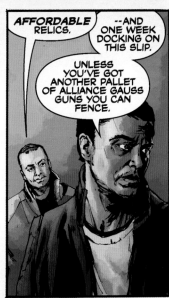

AFFORDABLE RELICS.

--AND ONE WEEK DOCKING ON THIS SLIP.

UNLESS YOU'VE GOT ANOTHER PALLET OF ALLIANCE GAUSS GUNS YOU CAN FENCE.

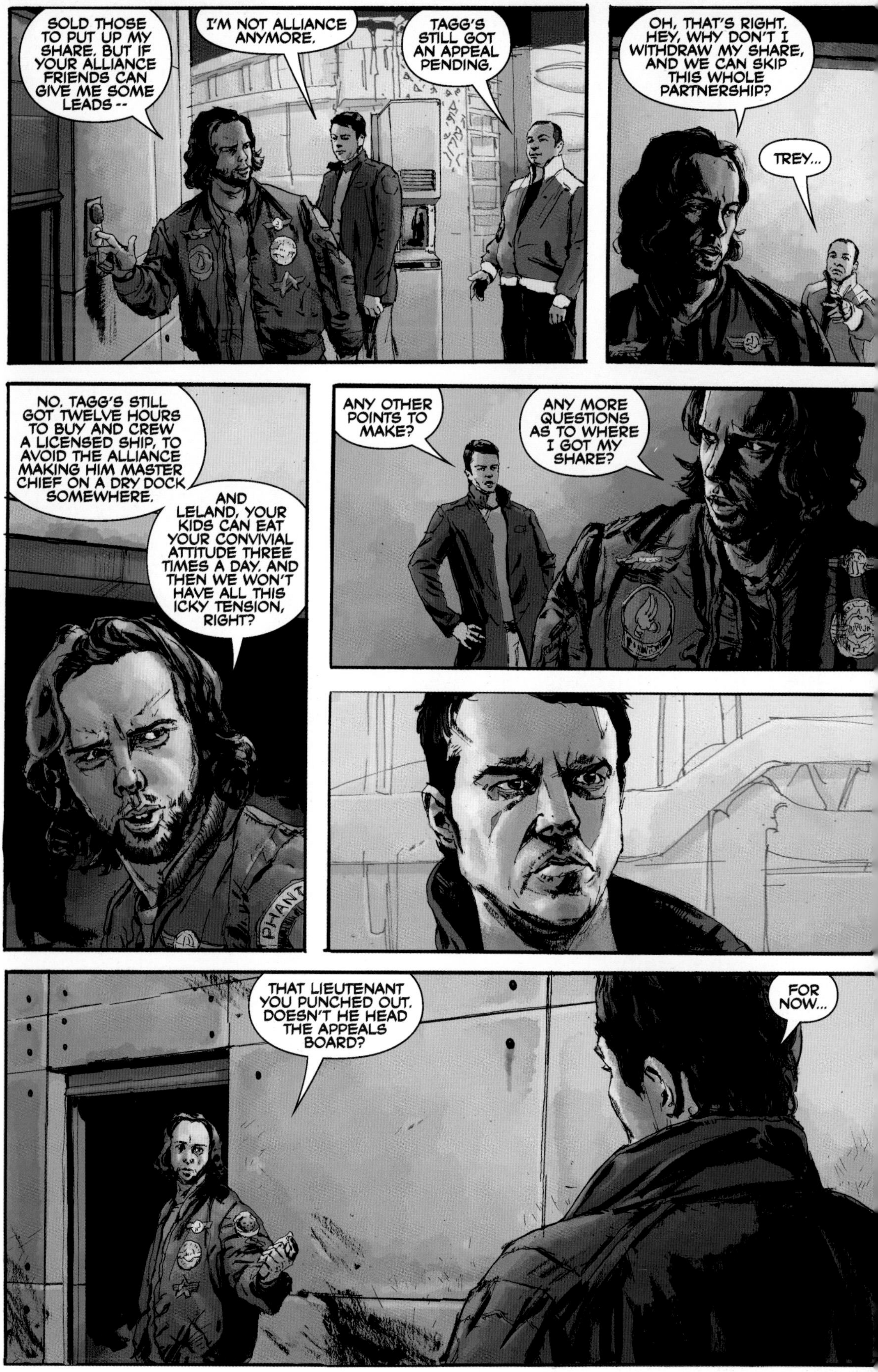

SOLD THOSE TO PUT UP MY SHARE. BUT IF YOUR ALLIANCE FRIENDS CAN GIVE ME SOME LEADS --
I'M NOT ALLIANCE ANYMORE.
TAGG'S STILL GOT AN APPEAL PENDING.
OH, THAT'S RIGHT. HEY, WHY DON'T I WITHDRAW MY SHARE, AND WE CAN SKIP THIS WHOLE PARTNERSHIP?
TREY...
NO. TAGG'S STILL GOT TWELVE HOURS TO BUY AND CREW A LICENSED SHIP, TO AVOID THE ALLIANCE MAKING HIM MASTER CHIEF ON A DRY DOCK SOMEWHERE.
AND LELAND, YOUR KIDS CAN EAT YOUR CONVIVIAL ATTITUDE THREE TIMES A DAY, AND THEN WE WON'T HAVE ALL THIS ICKY TENSION, RIGHT?
ANY OTHER POINTS TO MAKE?
ANY MORE QUESTIONS AS TO WHERE I GOT MY SHARE?
THAT LIEUTENANT YOU PUNCHED OUT. DOESN'T HE HEAD THE APPEALS BOARD?
FOR NOW...

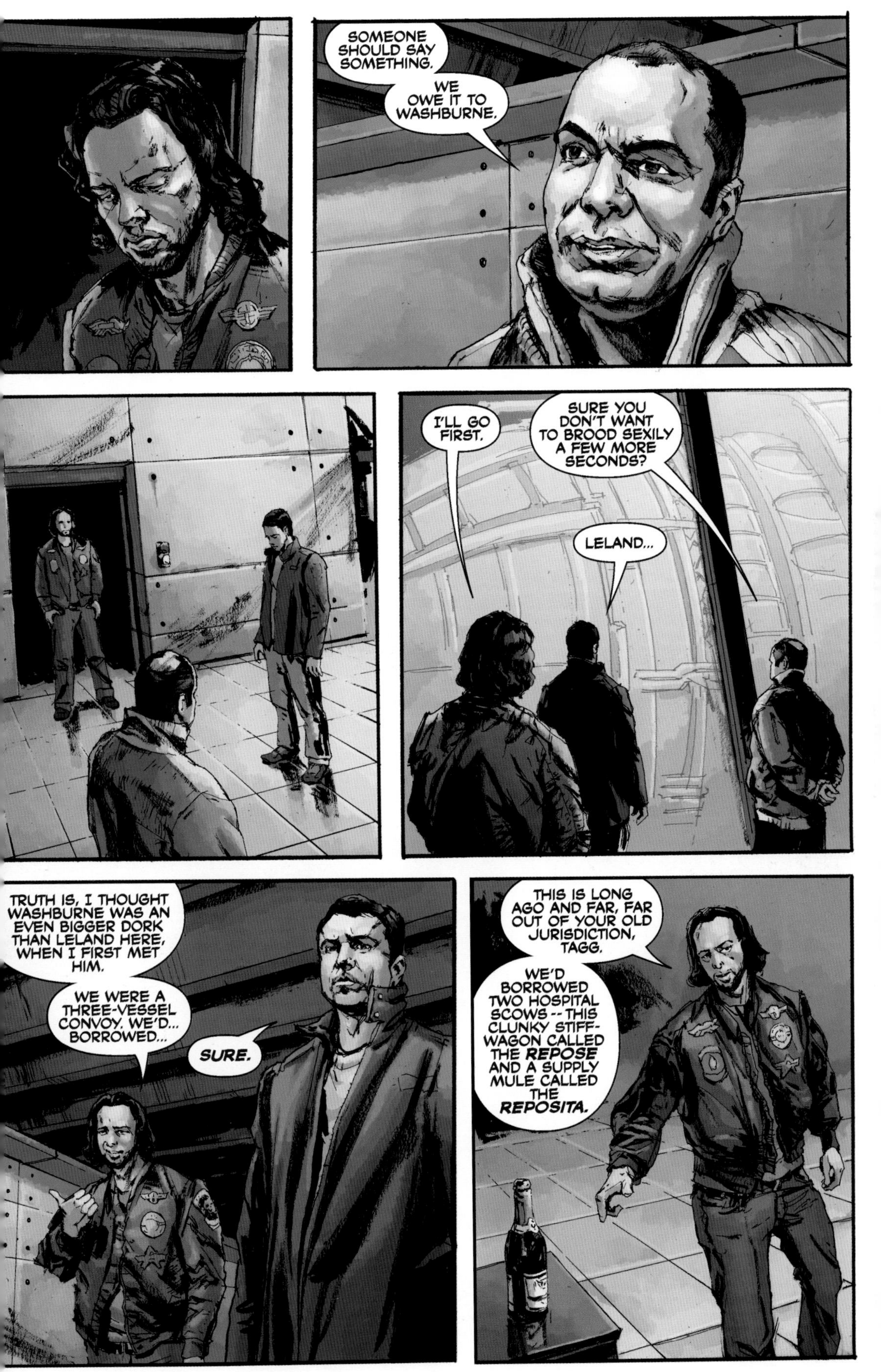
SOMEONE SHOULD SAY SOMETHING.
WE OWE IT TO WASHBURNE.
I'LL GO FIRST.
SURE YOU DON'T WANT TO BROOD SEXILY A FEW MORE SECONDS?
LELAND...
TRUTH IS, I THOUGHT WASHBURNE WAS AN EVEN BIGGER DORK THAN LELAND HERE, WHEN I FIRST MET HIM.
WE WERE A THREE-VESSEL CONVOY. WE'D... BORROWED...
SURE.
THIS IS LONG AGO AND FAR, FAR OUT OF YOUR OLD JURISDICTION, TAGG.
WE'D BORROWED TWO HOSPITAL SCOWS -- THIS CLUNKY STIFF-WAGON CALLED THE REPOSE AND A SUPPLY MULE CALLED THE REPOSITA.

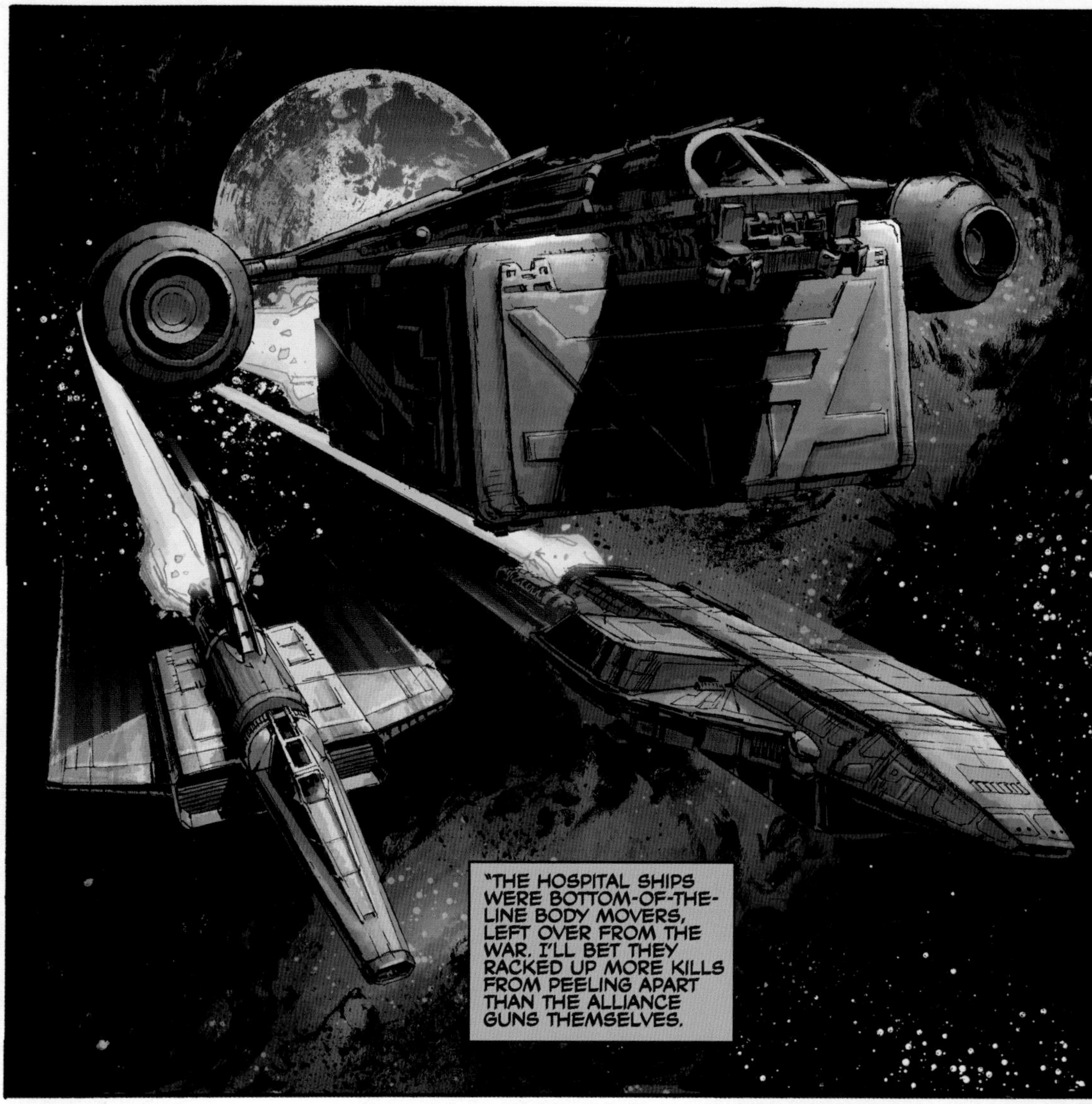
"THE HOSPITAL SHIPS WERE BOTTOM-OF-THE-LINE BODY MOVERS, LEFT OVER FROM THE WAR. I'LL BET THEY RACKED UP MORE KILLS FROM PEELING APART THAN THE ALLIANCE GUNS THEMSELVES.

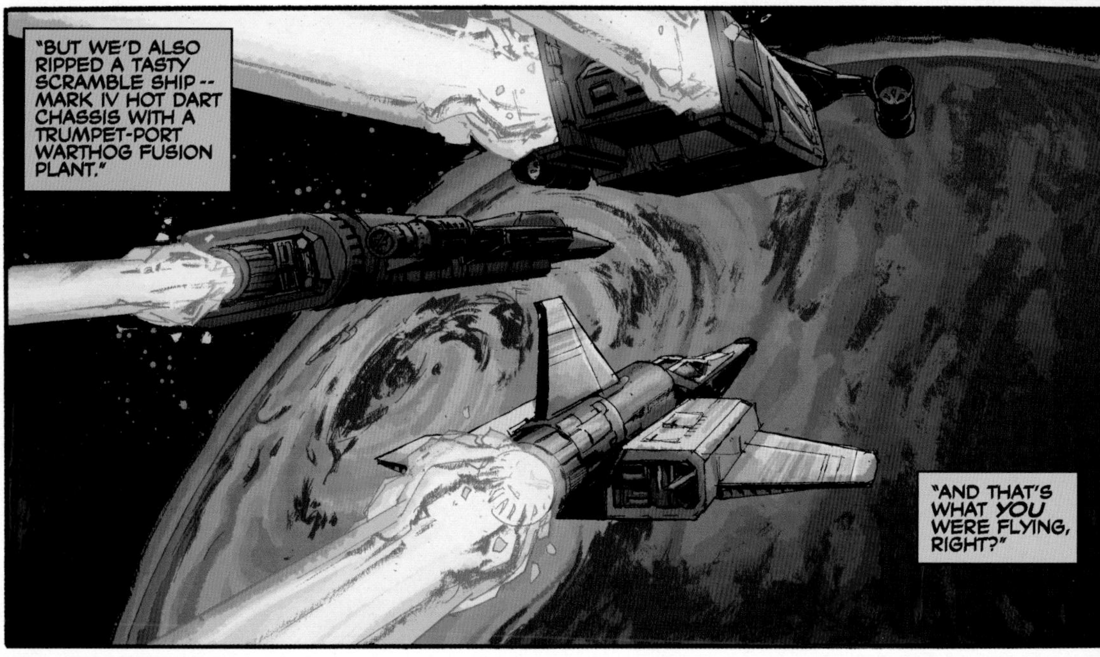
"BUT WE'D ALSO RIPPED A TASTY SCRAMBLE SHIP -- MARK IV HOT DART CHASSIS WITH A TRUMPET-PORT WARTHOG FUSION PLANT."
"AND THAT'S WHAT *YOU* WERE FLYING, RIGHT?"

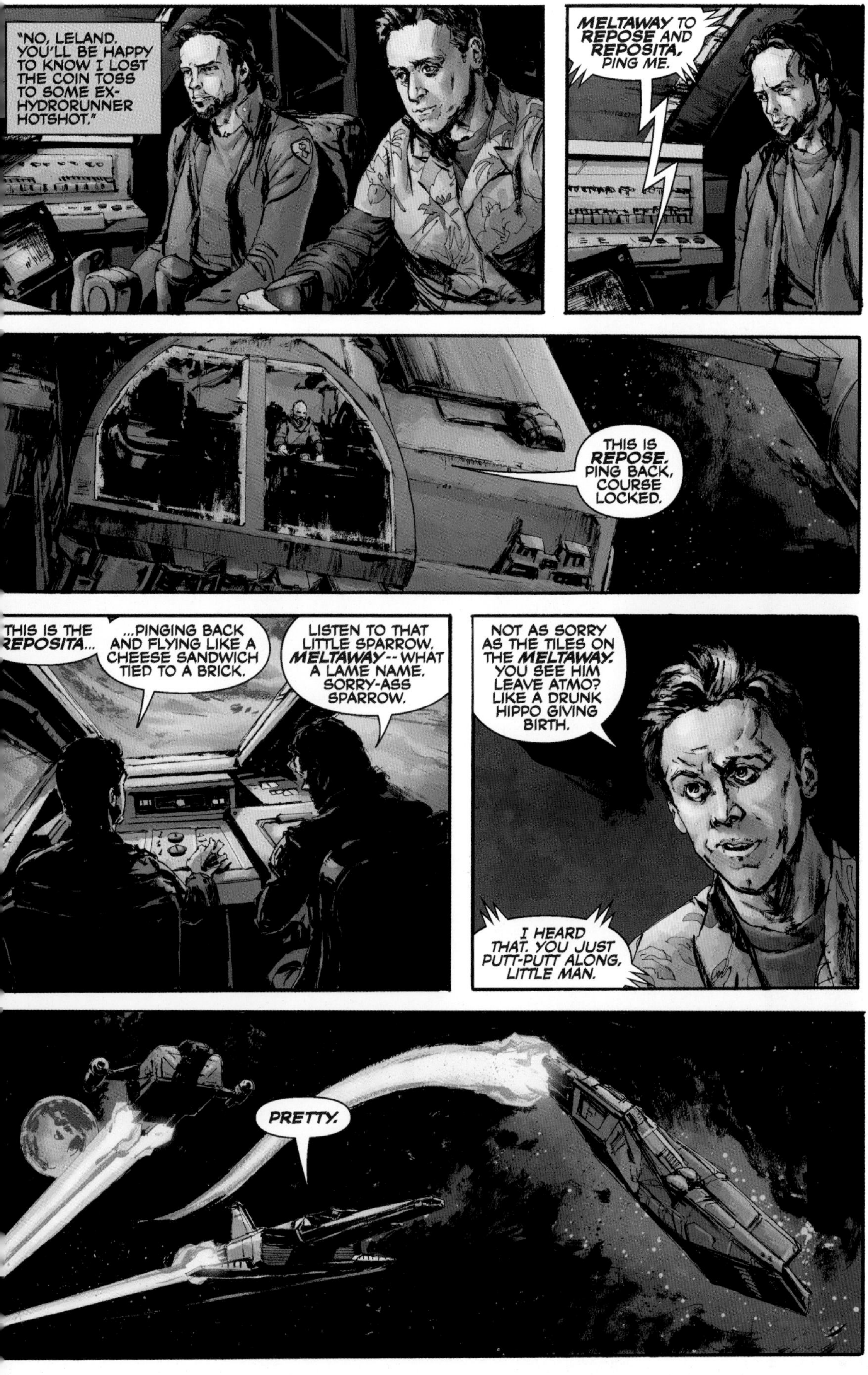
"NO, LELAND. YOU'LL BE HAPPY TO KNOW I LOST THE COIN TOSS TO SOME EX-HYDRORUNNER HOTSHOT."
MELTAWAY TO REPOSE AND REPOSITA, PING ME.
THIS IS REPOSE. PING BACK, COURSE LOCKED.
THIS IS THE REPOSITA...
...PINGING BACK AND FLYING LIKE A CHEESE SANDWICH TIED TO A BRICK.
LISTEN TO THAT LITTLE SPARROW. MELTAWAY-- WHAT A LAME NAME. SORRY-ASS SPARROW.
NOT AS SORRY AS THE TILES ON THE MELTAWAY. YOU SEE HIM LEAVE ATMO? LIKE A DRUNK HIPPO GIVING BIRTH.
I HEARD THAT. YOU JUST PUTT-PUTT ALONG, LITTLE MAN.
PRETTY.

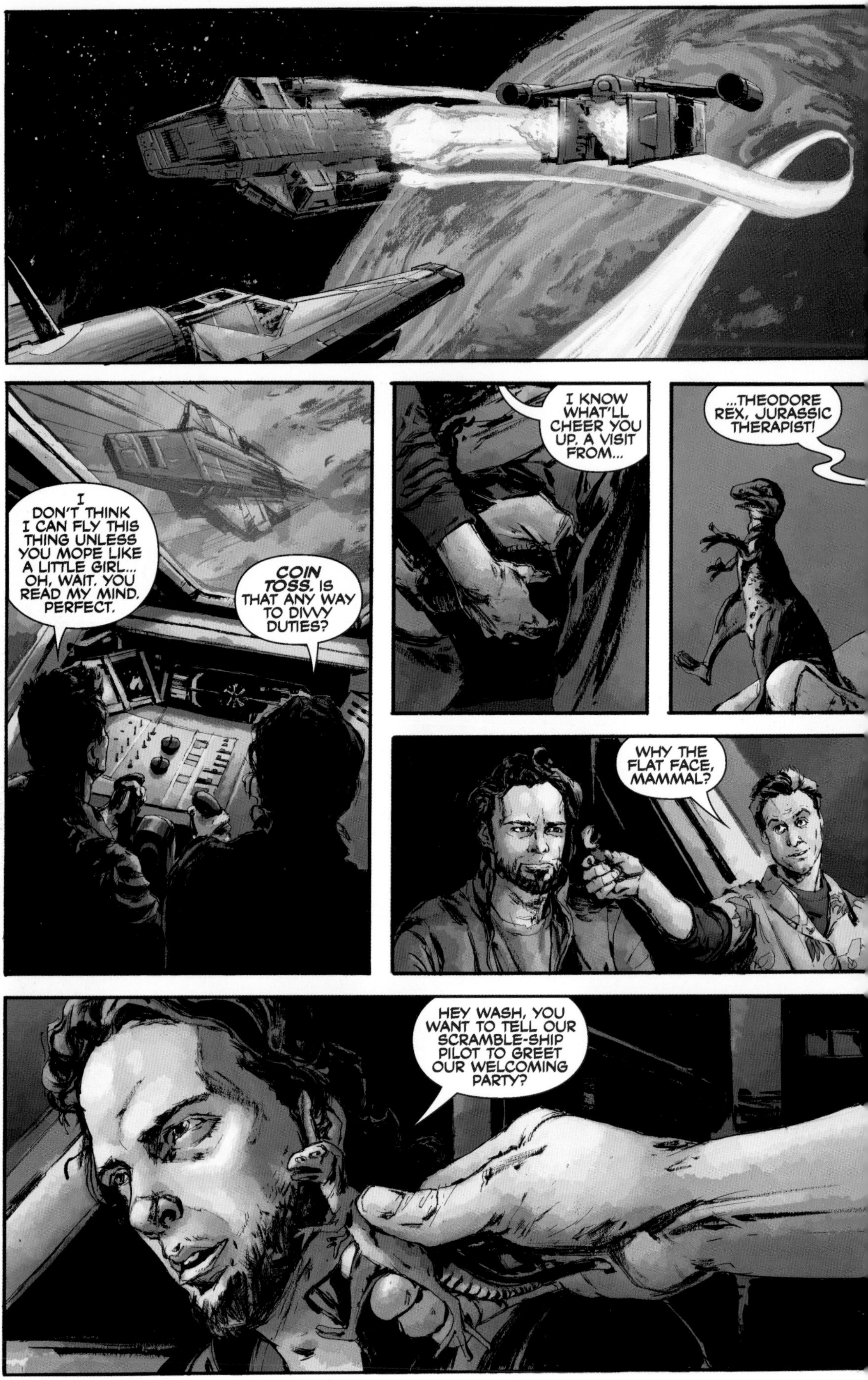
I DON'T THINK I CAN FLY THIS THING UNLESS YOU MOPE LIKE A LITTLE GIRL... OH, WAIT. YOU READ MY MIND. PERFECT.
COIN TOSS. IS THAT ANY WAY TO DIVVY DUTIES?
I KNOW WHAT'LL CHEER YOU UP. A VISIT FROM...
...THEODORE REX, JURASSIC THERAPIST!
WHY THE FLAT FACE, MAMMAL?
HEY WASH, YOU WANT TO TELL OUR SCRAMBLE-SHIP PILOT TO GREET OUR WELCOMING PARTY?

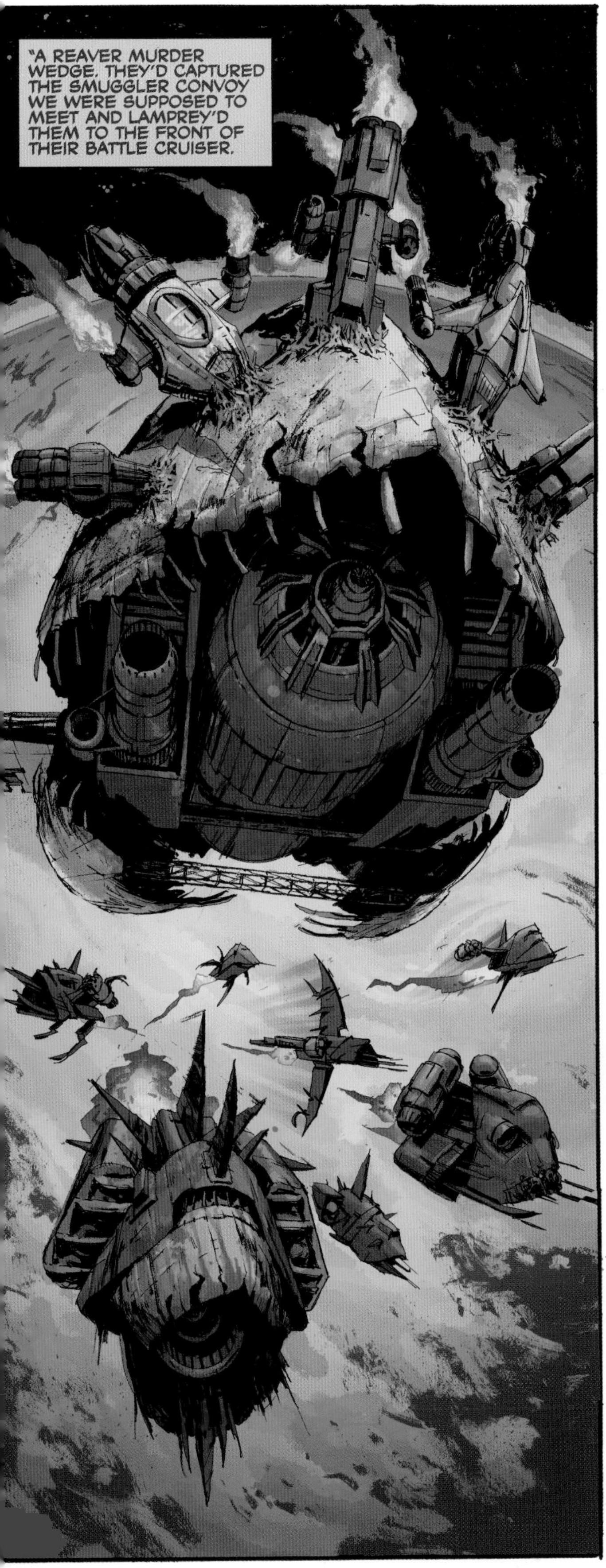
"A REAVER MURDER WEDGE. THEY'D CAPTURED THE SMUGGLER CONVOY WE WERE SUPPOSED TO MEET AND LAMPREY'D THEM TO THE FRONT OF THEIR BATTLE CRUISER.

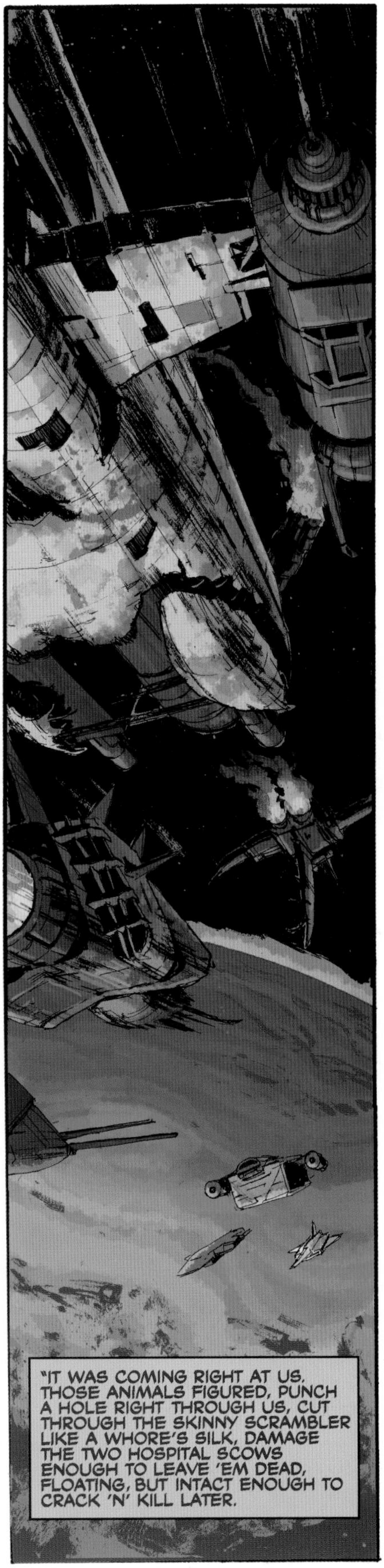
"IT WAS COMING RIGHT AT US. THOSE ANIMALS FIGURED, PUNCH A HOLE RIGHT THROUGH US, CUT THROUGH THE SKINNY SCRAMBLER LIKE A WHORE'S SILK, DAMAGE THE TWO HOSPITAL SCOWS ENOUGH TO LEAVE 'EM DEAD, FLOATING, BUT INTACT ENOUGH TO CRACK 'N' KILL LATER.

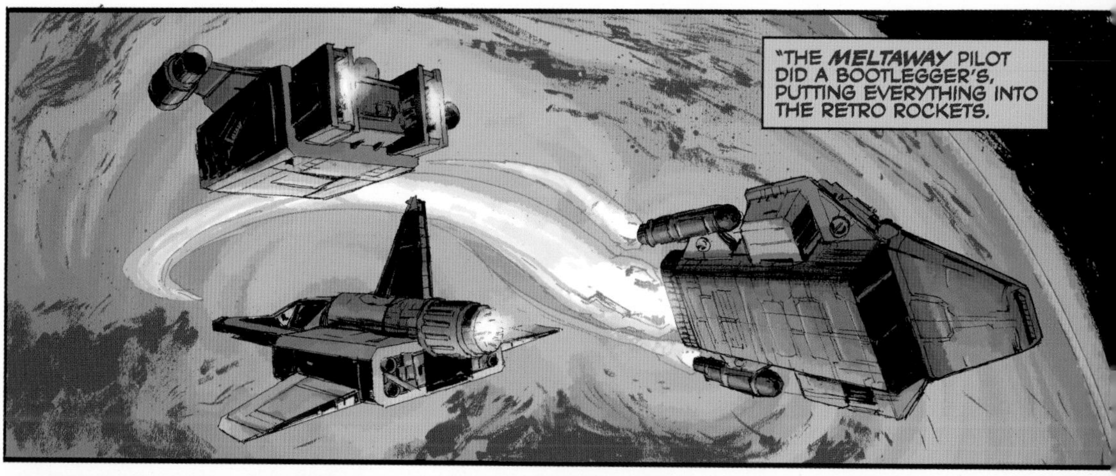
"THE MELTAWAY PILOT DID A BOOTLEGGER'S, PUTTING EVERYTHING INTO THE RETRO ROCKETS.

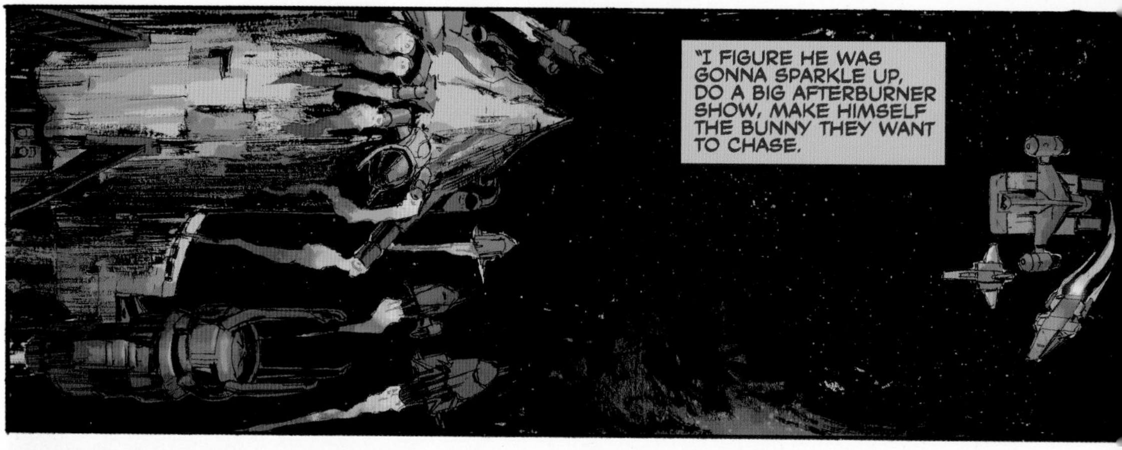
"I FIGURE HE WAS GONNA SPARKLE UP, DO A BIG AFTERBURNER SHOW, MAKE HIMSELF THE BUNNY THEY WANT TO CHASE.

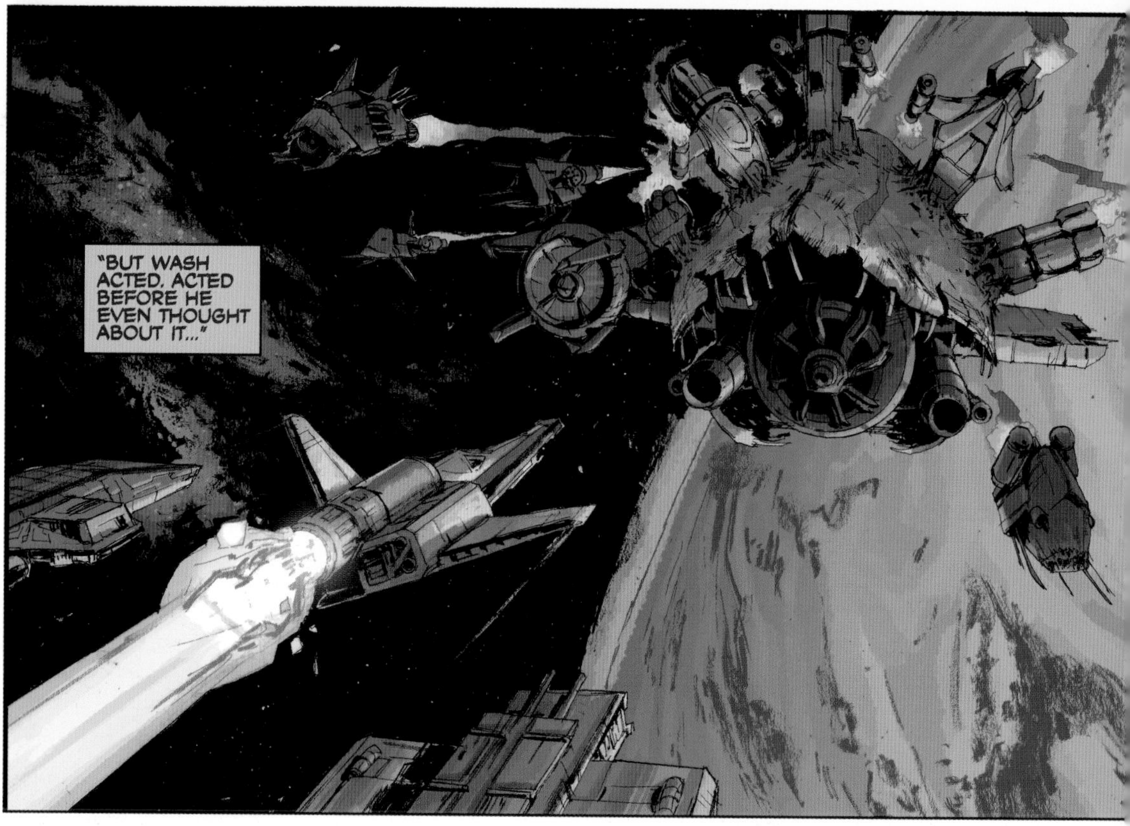
"BUT WASH ACTED. ACTED BEFORE HE EVEN THOUGHT ABOUT IT..."

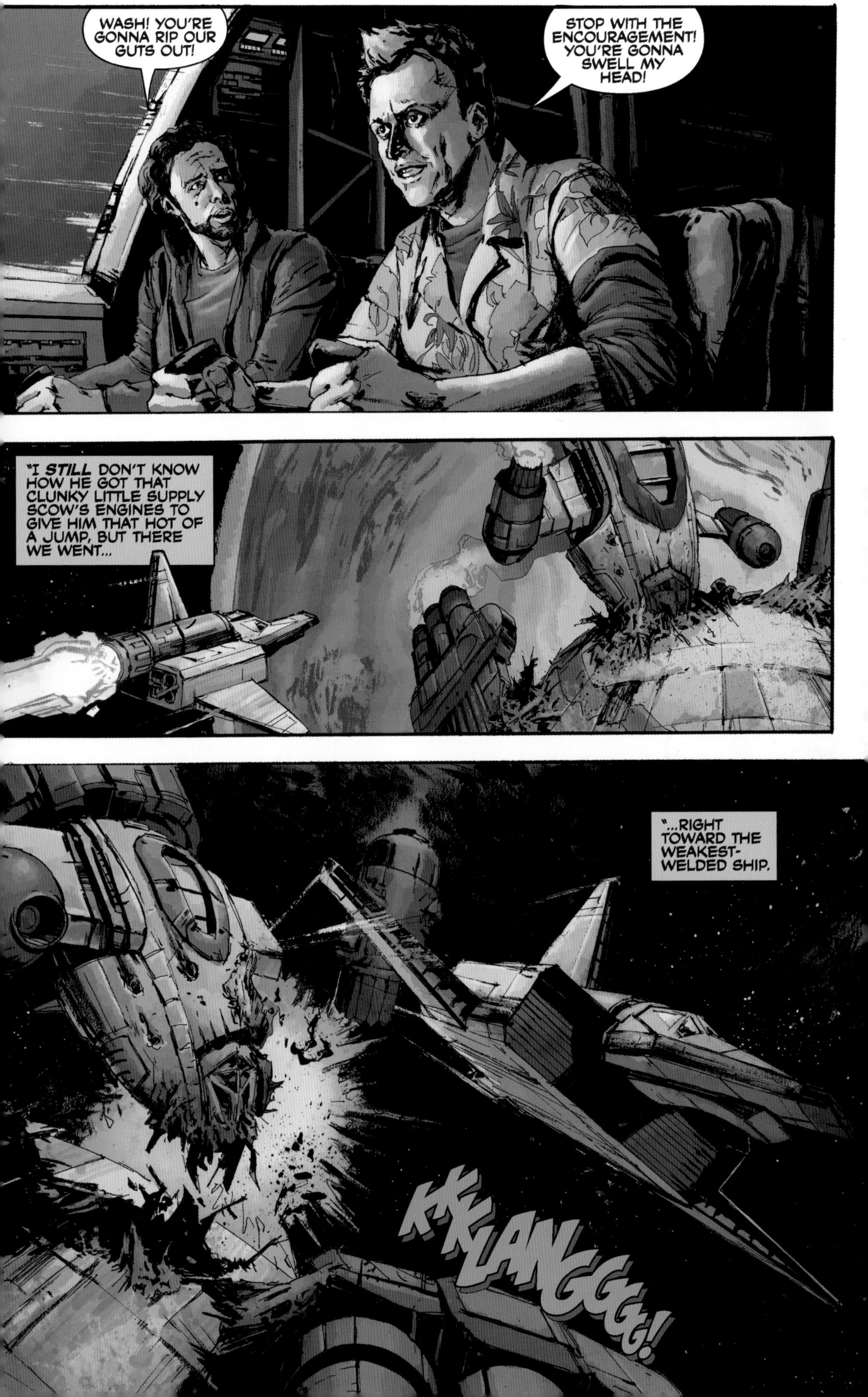
WASH! YOU'RE GONNA RIP OUR GUTS OUT!
STOP WITH THE ENCOURAGEMENT! YOU'RE GONNA SWELL MY HEAD!
"I *STILL* DON'T KNOW HOW HE GOT THAT CLUNKY LITTLE SUPPLY SCOW'S ENGINES TO GIVE HIM THAT HOT OF A JUMP, BUT THERE WE WENT...
"...RIGHT TOWARD THE WEAKEST-WELDED SHIP.
KKKLANGGGG!

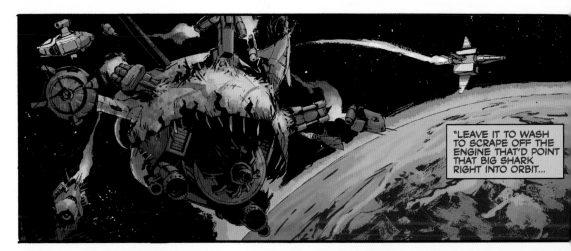

"LEAVE IT TO WASH TO SCRAPE OFF THE ENGINE THAT'D POINT THAT BIG SHARK RIGHT INTO ORBIT..."

"...AND YANK IT INTO THE GRAVITY WELL."

"AND SINCE REAVERS HAVE A HORNET'S CODE..."

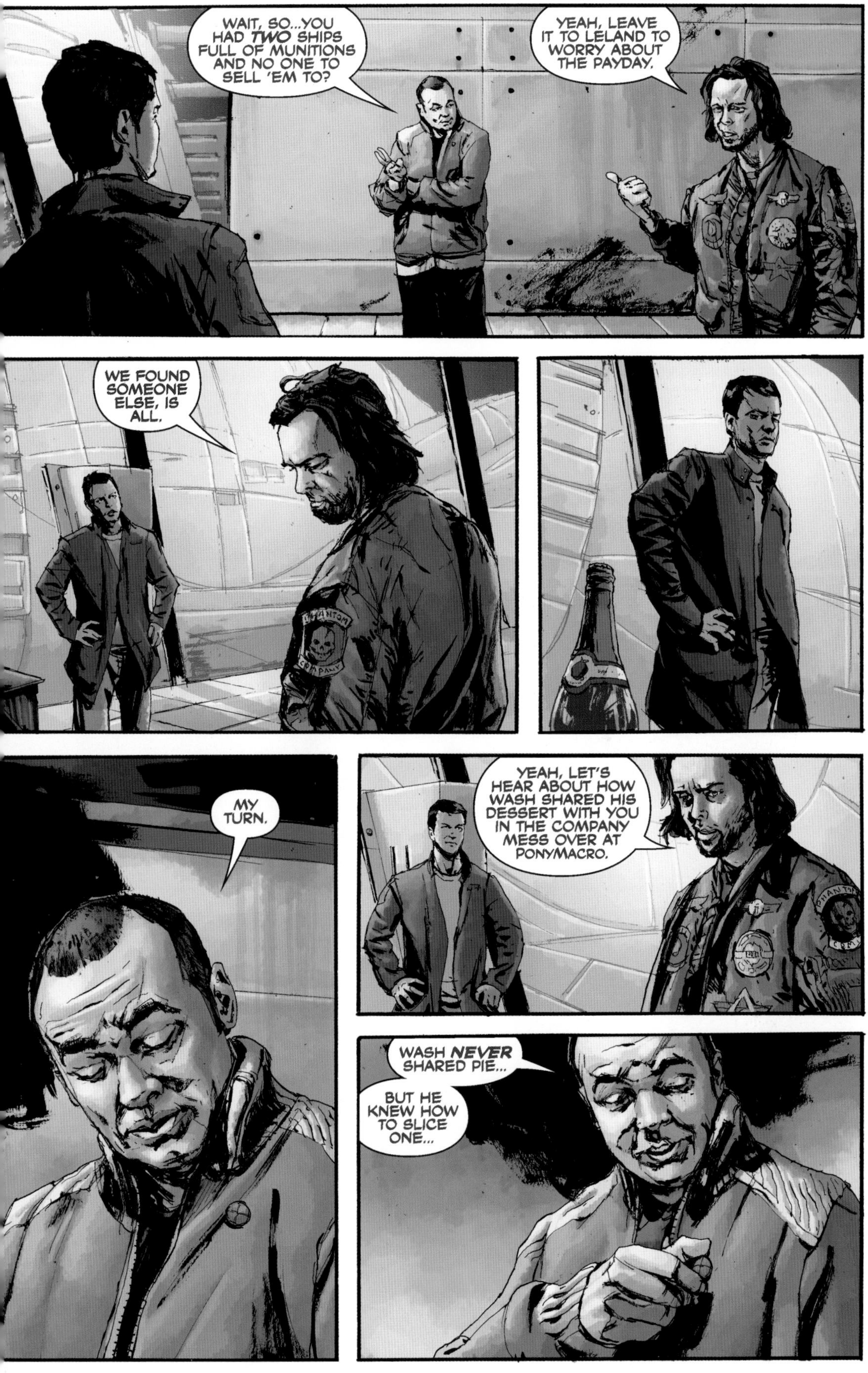
WAIT, SO...YOU HAD TWO SHIPS FULL OF MUNITIONS AND NO ONE TO SELL 'EM TO?
YEAH, LEAVE IT TO LELAND TO WORRY ABOUT THE PAYDAY.
WE FOUND SOMEONE ELSE, IS ALL.
PHANTOM COMPANY
MY TURN.
YEAH, LET'S HEAR ABOUT HOW WASH SHARED HIS DESSERT WITH YOU IN THE COMPANY MESS OVER AT PONYMACRO.
WASH NEVER SHARED PIE...
BUT HE KNEW HOW TO SLICE ONE...

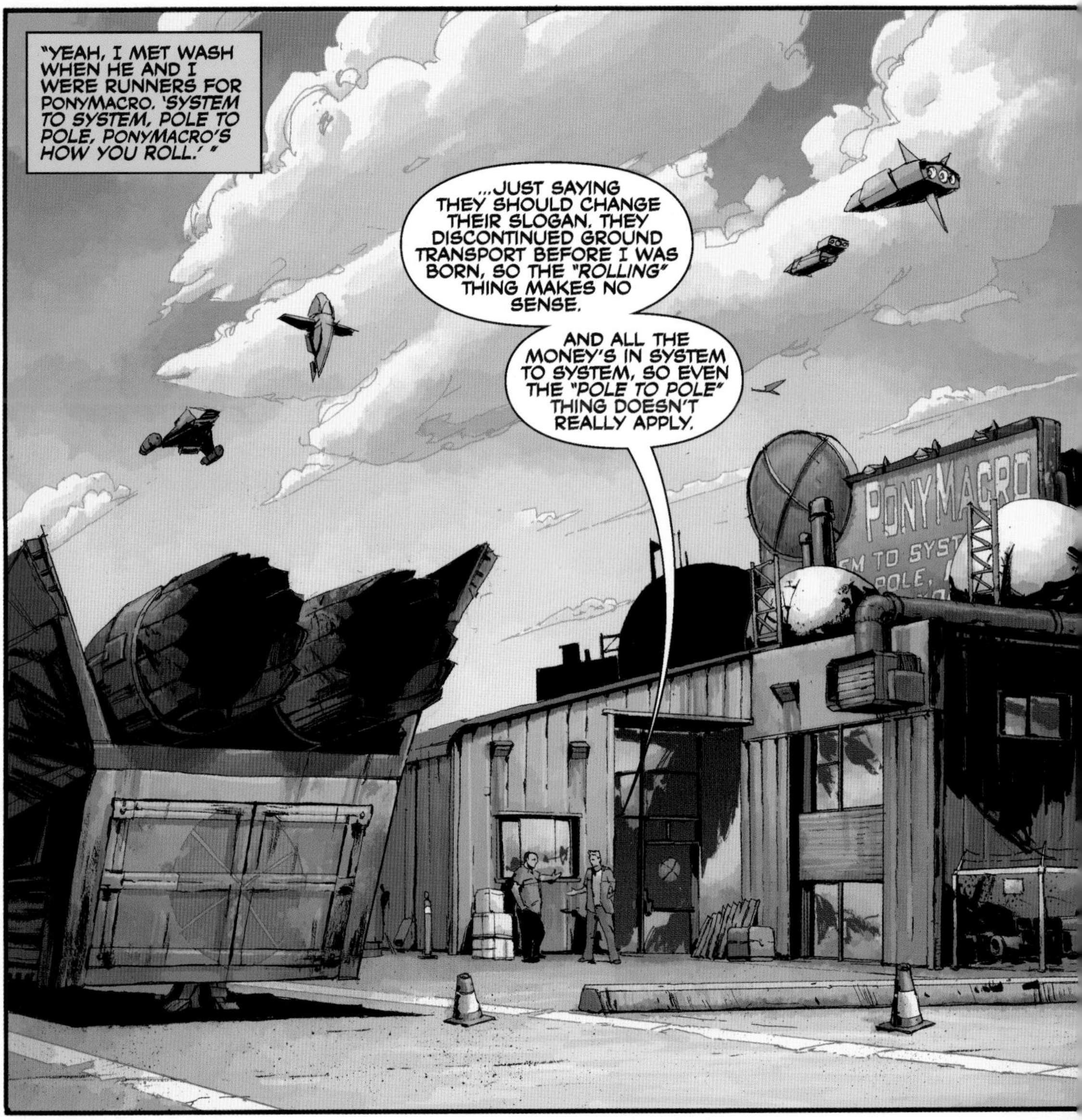
"YEAH, I MET WASH WHEN HE AND I WERE RUNNERS FOR PONYMACRO. '*SYSTEM TO SYSTEM, POLE TO POLE, PONYMACRO'S HOW YOU ROLL.*' "
...JUST SAYING THEY SHOULD CHANGE THEIR SLOGAN. THEY DISCONTINUED GROUND TRANSPORT BEFORE I WAS BORN, SO THE "*ROLLING*" THING MAKES NO SENSE.
AND ALL THE MONEY'S IN SYSTEM TO SYSTEM, SO EVEN THE "*POLE TO POLE*" THING DOESN'T REALLY APPLY.
PONYMACRO

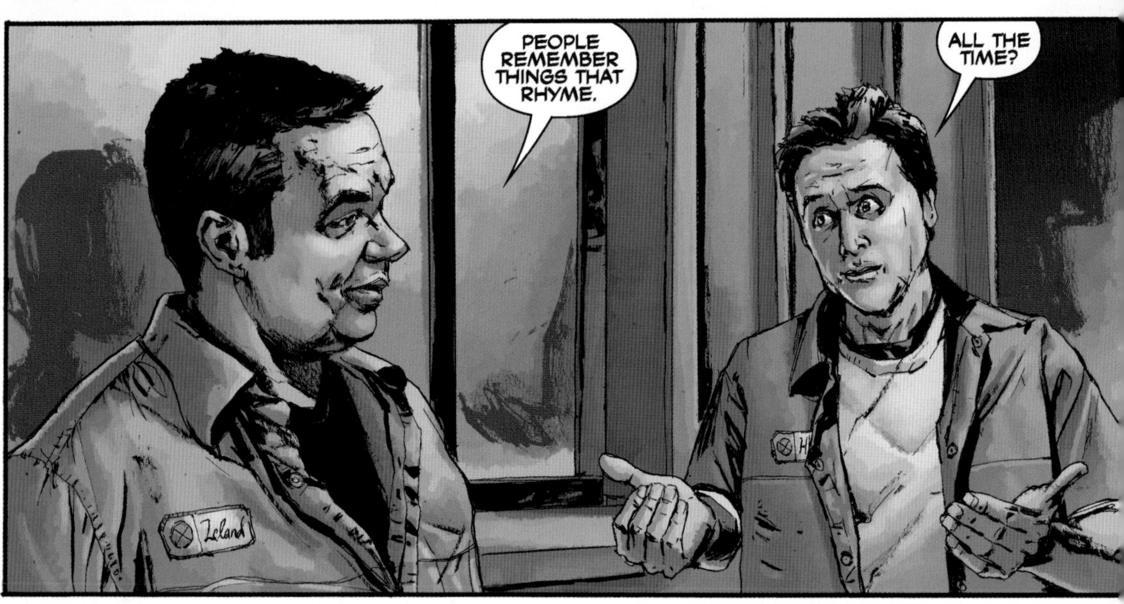
PEOPLE REMEMBER THINGS THAT RHYME.
ALL THE TIME?
Zeland

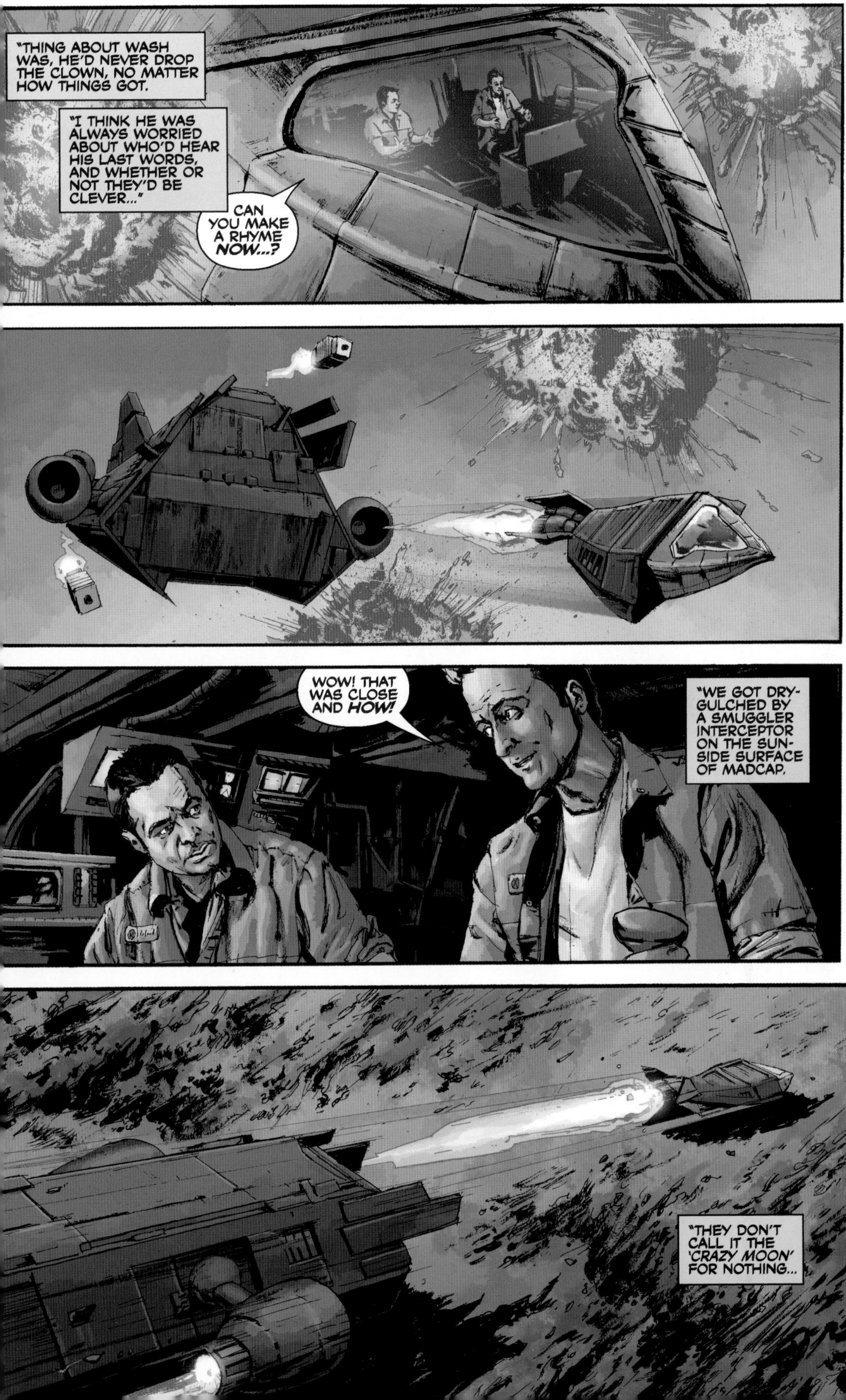
"THING ABOUT WASH WAS, HE'D NEVER DROP THE CLOWN, NO MATTER HOW THINGS GOT.
"I THINK HE WAS ALWAYS WORRIED ABOUT WHO'D HEAR HIS LAST WORDS, AND WHETHER OR NOT THEY'D BE CLEVER..."
CAN YOU MAKE A RHYME *NOW...?*
WOW! THAT WAS CLOSE AND *HOW!*
"WE GOT DRY-GULCHED BY A SMUGGLER INTERCEPTOR ON THE SUN-SIDE SURFACE OF MADCAP.
"THEY DON'T CALL IT THE *'CRAZY MOON'* FOR NOTHING...

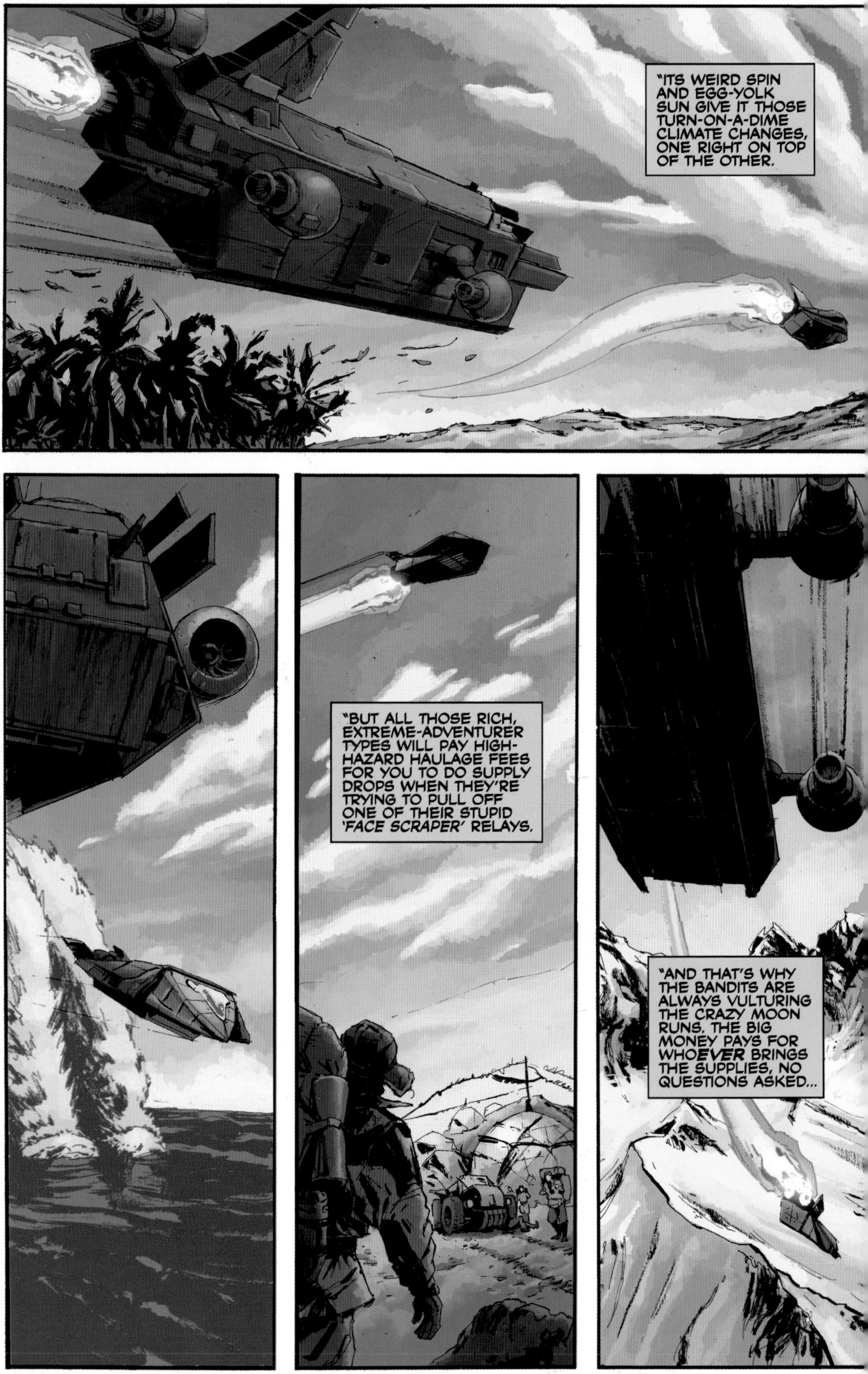
"ITS WEIRD SPIN AND EGG-YOLK SUN GIVE IT THOSE TURN-ON-A-DIME CLIMATE CHANGES, ONE RIGHT ON TOP OF THE OTHER.
"BUT ALL THOSE RICH, EXTREME-ADVENTURER TYPES WILL PAY HIGH-HAZARD HAULAGE FEES FOR YOU TO DO SUPPLY DROPS WHEN THEY'RE TRYING TO PULL OFF ONE OF THEIR STUPID '*FACE SCRAPER*' RELAYS.
"AND THAT'S WHY THE BANDITS ARE ALWAYS VULTURING THE CRAZY MOON RUNS. THE BIG MONEY PAYS FOR WHO*EVER* BRINGS THE SUPPLIES, NO QUESTIONS ASKED...

"WHILE I WAS CURSING THE PONYMACRO COMPANY FOR NOT EQUIPPING THE DELIVERY SCOUTS WITH SO MUCH AS A SCREAM-BLANKET, WASH USED THE *PLANET* AS AN ARSENAL.

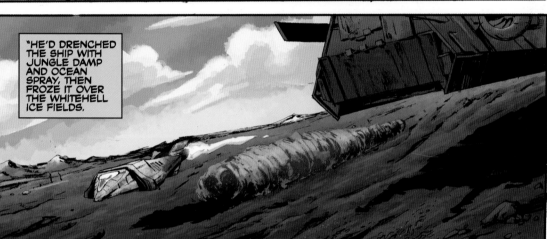

"HE'D DRENCHED THE SHIP WITH JUNGLE DAMP AND OCEAN SPRAY, THEN FROZE IT OVER THE WHITEHELL ICE FIELDS.

"ON A SMALL SHIP LIKE OURS, STEAMING OFF ALL THAT ICE OVER THE BLACK SAND FLATS GAVE US A LITTLE SHIMMY.

"BUT ON A BIG-ASS BOMBER DREADNAUGHT? WITH ALL THAT HOT STEAM INTO ITS INTAKES ALL AT ONCE?

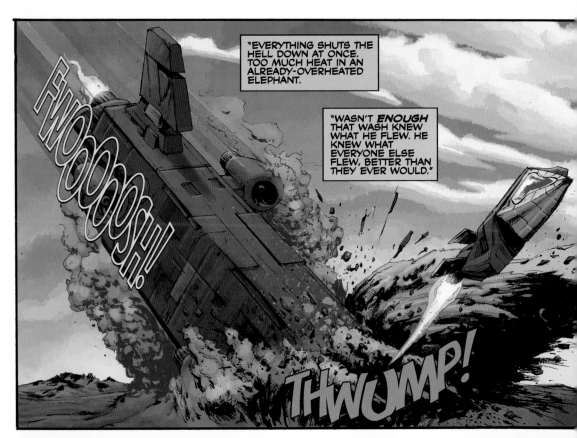

"EVERYTHING SHUTS THE HELL DOWN AT ONCE. TOO MUCH HEAT IN AN ALREADY-OVERHEATED ELEPHANT.

"WASN'T *ENOUGH* THAT WASH KNEW WHAT HE FLEW. HE KNEW WHAT EVERYONE ELSE FLEW, BETTER THAN THEY EVER WOULD."

FWOOOOSH!

THWUMP!

AND HE *NEVER* LOST A SHIPMENT.

YOUR TURN, TAGG.

"NEVER LOST A SHIPMENT."

NOT... NECESSARILY TRUE.

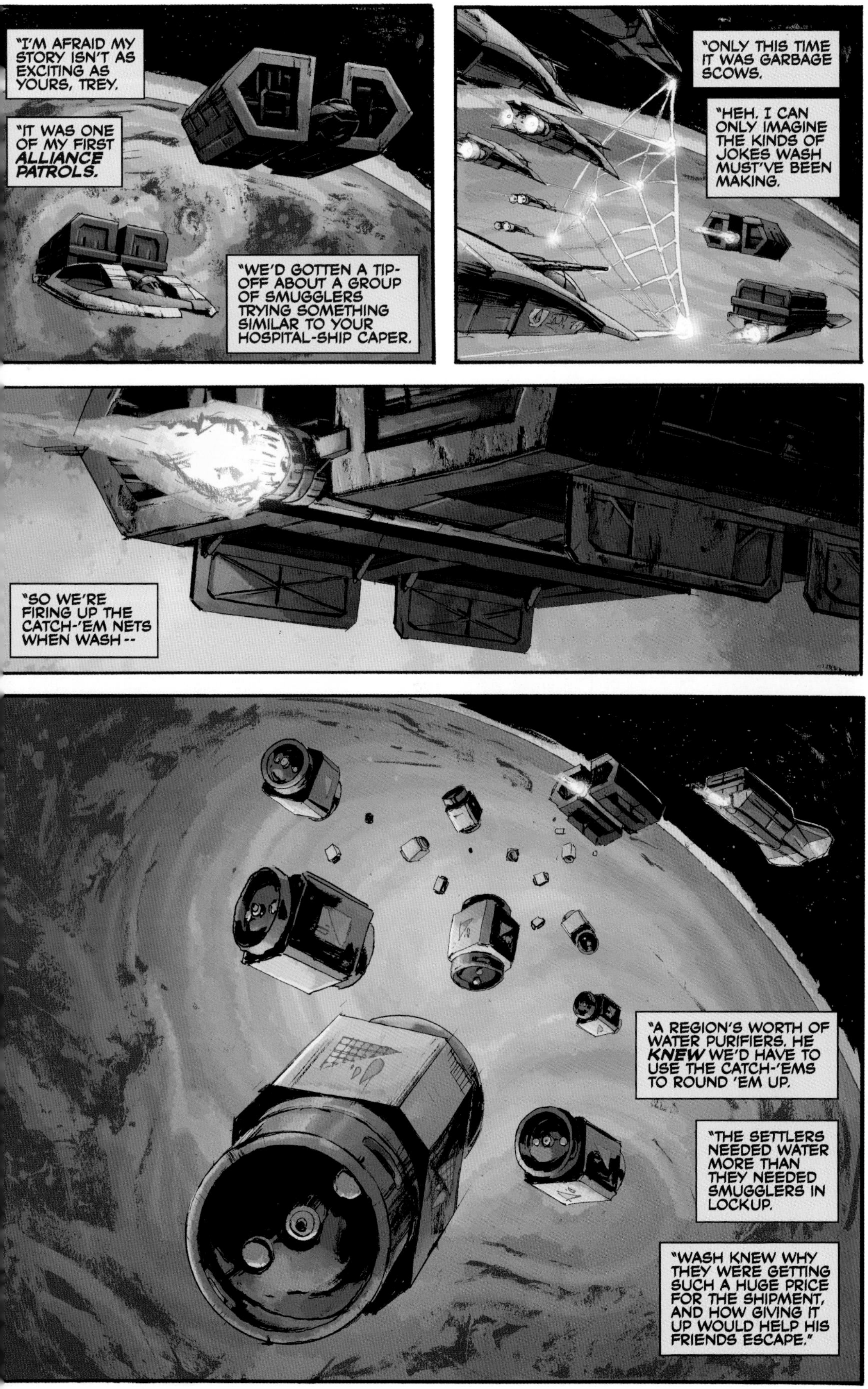
"I'M AFRAID MY STORY ISN'T AS EXCITING AS YOURS, TREY.
"IT WAS ONE OF MY FIRST ALLIANCE PATROLS.
"WE'D GOTTEN A TIP-OFF ABOUT A GROUP OF SMUGGLERS TRYING SOMETHING SIMILAR TO YOUR HOSPITAL-SHIP CAPER.
"ONLY THIS TIME IT WAS GARBAGE SCOWS.
"HEH. I CAN ONLY IMAGINE THE KINDS OF JOKES WASH MUST'VE BEEN MAKING.
"SO WE'RE FIRING UP THE CATCH-'EM NETS WHEN WASH --
"A REGION'S WORTH OF WATER PURIFIERS. HE KNEW WE'D HAVE TO USE THE CATCH-'EMS TO ROUND 'EM UP.
"THE SETTLERS NEEDED WATER MORE THAN THEY NEEDED SMUGGLERS IN LOCKUP.
"WASH KNEW WHY THEY WERE GETTING SUCH A HUGE PRICE FOR THE SHIPMENT, AND HOW GIVING IT UP WOULD HELP HIS FRIENDS ESCAPE."

I *REMEMBER* HEARING ABOUT THAT. A KING'S RANSOM IN CARGO, AND HE TOSSED IT?

SO HIS FRIENDS COULD GET AWAY.

HOW'D YOU KNOW IT WAS WASH?

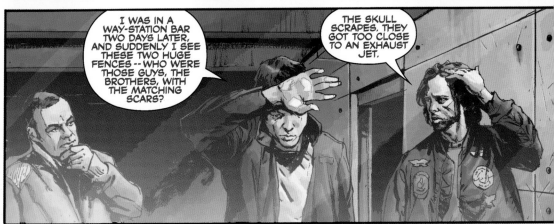

I WAS IN A WAY-STATION BAR TWO DAYS LATER, AND SUDDENLY I SEE THESE TWO HUGE FENCES -- WHO WERE THOSE GUYS, THE BROTHERS, WITH THE MATCHING SCARS?

THE SKULL SCRAPES. THEY GOT TOO CLOSE TO AN EXHAUST JET.

"THE SCRAPES ARE SCREAMING ABOUT THE WATER FILTERS, AND I KNOW, I *KNOW* THIS IS THE PILOT WHO DUMPED THEM.

"AND...I COULD'VE JUMPED RIGHT TO FIRST LIEU-TENANT, SKIPPED ALL THE NONOFFICER GRADES IF I'D SLAPPED BRACELETS ON HIM. BUT..."

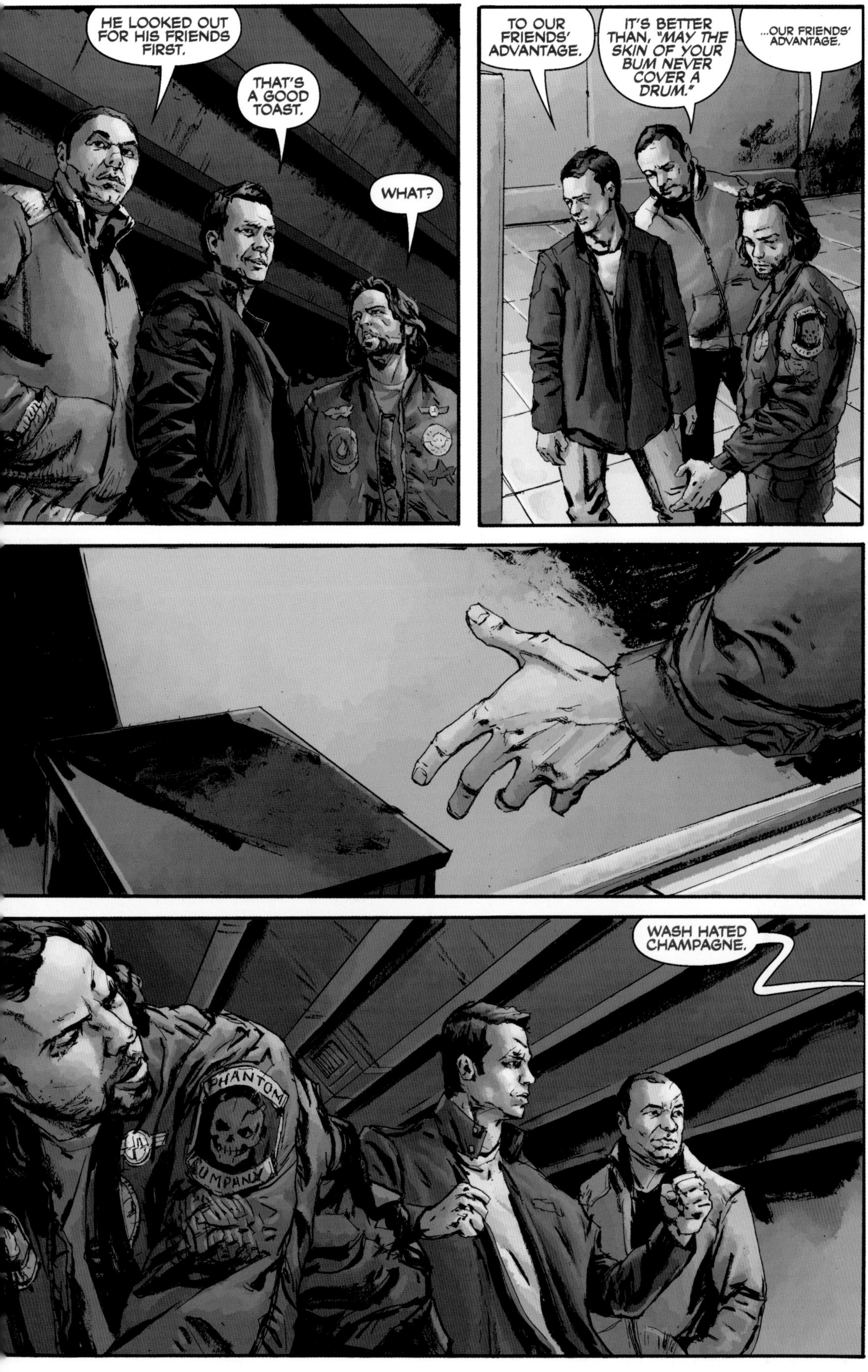
HE LOOKED OUT FOR HIS FRIENDS FIRST.
THAT'S A GOOD TOAST.
WHAT?
TO OUR FRIENDS' ADVANTAGE.
IT'S BETTER THAN, "MAY THE SKIN OF YOUR BUM NEVER COVER A DRUM."
...OUR FRIENDS' ADVANTAGE.
WASH HATED CHAMPAGNE.
PHANTOM

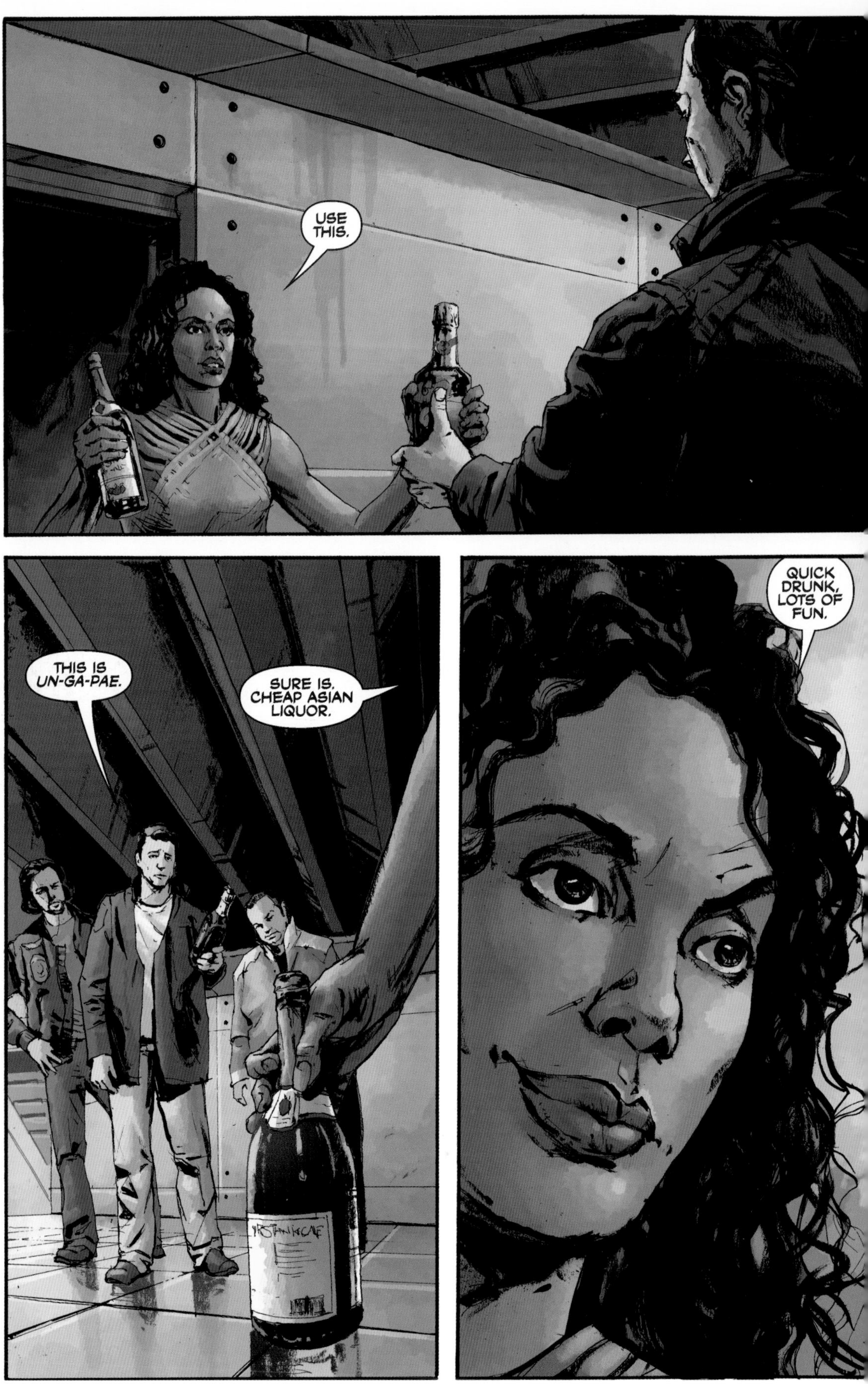
USE THIS.
THIS IS UN-GA-PAE.
SURE IS. CHEAP ASIAN LIQUOR.
QUICK DRUNK, LOTS OF FUN.

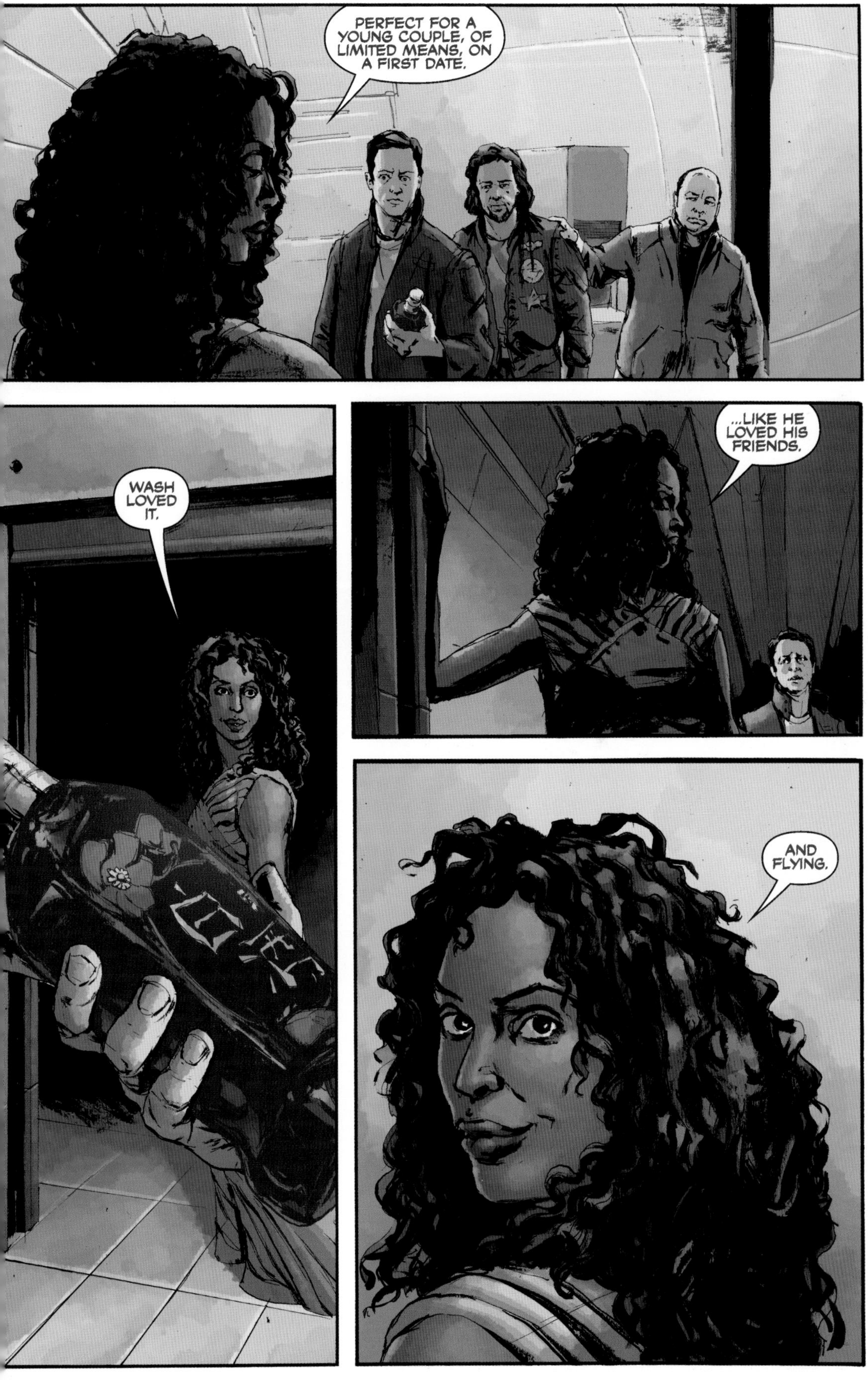
PERFECT FOR A YOUNG COUPLE, OF LIMITED MEANS, ON A FIRST DATE.
WASH LOVED IT.
...LIKE HE LOVED HIS FRIENDS.
AND FLYING.

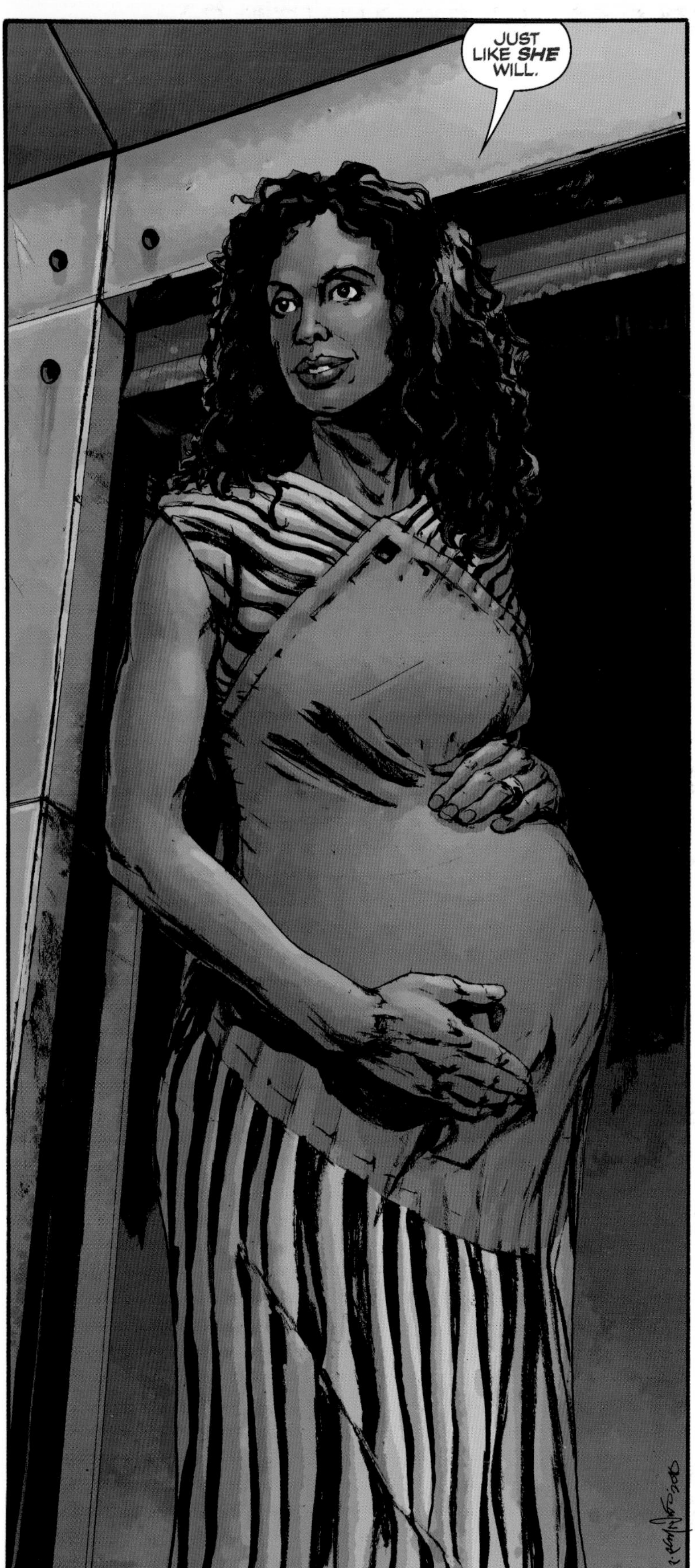
JUST LIKE SHE WILL.

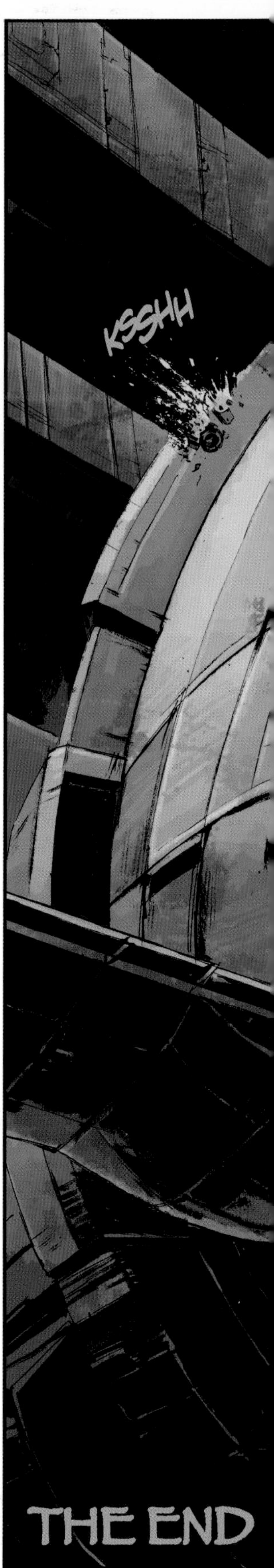
KSSHH
THE END

ALSO FROM JOSS WHEDON

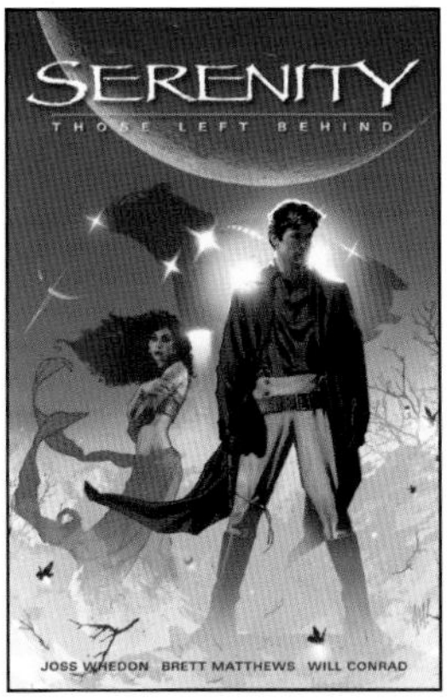
SERENITY
THOSE LEFT BEHIND
JOSS WHEDON BRETT MATTHEWS WILL CONRAD

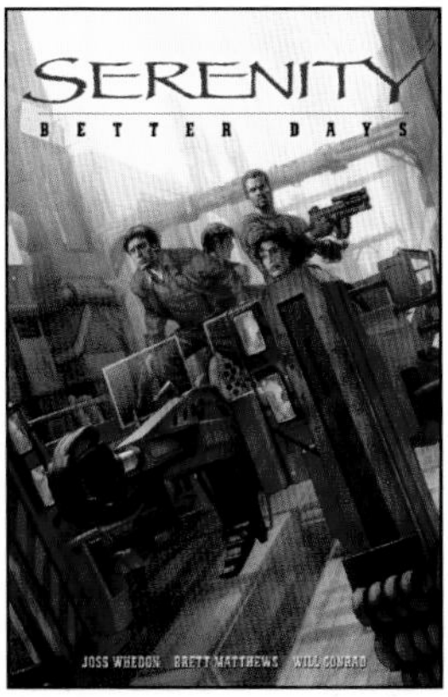
SERENITY
BETTER DAYS

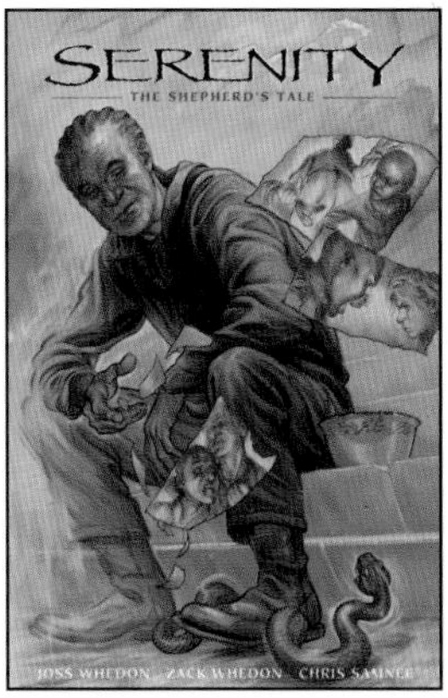
SERENITY
THE SHEPHERD'S TALE

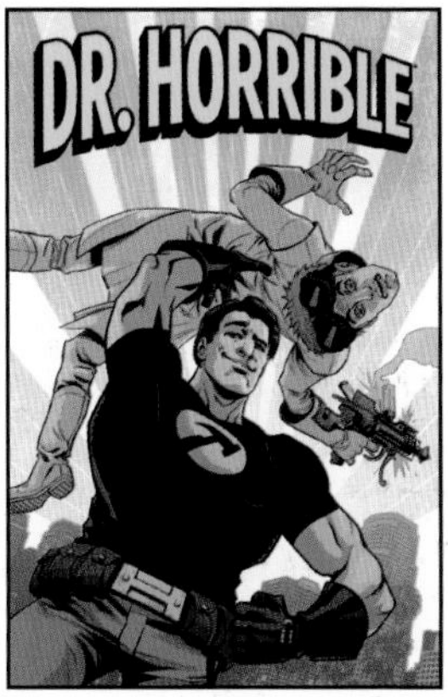
DR. HORRIBLE

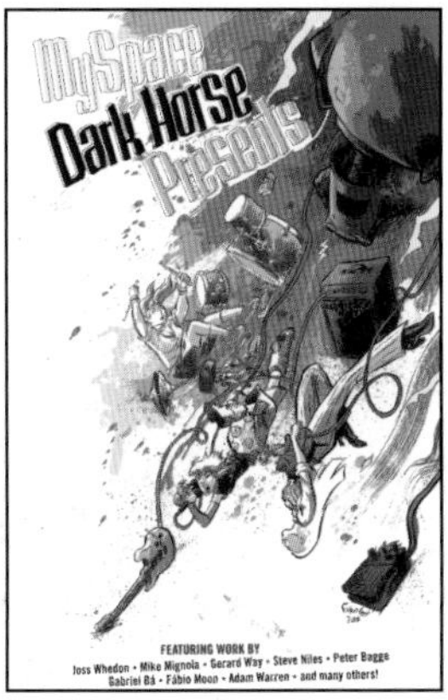
MySpace
Dark Horse
Presents
FEATURING WORK BY

SERENITY VOLUME 1: THOSE LEFT BEHIND
Joss Whedon, Brett Matthews, and Will Conrad
ISBN 978-1-59307-449-4 $9.99

SERENITY VOLUME 2: BETTER DAYS
Joss Whedon, Brett Matthews, and Will Conrad
ISBN 978-1-59582-162-1 $9.99

SERENITY VOLUME 3: THE SHEPHERD'S TALE
Joss Whedon, Zack Whedon, and Chris Samnee
ISBN 978-1-59582-561-2 $14.99

DR. HORRIBLE
Zack Whedon, and Joëlle Jones
ISBN 978-1-59582-577-3 $9.99

MYSPACE DARK HORSE PRESENTS VOLUME 1
Featuring Sugarshock *by Joss Whedon and Fábio Moon*
ISBN 978-1-59307-998-7 $19.99

DARK HORSE BOOKS
DarkHorse.com

AVAILABLE AT YOUR LOCAL COMICS SHOP OR BOOKSTORE!
TO FIND A COMICS SHOP IN YOUR AREA, CALL 1-888-266-4226.
For more information or to order direct visit DarkHorse.com or call 1-800-862-0052 Mon.–Fri. 9 AM to 5 PM Pacific Time.

FROM JOSS WHEDON

Buffy the Vampire Slayer™

BUFFY THE VAMPIRE SLAYER SEASON 8:

VOLUME 1: THE LONG WAY HOME
Joss Whedon and Georges Jeanty
ISBN 978-1-59307-822-5 | $15.99

VOLUME 2: NO FUTURE FOR YOU
Brian K. Vaughan, Georges Jeanty, and Joss Whedon
ISBN 978-1-59307-963-5 | $15.99

VOLUME 3: WOLVES AT THE GATE
Drew Goddard, Georges Jeanty, and Joss Whedon
ISBN 978-1-59582-165-2 | $15.99

VOLUME 4: TIME OF YOUR LIFE
Joss Whedon, Jeph Loeb, Georges Jeanty, and others
ISBN 978-1-59582-310-6 | $15.99

VOLUME 5: PREDATORS AND PREY
Joss Whedon, Jane Espenson, Cliff Richards, Georges Jeanty, and others
ISBN 978-1-59582-342-7 | $15.99

VOLUME 6: RETREAT
Joss Whedon, Jane Espenson, Cliff Richards, Georges Jeanty, and others
ISBN 978-1-59582-415-8 | $15.99

VOLUME 7: TWILIGHT
Joss Whedon, Brad Meltzer, and Georges Jeanty
ISBN 978-1-59582-558-2 | $16.99

VOLUME 8: LAST GLEAMING
Joss Whedon, Scott Allie, and Georges Jeanty
ISBN 978-1-59582-610-7 | $16.99

TALES OF THE SLAYERS
Joss Whedon, Amber Benson, Gene Colan, P. Craig Russell, Tim Sale, and others
ISBN 978-1-56971-605-2 | $14.99

TALES OF THE VAMPIRES
Joss Whedon, Brett Matthews, Cameron Stewart, and others
ISBN 978-1-56971-749-3 | $15.99

BUFFY THE VAMPIRE SLAYER: TALES
ISBN 978-1-59582-644-2 | $29.99

FRAY: FUTURE SLAYER
Joss Whedon and Karl Moline
ISBN 978-1-56971-751-6 | $19.99

ALSO FROM DARK HORSE . . .

BUFFY THE VAMPIRE SLAYER OMNIBUS

VOLUME 1
ISBN 978-1-59307-784-6 | $24.99

VOLUME 2
ISBN 978-1-59307-826-3 | $24.99

VOLUME 3
ISBN 978-1-59307-885-0 | $24.99

VOLUME 4
ISBN 978-1-59307-968-0 | $24.99

VOLUME 5
ISBN 978-1-59582-225-3 | $24.99

VOLUME 6
ISBN 978-1-59582-242-0 | $24.99

VOLUME 7
ISBN 978-1-59582-331-1 | $24.99

ANGEL OMNIBUS
Christopher Golden, Eric Powell, and others
ISBN 978-1-59582-706-7 | $24.99

BUFFY THE VAMPIRE SLAYER: PANEL TO PANEL
ISBN 978-1-59307-836-2 | $19.99

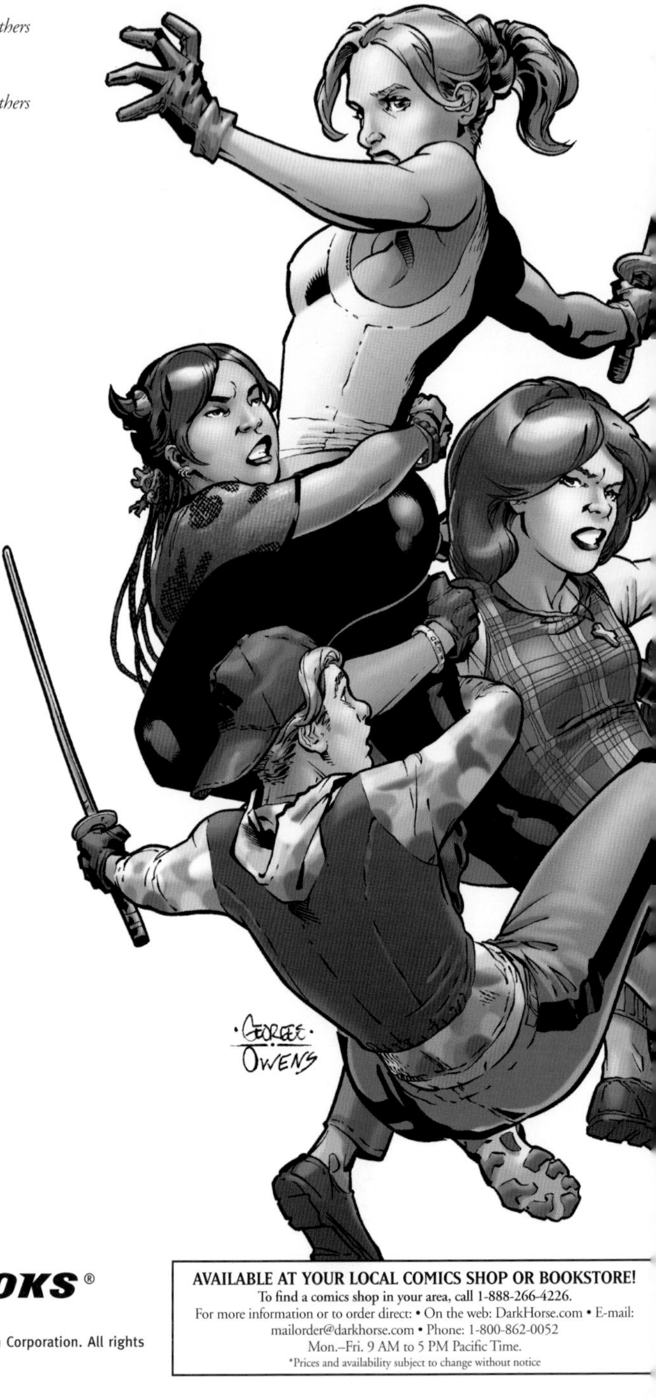
·GEORGE·
OWENS

DARK HORSE BOOKS®
DarkHorse.com

AVAILABLE AT YOUR LOCAL COMICS SHOP OR BOOKSTORE!
To find a comics shop in your area, call 1-888-266-4226.
For more information or to order direct: • On the web: DarkHorse.com • E-mail: mailorder@darkhorse.com • Phone: 1-800-862-0052
Mon.–Fri. 9 AM to 5 PM Pacific Time.
*Prices and availability subject to change without notice